BT 22.00

**W9-BCR-781**

# Ethics in
# the Sanctuary

MARGARET P. BATTIN

# Ethics

## in the Sanctuary

*Examining the Practices of*
*Organized Religion*

*Yale University Press   New Haven & London*

Designed by Richard Hendel
Set in Galliard type by The Composing
Room of Michigan, Inc.
Printed in the United States of America.
The paper in this book meets the
guidelines of permanence and durability
of the Committee on Production
Guidelines for Book Longevity of the
Council on Library Resources.

10 9 8 7 6 5 4 3 2 1

Library of Congress Cataloging-in-
Publication Data
Battin, M. Pabst.
   Ethics in the sanctuary / Margaret P.
Battin.
      p.    cm.
   Includes bibliographical references.
   ISBN 0–300–04547–6 (alk. paper)
   1. Clergy—United States—
Professional ethics. 2. Religious and
ecclesiastical institutions—Moral and
ethical aspects. 3. Religious and
ecclesiastical institutions—
Employees—Professional ethics. I.
Title.
BV4011.5.B38    1990
174'.1—dc20    89–29675
                    CIP

*For Bill and Glendy Pabst*

# CONTENTS

If you live in the West, as I have for over a dozen years, you begin to treasure a curious form of recreation: long, long drives through the basin-and-range country, two hundred miles in one direction, four hundred miles in another. It is empty country: dry lunar valleys ridged every hundred miles or so by arid, unused mountains, inhabited only by the thin strip of the highway and an occasional crossroads: two or three bleak wooden houses and a couple of rusting gasoline pumps. What you see out the window, after conversation in the car has exhausted itself and the radio stations you can trust are long out of reach, is a country of almost nothing: utterly empty land, only sparsely stubbled with sagebrush, with a few isolated cattle and maybe, perched on a random fencepost, a hawk.

There is a reason for treasuring such drives. Unlike the more vivid, sophisticated, and teemingly peopled parts of the world, where there is always something to attract one's attention, this bare landscape is good for thinking. It is where rumination begins, where a train of thought is measured in miles, where ideas for which one would never have patience in a busier part of the world strike without warning. That is how this book was born: it began with an instantaneous idea, like the proverbial light bulb turning on, which occurred four or five hours into a drive somewhere out in nowhere, hundreds of miles beyond anything that might pass as a town.

As we often do on these drives, my husband and I had been talking about the things we'd been working on: the things we write, think about, teach. Fifty miles earlier, I'd been ruminating about matters in bioethics (where I do most of my work), about business ethics and professional ethics generally (which I also teach), and about the structures that are common among all the professions and the kinds of moral problems they raise. My husband, an English professor, had talked about a problem in the interpretation of Wordsworth. Then that silence had set in, where you are too consumed with thinking to put any of it into words, and a single, seemingly perfectly simple idea occurred: if applied ethics has enlarged and enriched our understanding of professional institutions like medicine and law, not by rejecting them but by showing how their characteristic structures unavoidably give rise to moral problems, why couldn't this kind of analysis be extended to organized religion, too? After all, organized religion also has much of the structure of a professional institution; can one not expect that this structure will also give rise to moral problems that are much the same?

That put an end to the silence on this long, empty drive. Within the next fifty miles, we'd argued through all the obstacles to such a project. By the end of the trip, I understood both why it is important for a society to critique its religious institutions in this way and, at the same time, why a book about these matters could only be half about ethics, while the other half would need to confront methodological issues. Indeed, that is the way this book has taken shape.

Over the next several years, as I've worked on this book, I've begun to see what is interesting about this project in another way. After developing a course syllabus and set of readings for use in teaching, I've had the pleasure of seeing the same light bulb go on in classfuls of undergraduate minds, suddenly illuminated by the possibility of looking at religious institutions critically—including the ones of which they are part. This field is a particular challenge to the student: since it is virtually unencumbered by a preexisting academic literature that formulates the issues, the student soon finds that it is necessary not only to think a problem through afresh but that it is necessary to begin by figuring out what the problem is. Students often have quite close exposure to religious groups of various sorts, both their own and those of their friends, and they move through various degrees of affiliation and disaffiliation; they are a wonderful stimulus in this project, since they are often alert to problems others of us might not see.

A few remarks are in order about this book. For the most part, I've called religious groups and their members by their colloquial names rather than their full titles: for instance, "Catholic church" for "Roman Catholic Church," "Moonies" for the Unification Church, "Mormons" for Church of Jesus Christ of Latter-day Saints, "Quakers" for Society of Friends. Some of these nicknames are pejorative (as most religious nicknames were originally); I use them, without wishing to convey these negative connotations, because it is under these names that the groups are best known.

The Bible translation used is the New Revised Standard Version (copyright 1989, Division of Christian Education of the National Council of the Churches of Christ in the United States of America, used by permission). Many groups welcome the use of a variety of Bible translations; however, where it is relevant that a group uniformly uses a single one—for instance, as is common in fundamentalist groups, the King James version—I have so indicated.

A few parts of this book bear some resemblance to work I've published elsewhere. Portions of the introduction resemble my paper "Applied Professional Ethics and Institutional Religion: The Methodological Issues," which appeared in *The Monist* (vol. 67, no. 4, Oct. 1984, pp. 569–83), though there are considerable differences. A (much) earlier version of chapter 1, called " Telling Confessions: Confidentiality in the Practice of Religion," appeared in *Sunstone* (vol. 8, no. 6, Nov.–Dec. 1983, pp. 23–33). Chapter 2 has appeared under the title "High-Risk Religion" in *Philosophical Exchange* (double issue, vols. 19–20, 1988–89), and a few paragraphs of the conclusion are drawn from my "Professional Ethics and the Practice of Religion: A Philosopher's View," in *Ethical Issues in the Practice of Ministry*, edited by J. Boyajian (Minneapolis, Minn.: United Theology Seminary of the Twin Cities, 1984). Some of the differences between this earlier work and the current book reflect not only my own changes in thinking but shifts in the practices of the groups under discussion. I have been astonished in working on this book at the fluidity and change in religious practice as a human institution, though I suspect that the rapid evolution in some of the practices examined here is to be explained by the fact that these are the areas where tension between them and the expectations of ethics is greatest.

I owe debts of gratitude to an enormous number of people who have been involved in various ways with this book. First my husband,

Brooke Hopkins, was there not only at its inception, hundreds of miles out in the barren countryside, but has seemed to enjoy every further step of the way. My colleagues in the Philosophy Department at the University of Utah, especially Bruce Landesman, Leslie Francis, Peter Appleby, Peter Windt, Mendel Cohen, Max Rogers, Virgil Aldrich, Pat Hanna and Don Garrett, have provided varying degrees of sustained critique. So have colleagues in philosophy at other institutions: Karen Lebacqz, Philip Quinn, Stanley Godlovitch, Anita Silvers, and Alan Gewirth—some on parts of the book, others on the whole thing. Michael Harris has been of invaluable help in checking the final manuscript for accuracy. John Davis and Glendy Pabst have at various points attempted to civilize its prose, and Lorraine Alexson has been ruthless, as a manuscript editor should be, in imposing economy and order. Jeanne Ferris enhanced the book, as its acquiring editor at Yale University Press. I've profited from discussions of various points—some brief, some extended—with Herman Luben, Jeff Gros, Richard Ostling, Russell Chandler, Ruth Wallace, Frank Flinn, Bill Zlatos, Daniel Ellsberg, Rita Swan, Thomas Johnsen, Christine Liu, Reba Keele, David Green, Steven Durrant, Delmont Oswald, Michael Quinn, Karlynn Hinman, C. Roy Woodruff, R. J. Ross, Ron French, Cathleen Stewart, Elke Schmidt, Don Scheid, Rev. Bob Randolf, Rev. Donald Baird, Father Lewis Fischer, Rev. Robert J. Schrank, Rev. Bill Hearns, Rev. Margaret Lacey, Rev. Tom Goldsmith, and Rev. Rodney Dorsey. I've enjoyed talking with some of those involved in the *Guinn* and *Nally* cases, including Rev. Ron Witter, Tommy Frazier, Tony Graham, David Cooksey, and Ed Barker. I've also discussed with a number of people who would prefer that their names not be mentioned their experiences with religious groups; I'd like to thank them for their candor. I'd like to thank the audiences for papers drawn from various parts of this book at the University of Alabama, the University of Chicago, the University of Colorado, the University of Hawaii, the University of Utah, the Sunstone Theological Conference, and the Society for the Scientific Study of Religion, as well as my students in Philosophy 379 and Liberal Education 110. I am grateful to the University of Utah Research Fund and the National Endowment for the Humanities, which have provided some of my leave time, to the libraries at the Pacific School of Religion and Union Theological Seminary, and to the Hastings Center, where I did some of the earliest work. And finally, I'd like to thank three people whose contribution was encouragement of a project I wasn't always sure would succeed: Sam Gorovitz, Dan Wikler, and Joseph Fletcher.

# Applied Professional Ethics
# and Organized Religion

Within the past twenty years, enthusiasm for applied professional ethics has spread from its origins in medicine to a broad variety of other professions, including law, business, education, engineering, journalism, and other professional and semiprofessional fields. Each involves an institutional structure within which practitioners provide specific services to clients and within which the behavior of the practitioners in providing services is regulated by both formal and informal institutional codes and conventions. As interest in applied ethics has spread, philosophers examining the various professions have largely succeeded in describing and addressing—though perhaps not resolving—the characteristic moral dilemmas associated with their structures and practices. In the process, applied professional ethics has matured sufficiently to be able to scrutinize its own structure and functions, to reflect on its roots in ethical theory, and to concern itself with the relation between ethical theory and applications of theory to concrete problems. But in spite of the broad spread of interest in professional ethics and its increasing sophistication as a field, one area of institutional practice has nearly completely escaped its notice: organized religion. Inasmuch as the ministry, priesthood, or pastorate—called "divinity" in earlier periods—has traditionally been counted among the principal professions, this is a startling omission.

In this book, I take advantage of the remarkable opportunity this circumstance presents. Applied professional ethics, which will be understood here to cover both the professions proper and business, supplies a highly developed critical apparatus for the exploration of concrete moral problems. At the same time, organized religion presents a new, completely untouched area for exploration, one that applied ethicists have simply not yet examined.[1] This opportunity is remarkable because it not only lets us weigh the capacities of professional ethics as it has developed so far but invites the inauguration of a virtually unexplored field. To be sure, this new field covers a vast and highly varied range of problems, involving issues arising in religious groups from the plainest mainstream to the most colorful sects and cults at the fringes. But it also poses extremely difficult and interesting methodological problems of a sort professional ethics has not yet had to face. Consequently, my intention here in marking out this new field is twofold: both to identify and examine some of the central moral issues to which the practices of organized religion give rise and, in doing so, to reflect on the methodological issues this examination raises.

That organized religion has thus far escaped the scrutiny of contemporary applied ethics is to be explained, at least in part, by our traditional respect for freedom of religion, by our desire to avoid interference in the religious beliefs or practices of others, and by our legally reinforced, politically and culturally entrenched tendency to separate church and state. Added to this is the widespread belief that ethics, however rigorously formulated its requirements may be in secular moral theory, is ultimately derived from religion and hence cannot be used to critique religion itself. It may seem odd to launch a moral critique of a respected institution whose central professional claims include the custodianship of morality itself. But, just as our traditional respect for doctors earlier led us to overlook important moral problems in the practice of medicine and just as our confidence in the legal system led us to ignore what lawyers actually do, so our respect for the inviolability of religious belief and our uncertainty about the basis upon which we might critique it still lead us to "screen off" moral problems that arise within the institution of religion. Of course, we continuously scrutinize organized religion from a variety of other perspectives—sociological, psychological, political, and many others. We are also intuitively familiar with the possibility of moral criticism of institutional religion and its officials at a superficial level: we denounce mass marriages and snake handling, hard-sell convert-seeking techniques and slick solicitation methods in the media ministry, and the behavior of various religious operatives whose personal transgressions are publicly exposed. However, in spite of the traditional view of the ministry as a profession (a view prevalent at least through the nineteenth century), it simply has not occurred to moral theorists and philosophers concerned with applied professional ethics to examine the institution of religion in the same sustained way that the institutions of medicine and law are examined, though these institutions are all very much alike in many ways and exhibit many of the same characteristic moral problems.

To embark on this examination, I propose to begin by looking at three central ethical issues in organized religion. The first, confidentiality, is a familiar issue in medicine, psychiatry, law, accounting, and many secular fields. It also arises in pastoral work and, with considerable frequency, in religious marriage counseling. But it develops with particular force where religious practice encourages or requires the confession of sins, especially in private, personal disclosure to an official of the church. In chapter 1, I examine this issue with respect to three groups whose practices concerning confidentiality differ dramatically: the Roman Catholic Church, the Church of Jesus Christ of Latter-day Saints, or Mormon church, and the independent fundamentalist Church of Christ in Collinsville, Oklahoma.

The second issue concerns risk taking, where religious groups permit, encourage, or require their adherents to engage in practices that pose serious risks to life or health. This issue, which has analogues both in the specific problem of "informed consent" in medicine and in general problems of consent in law, engineering, investment management, education, and other secular professions, arises whenever professionals provide services that involve risks to clients but at the same time advise their clients on the prudence of taking these risks. To explore this issue, I discuss in chapter 2 factors that shape risk-taking choice in three religious groups whose practices involve the refusal of medical treatment or some component of it—Christian Science, Jehovah's Witnesses, and a small fundamentalist group in the north central states, the Faith Assembly—as well as a fourth group whose practices in addition pose direct risks to life, the pentecostal serpent-handling groups within the Holiness churches.

The third of the three initial problems to be discussed in this study appears in a much starker form in religion than in the secular professions, although it bears some similarity to issues of paternalism in standard professional areas. This is the problem of convert seeking; it concerns whether manipulative, duplicitous, or coercive conversion techniques can be justified in the light of claims concerning a strongly positive or negative afterlife outcome, that is, salvation or damnation. In chapter 3, I will discuss a broad range of groups whose strategies in seeking converts raise these issues, including the Protestant and Catholic foreign missions of the nineteenth and twentieth centuries, the contemporary Campus Crusade for Christ, the Children of God, the Unification Church or Moonies, the present-day mainline and evangelical groups, and others.

In each of these extended discussions, sustained attention is given to methodological issues. The discussion in chapter 1 on confidentiality in confession yields a broad, general methodological principle for the moral analysis of religious practice, a principle that serves to identify what can and what cannot be a target of such analysis and that addresses the issue of the role of doctrinal claims in moral argumentation. It is supplemented by a second principle, developed during the discussion of risk taking in chapter 2, which identifies a central role obligation of the religious professional and more precisely limits the range of religious practices open to moral critique. Chapter 3, concerning convert seeking, confronts the issue of what weight faith-based claims about afterlife outcomes should be given in controlling present behavior and introduces a third principle, which, while it does not further limit the range of candidates for analysis, points a finger more strongly at some phenomena than others. These methodological issues—the function of doctrinal claims, the role obligations of the religious professional, and the weight of faith-based claims—are what make "ecclesioethics" (as we might call this new field) a still more difficult area of inquiry than secular fields like bioethics or legal ethics, since these methodological issues are extremely complex but cannot be ignored. I will examine these methodological issues in a sustained, "nested" way in chapters 1–3; they are supplemented in chapter 4, which treats issues in mainstream groups, with an additional general principle that permits the consolidation of specific analyses of individual practices into a moral characterization of a given religious group as a whole. These methodological principles, developed in this nested way over the first four chapters, are then exhibited in operation in chapter 5, where they are employed to conduct a sustained analysis of a single specimen case. Thus, though the subject matters of the various chapters are more or less independent and could be examined in any order, the methodological concerns discussed in each are developed in a cumulative, progressive manner.

## *The Nature of Professional Ethics*

In order to pursue an inquiry that takes professional ethics as its starting point for exploring a new and different sort of field, it is important to see why *professional* ethics provides a suitable apparatus for inquiry, as well as what its capacities and limitations are. Professional ethics, as a subdiscipline of applied ethics or normative philosophy, begins with principles derived from background ethical theory—especially utilitarianism and the deontological theory primarily associated with Immanuel Kant—and applies them in situations characteristic of professional practice. Utilitarian theory, usually attributed to Jeremy Bentham and John Stuart Mill, supplies what is known as the principle of utility or, loosely, the requirement that the agent act so as to bring about "the greatest balance of happiness over unhappiness" or "the greatest good for the greatest number." In contemporary professional ethics, the principle of utility is usually deployed by means of the two component principles of nonmaleficence and beneficence, the requirements that the agent "do no harm" and that the agent act to bring about good, principles that attend to the consequences of the agent's acts for all persons affected. In addition, though its roots may be partly or even largely incompatible with utilitarianism, professional ethics also draws on Kantian deontology for its principle of autonomy, that principle which requires respect for persons and for their unencumbered

choices. This is a nonconsequentialist principle, which, unlike the utilitarian ones, does not take the outcomes of the agent's act as determina-
tive of its moral character; it is concerned with the nature of an act.
Professional ethics further draws on sources from Aristotle to John
Rawls in its consideration of the principle of justice, which governs the
equitable distribution of goods in a situation of scarcity. It also often
draws on Aristotelian and contemporary accounts of the virtues in
human character. Among those who work in the field of professional
ethics, whether in bioethics, legal ethics, business ethics, or elsewhere,
there is little consensus about how these principles are to be prioritized
when they conflict with one another, as they often do in "hard cases,"
or about whether additional principles such as loyalty and gratitude
must be introduced independently. Nor is there agreement about
whether any or all of the professions can be said to be "strongly
differentiated"[2]—that is, whether any or all of the professions are
governed by a different set of moral principles or are exempt from
some of them.

Nevertheless, professional ethics as a field of philosophic inquiry is
comparatively unified in its concerns, in its canons of argumentation,
and in the problems it regards as central; to this extent it supplies a
coherent apparatus for moral inquiry. At least in its earlier stages,
professional ethics primarily addressed moral dilemmas concerning
matters of how the professional practitioner should or should not treat
a client—particularly issues of truth telling, confidentiality, and informed consent. These have been examined exhaustively in the context
of medicine and law. But as professional ethics had broadened its scope
to examine a wider range of professions, it is becoming evident that
where a particular institutional structure gives rise to a certain kind of
problem in one professional area, other professional areas with similar
institutional structures and with professional practitioners assigned
similar roles also face similar moral problems. To be sure, although
different professional areas have developed quite different ways of
responding to endemic problems and have adopted radically different
practical solutions, the central features of the underlying issues typically remain the same. This is because the central problems are structurally generated; they are systemic moral dilemmas, not adventitious

ones. It is this that gives professional ethics its coherence as a field of inquiry.

Consequently, since it is as a function of particular institutional structures and professional roles that certain characteristic problems arise, where organized religion exhibits structures that resemble those of the secular professions or assigns its practitioners similar roles, it too will give rise to similar ethical issues. By making use of those recurrent concerns that are central to secular professional ethics and by observing the characteristic institutional junctures at which they arise, we can discern certain quite troubling ethical issues within religion that we might not otherwise see.

## *The Structure of Professions*

The first question to consider, then, are whether and to what degree organized religion employs the same institutional structures as the secular professions or assigns its practitioners similar roles. What is of interest is not so much whether organized religion *is* a profession— though it has traditionally been regarded that way—but what specific institutional structures and professional roles it shares with some or all of the secular professions.[3]

Among the features usually thought to be characteristic of the secular professions and hence features to look for in organized religion are at least the thirteen listed below. While not all of these features are found in all of the secular professions, and while some professions exhibit additional important, distinctive features, these are the principal features of those background institutional structures and roles that in general characterize the secular professions. They include:

1. an identifiable class of practitioners or providers of services, distinct from the class of clients or recipients of services
2. a federation, association, or collegial relationship among identified professional practitioners
3. a publicly recognized role for practitioners
4. a specialized body of theoretical knowledge to which the practitioners have access

5. a common set of services, based on this specialized body of knowledge, that practitioners provide to clients
6. a monopoly, or virtual monopoly, on providing services of that kind
7. pay for services provided, whether in salary, fee, retainer, contingency fee, or other form
8. an extended period of formal education and training to which prospective new practitioners are subject
9. a selective procedure for new practitioners to obtain credentials; practitioners are institutionally appointed and volunteer practitioners without credentials are not admitted
10. rules, regulations, and codes, written or unwritten, that govern the behavior of practitioners, both among themselves and in providing services to clients
11. disciplinary procedures for controlling deviant practitioners
12. expectations that practitioners will be loyal to the institution
13. inequalities of authority and power between the practitioners and their clients

Clearly, organized religion shares with the secular professions many of these thirteen features. For example: *Item 1:* Its "practitioners" or "professionals"—variously called "ministers," "priests," "pastors," "rabbis," and so on, depending on their specific denominational affiliation—form an identifiable class, distinct from those persons to whom they provide services—variously called "parishioners," "churchgoers," "members of the congregation," "the laity," and so on. *Item 2:* At least within their own denominations or affiliations, members of the group of practitioners enjoy associational and collegial relations. *Item 3:* They also enjoy a public role, sometimes reinforced with special clothing such as clerical collars and vestments or by special duties such as offering invocations at public functions. *Item 4:* Whether they have a specialized body of theoretical knowledge, comparable to that of the physician and the attorney, may be a matter of doctrinal dispute, but these practitioners are usually regarded as authoritative interpreters of their denomination's teachings, including its scriptures, together with related historical, linguistic, and cultural material. *Item 5:* They provide services for their clientele, including the guidance or leading of worship, both in group worship and individual prayers, the performance of specific rites such as marriages or funerals, counseling and confession-hearing services, consolation and bereavement services, and so on. *Item 6:* At least within a specific religious group, they have a monopoly on the services they provide. Although different groups make such things as worship services, marriages, and funerals available, a prospective "client" can only get a Presbyterian worship service from the Presbyterian clergy, a Catholic marriage from a Catholic priest, a Jewish funeral from a rabbi. The provision of these services, as in any true monopoly, is entirely within institutional control. *Item 7:* With the exception of honoraria for performing special services such as officiating at marriages, members of the clergy typically are not paid individually by the members of their congregations for specific services rendered; rather, contributions to the church are solicited from church members by the clergy (for instance, in the offertory or collection) and then distributed by the church as salaries or livings to individual clergy. (These arrangements vary considerably among different religious groups.) *Item 8:* There is typically a substantial period of training for prospective new members of the clergy, usually taking place in a seminary or similar institution. *Item 9:* Admission to practice is marked by a procedure involving the award of credentials, usually called ordination, and installation in a post. *Item 10:* Various religious groups typically have both written and unwritten rules, regulations, and codes that govern the behavior of their practitioners, including church constitutions, books of discipline, canon law, and so on. *Item 11:* Disciplinary procedures exist for practitioners who fail to follow those rules, regulations, and codes. *Item 12:* Expectations are very strong that the priest or minister will remain loyal to the church. *Item 13:* Inequalities of authority and power between practitioners and clients—that is, between the clergy and church members—are often pronounced and are sometimes (though not always) great. In all of these ways, religious institutions resemble secular professional institutions.

## *Mainstream and Fringe Religious Groups*

Of course, the resemblance is strongest in the mainstream religious groups and especially in the liberal, traditionally white Protestant denominations within the National Council of Churches that are descended from colonial times, usually called the mainline, since their institutional structures tend to be most like those of the secular professions. The resemblance becomes increasingly tenuous as one moves further out among the fringe cults and sects, especially among the new religions. Not only does it seem less plausible to describe fringe cults and sects as religious *institutions,* but it also seems implausible to describe religious operatives at the fringes—various cult leaders, gurus, revivalists, self-appointed messiahs, and divines—as professionals in the same way that this term is applied to doctors, lawyers, and mainstream clergy. As these parallels become increasingly stretched, the use of the analytic apparatus of applied *professional* ethics—with its characteristic concern with role expectations and institutional structures— may seem less and less feasible.

However, in assessing fringe groups, ordinary moral intuitions typically come into greater play. As a public, we intuitively criticize institutional religion and its officials rather readily, at least in superficial ways. For instance, it is often said that arranged mass marriages, such as the October 1988 Unification Church marriage of 6,516 couples—many of whom did not speak the same language and had been introduced only a day or two before—are wrong, since they involve manipulation and the violation of privacy in an intimate personal relationship. Serpent handling is often said to be wrong because it imposes a deliberate risk of death. The solicitation methods of televangelists like Oral Roberts—who claimed in January 1987 that God would "call him home" if the additional $4.5 million needed to meet his $8 million goal was not raised by March 31—have been widely ridiculed because, like other media pitches, they are believed to involve phony threats, false promises, and other unsavory strategies. These are widespread public criticisms that, although they do not involve overt appeal to background moral theory, nevertheless employ the same nonspecialized, ordinary normative principles that form a culture's common general body of moral reasoning.

This body of moral reasoning employs all of the core principles of professional ethics, including nonmaleficence, beneficence, autonomy, and justice; it, too, can appeal for justification to background moral theory, including the partly incompatible theories of utilitarianism, Kantian deontology, and sometimes virtue ethics and divine-command theories, though it rarely makes explicit reference to them. However, in contrast to professional ethics, the insights of ordinary moral reasoning are developed with respect to a rather different range of characteristic problems. Role expectations are much less conspicuous as a focus of ethical scrutiny, despite attention to such roles as those of parent and friend. Problems that arise from the conflict of individual wants and interests with those of an institution occupy a much smaller role. In general, however, though there are very conspicuous differences in the way they are pursued, professional ethics and ordinary normative ethics differ more in their foci of concern and in the morally relevant phenomena to which they are sensitive than in their theoretical foundations.

Perhaps because it is not centrally concerned with professional roles and institutional structures, ordinary morality is the analytic apparatus we typically use in the casual critique of religion. It is often theoretically unsophisticated, but its pronouncements nevertheless function as genuine moral critique. Moral critique using ordinary morality, though comparatively crude, is what is going on when the news media hold the "bizarre" practices of fringe religious groups up to view. This is why such practices make good press: the public responds to these reports on the basis of moral views it already generally holds and which it is accustomed to employing in other contexts. For instance, the press gave front-page coverage several years ago to reports of disciplinary practices in the Northeast Kingdom Community Church in Island Pond, Vermont. Children were being whipped and beaten, the press reported, for very minor offenses. It described such occasions as the whipping of a thirteen-year-old girl with a slim wooden rod at intervals over seven-hour period and the beatings of small children who continued to cry after a single warning. A four-year-old boy, the press also reported, was disciplined for violating the group's rule against toys by pretending that the block he was playing with was a truck; he was struck fifteen or twenty times with a rod with his pants pulled down; and when he persisted in playing with the block as a toy, he was "scourged"—given two long beatings in two days.[4] We respond to such reports almost entirely on the basis of the same moral principles we employ in assessing ordinary cases of cruelty to children and child abuse—particularly the principle of nonmaleficence, prohibiting harm—often without reflection on what difference it makes, if any, that these beatings are a form of *religious* discipline.

That we are used to critiquing fringe religious practices in these crude, familiar ways does not, of course, entail that any or all of these practices—including mass marriages, serpent handling, media solicitation, child beating, or even more flagrant cases such as ritual sacrifices and the enforced suicides at Jonestown—are actually morally wrong. It is just that we are quite accustomed already to assessing them on ordinary moral grounds. However, while we often view practices in the fringe groups in this way, we tend not to make explicit moral assessments of the practices of mainstream groups. Of course, we do respond to scandals involving individual mainstream practitioners. Yet although we criticize deviant clergy, we do not pursue moral critique of the churches from which they deviate. This, no doubt, results at least in part from a kind of moral favoritism in religion: public attitudes have tended to give the benefit of any doubt to the mainstream groups but have regarded cults and new religions with suspicion. Yet surely it cannot be supposed that the moral problems of organized religion are all at the fringes, while the mainstream is above reproach; such judgments can be made only after careful ethical critique of both mainstream and fringe groups.

In effect, then, what I shall be using to examine moral problems in organized religion is a kind of critical "pincer" apparatus. It moves in on the one hand with a set of questions originating in professional ethics and a strategy of focusing on role expectations and institutionally generated problems. But it also presses in on the other with broadly accepted, common-sense, precritical judgments based in ordinary morality, even where universal agreement and consistency are not forthcoming, necessitated when the focus is on ordinary human relationships, not on the specialized roles and institutions of the professions. This dual approach can be employed whether or not it is supposed that professional ethics is strongly differentiated or involves a different set of principles than those of ordinary normative ethics. It need only be observed that professional ethics and ordinary morality typically focus on different sets of roles and situations; hence, the two prongs of the pincer tend to concentrate on the different types of moral problems familiar to each. Of course, the differences between professional ethics and ordinary morality are not just a matter of focus, but of many other associated matters: they have different historical concerns, literatures, academic bases, spokespersons, and so on. Furthermore, these two prongs of the pincer may not mesh perfectly and both have limitations—among them the tendency to fail to see all aspects of a situation. Nevertheless, this pincer approach, as an interactive strategy for moral inquiry, can greatly improve our view of specific morally relevant features of organized religion. It works in part by setting problems in the mainstream groups up against problems in the fringe cults and sects, thus sharpening our perceptions of each—even if, because their "professional" and institutional structures are not fully analogous, they cannot be analyzed in quite the same way. Thus in organized religion the view from the mainstream may tell us what to look for in the fringes and vice versa—even though one is viewed primarily through the eyes of professional ethics and the other through the eyes of ordinary morality.

Hence, even though the rationale for using the critical apparatus of professional ethics in examining organized religion is based on the similarity of institutional structures between the secular professions and mainstream religion, strongest in the mainline denominations, it is not necessary to determine which denominational ministries should count as professions or where the line between mainstream and fringe religious groups falls. This would be a loose boundary at best, but it is one that for our purposes there is little point in drawing. The insights of professional ethics often have considerable bearing on situations well outside mainstream bounds, and gut moral judgments about fringe groups often prove relevant to comparatively mainstream denominations. Indeed, several of the specific issues to be discussed here arise in both mainstream and fringe groups, though the more flagrant examples in the fringe groups lead us to look there for problems first.

## Additional Methodological Problems

A variety of other methodological problems challenge a project like this. Some are minor: for instance, there is no conveniently general term to cover the full range of religious functionaries from minister, priest, pastor, rabbi, and imâm to guru and cult leader—even though all of these hold institutionally assigned roles in religious organizations. Nor is there a convenient term for the adherents of the respective groups. I will variously use such constructs as "religious professional," "religious practitioner," "spiritual provider," and so on for the occupants of designated institutional roles, and "parishioner," "church member," "adherent," "laity," "the faithful," and so forth for the "clients" of various groups within organized religion. Nevertheless, all these labels will prove inadequate in the end.

Some of the methodological problems confronting a project such as this are neither trivial nor purely theoretical but involve pragmatic impediments. It is remarkably difficult to obtain reliable sources or to find reliable informants about some groups, especially those at the fringes. Nor is it easy to determine what counts as a reliable source or informant, even in the mainstream, since there are varying degrees of orthodoxy, loyal belief, and participant and practitioner informedness. Then, too, prejudice—both one's own and that of many sources and informants—is a constant liability, difficult to detect and eradicate.

Some methodological problems are conceptual. Paramount among these is the issue of what is to count as a religion or a religious group and how to differentiate these from quasi- and nonreligious groups and organizations. Here discussion is confined largely to groups generally recognized as religious, though much of the critique to be pursued could be extended to organizations less clearly defined as religious.

Finally, the most severe methodological problems have to do with the apparatus of analysis itself. While professional ethics can be of enormous value in encouraging us to look at organized religion for specific problems analogous to those characterizing the secular professions, it has considerable limitations. For one thing, in its current stage of development as a discipline, professional ethics is completely unequipped to deal with the central religious concepts, including such notions as *God, salvation, sin,* and so on. Nor is professional ethics prepared to tell us how we should treat items of doctrine in moral argumentation, how much weight to give individual religious beliefs, or how to handle unprovable, though not disprovable, metaphysical claims. Its own recognized principles include such utilitarian principles as beneficence and nonmaleficence, the Kantian-influenced principle of autonomy and respect for persons, and various forms of the principle of justice. But it cannot tell us whether principles of religious morality, such as obedience to God or loyalty to a church, ever override these.

Consequently, an attempt to make use of professional ethics as a method of analysis also forces us to address the matter of the bearing of ethical theory on religion generally. To the degree that professional ethics functions as a subdivision of ordinary (secular) normative ethics and does not appeal to distinctive ethical principles, prioritizations of principle, or other claims not grounded in secular ethical theory in general—that is, to the degree that the ethical principles of the professions are not strongly differentiated—the bearing of (secular) *professional* ethics on religion will not be any stronger than that of (secular) ethics generally. Where professional ethics does adopt distinctive principles (if it does), justification must be produced. In general, using professional ethics as a way of seeing problems in an area that has effectively been screened from view, though an extraordinarily fruitful process, will also present us with a number of formidable methodological difficulties.

Two approaches, involving two valuations of religious claims, must be ruled out in advance. One of them accepts religious claims, beliefs, and teachings, together with practices and ethical principles based on them, as true and binding. While for the inquiry here we will not initially have reason to challenge fundamental religious claims—for instance, the reality of God or the promise of salvation—an approach that accepts religious claims generally as true would also accept as true precisely those religious claims that appear to settle (or disguise) the very kinds of moral problems within religious institutions that are to be examined here. Hence, a generally accepting approach is not compatible with this inquiry; it would simply preclude recognition that there is an issue.

Alternatively, a metaphysically skeptical approach would reject religious claims altogether as without foundation in reality, counting them all false. On this valuation, institutional religion is simply a crazy house of pretenders doing pointless, silly, or cruel things to each other. However, whether or not this latter approach is metaphysically correct, it too is unable to distinguish among various kinds of religious claims and, by dismissing all religious claims generally, makes it impossible to see how religious structures generate genuine moral dilemmas. Since it, too, precludes recognition that there is any issue, this position would also be incompatible with the inquiry to be pursued here. Instead of these essentially theist or atheist approaches, a neutral procedural rule will be adopted here: While the conventional Judeo-Christian metaphysical framework may be used for the purpose of discussion, no truthvalue, whether true or false, may be assigned or presupposed for any of its background metaphysical assumptions and religious claims. This will be a difficult policy to follow in practice, for while a genuine, thoroughgoing agnostic posture is perhaps intellectually possible, it is psychologically discomforting. Nevertheless, complete restraint from either affirmation or denial of the traditional metaphysical and religious claims forming the Judeo-Christian tradition is necessary to examine the moral problems generated by its varieties of institutional religion, without either dismissing or insulating them from critique. The further methodological problems this raises, of course, will be addressed as they arise.

Concern with methodological issues will remain paramount throughout this book. Because the issues are so complex, the methodology will be developed progressively, in "nested" stages, attending to each component as necessary for the type of problem at hand. This cumulative methodology is intended to yield a strategy for pursuing not only the issues actually discussed here, but many additional issues concerning other varieties of institutional religious practice.

## *What This Inquiry Is Not*

Ethical inquiry into the institutional practice of religion, however probing, need not be perceived as antecedently disloyal to religion in general. It is not a critique of religious *belief.* The normative issues focus on developed practices within characteristic institutional structures rather than on articles of faith or canons of theology, and consider these latter only where specifically relevant to the issues themselves. Inquiry into the ethics of organized religion does not attempt, as does traditional philosophy of religion, to examine the coherence or intelligibility of religious doctrines or teachings (except insofar as conceptual clarity is necessary for the discussion of moral issues), nor does it attempt to dismiss religious beliefs on atheist or other grounds. It neither asserts nor denies the existence of God, nor does it assert or deny the desirability of religious belief and practice in general, but treats these neutrally as objects for moral reflection and scrutiny. Indeed, a normative ethics of religious practice must focus on practical moral problems involved in the institutional practice of religion as far as possible independently of the content or correctness of religious belief. This does not mean that we can conduct our inquiry in ignorance of the beliefs and doctrine of the groups concerned but rather that those beliefs and doctrines will attract our moral concern only in a quite carefully limited way.

This sort of inquiry, moreover, is not a matter of what is usually called "Christian ethics," nor is it directed toward issues of how believers should live. Instead it is an inquiry into how religious groups should treat or refrain from treating their adherents. It is not an inquiry into what believers should or should not do for religion, but into what organized religion should or should not do to believers.

To be sure, this inquiry does not really touch the so-called invisible church of intimate, private belief and spiritual communion. Rather, it concerns itself only with externally observable, institutionally identifiable practices. Thus it remains in many ways an external critique. The practices considered, however, cannot simply be dismissed on the ground that they do not touch "the church"; they are certainly part, if not all, of it, and—in view of their traditionally protected status—eminently deserving of scrutiny.

It might be wondered whether an inquiry such as this must be restricted to Western or Judeo-Christian religious groups. Only such groups will be examined here, but similar normative inquiries could well be pursued within other world faiths. Certain issues might loom larger in other traditions—for example, the protection of such societal hierarchies as caste systems in Hinduism, the promotion of personal detachment in Buddhism, Islam's celebration of martyrdom in religious war, Shintoism's attribution of moral precedent in ancestor worship, and so on. In focusing attention in this study largely on Christian groups, I do not wish to suggest that Christianity has a monopoly on moral problems, nor that other traditions are free from them. However, because the analytic framework of applied professional ethics is based on and adapted to Western professional institutions, it is more likely to identify characteristic problems in Western, primarily Christian religious groups, since it is these groups that exhibit an institutional structure most like the secular, Western professions.

As a culture, we are heavy consumers of services offered by religion and heavy contributors to religion's support. The vast majority of Americans say they believe in God; 92 percent indicate a religious preference; nearly 60 percent are members of churches or other organized religious groups; and 40 percent say they go to church in a typical week.[5] Churches are the biggest recipients of charitable contributions, far outstripping organizations devoted to education, health, the arts, or political or social causes. Churches, including mainstream and, increasingly, evangelical and fundamentalist ones, have enormous political influence. Organized religion also affects persons who are nonbelievers and who have no direct contact with religious groups, since it remains a tremendous force in shaping the culture in which we live. After all, organized religion is at least as powerful a force in shaping the character of our culture as the institutions of medicine, law, and other secular professions. It is extraordinary, then, that we have not yet come to consider whether it is possible to examine the institution of religion in the same way that we examine the secular professions. I hope, in this exploratory book, to open this vast new area to the scrutiny of applied professional ethics, the kind of scrutiny to which I think organized religion is entitled and which it urgently deserves.

# CHAPTER 1

# Telling Confessions

## *Confidentiality in the*

## *Clergy-Church Member Relationship*

In many essential ways, the dilemmas of confidentiality confronting members of the clergy—whether priests, ministers, preachers, or rabbis—are much like those faced by doctors, lawyers, psychiatrists, accountants, and other practitioners in the secular consulting professions. Of course, the problem of confidentiality arises in interpersonal contexts in everyday secular life, but it arises with particular force in professional-client relationships. In the consulting professions, the practitioner typically has sustained, direct personal contact with the patient or client, and the usual course of professional practice requires the professional to make use of personal information provided by the patient or client. Disclosure is unidirectional, going from the client to the professional but not the other way around. The patient tells the doctor his symptoms and the client tells the lawyer her legal problems, but the doctor and the lawyer do not—as a matter of institutional practice—confide in their patients or clients. The problem of confidentiality is more acute in contexts in which confidential disclosure is not only institutionally elicited or required but where it is the central objective of the transaction, as, for instance, in psychiatry, and where the consequences to the client for failing to disclose personal information, as in medicine, and of having the information revealed, as in law, can be quite bad. If these things are so, however, the problem of confidentiality in the clergy-church member relationship will not only resemble that which arises in physician-patient, attorney-client, and other secular professional relationships, but will resemble it in its most acute forms.

These dilemmas will not be easy to resolve. Consider the following three cases, taken from three religious traditions. All three cases are true.

1. In a much-publicized case in Langenberg, West Germany, several years ago, Jürgen Bartsch, a fifteen-year-old butcher's apprentice, confessed to his priest that he had committed a murder. The priest attempted to persuade Bartsch to give himself up to the police. When he was unable to do so, the priest followed Roman Catholic church law requiring absolute confidentiality of the confessional and did not reveal information about the murder or Bartsch's intentions. Bartsch committed three more murders—all of them of eleven-year-old boys, all of whom he subjected to sexual torture prior to killing them—before he was caught four years later.[1]

2. In 1985 in Ogden, Utah, Clair Harward, a member of the Church of Jesus Christ of Latter-day Saints, learned that he had AIDS. Convinced he would go to hell when he died and seeking spiritual guidance, Harward admitted to his bishop that he was homosexual. The bishop, following official Mormon church policy, instituted internal church court proceedings leading to Harward's excommunication. The bishop also asked Harward for a list of people with whom he had had homosexual contact; soon afterward, Harward's roommate was also excommunicated.[2] Harward died on March 16, 1986, at the age of twenty-six.

3. In 1981 in Collinsville, Oklahoma, a rumor reached the elders of the Church of Christ that one of their members, a divorcee named Marian Guinn, was having an affair with the former town mayor, Pat Sharp. The elders summoned Guinn, insisted that she terminate the affair, and warned her that if she did not do so they would "tell it to the church." Guinn refused. She sent the church a letter of resignation and forbade the elders to mention her name in church except to say that she had withdrawn. Nev-

ertheless, the following Sunday, the elders denounced Guinn's "sins of fornication" to the entire congregation in the church.

All three cases involve a religious authority who comes to know that a member of the religious group has committed an act or is engaged in behavior that the group identifies as sinful. All three involve individual confession by the deviant member directly to the religious professional, and all three involve confessions that took place in private. It is safe to assume that in all three cases the individual making the confession did not want the matter publicly revealed, since otherwise he or she would have done so directly. In all three cases, revealing the matter posed grave consequences both for the person confessing and for others involved.

In spite of these similarities, the responses of the religious professionals in the three cases were radically different. Hearing the murder confession of the West German butcher's apprentice, the Catholic priest maintained absolute confidentiality, even at the cost of three additional lives. The Mormon bishop related not only Clair Harward's own confession but also information about his homosexual partner to an internal church court system. By announcing Marian Guinn's transgression to an entire congregation in a small, talkative town, the Church of Christ elders in effect made the details of her sexual life public.

These differing responses were by no means irregular in the traditions of each church. In each of the three cases the religious practitioners were conscientiously following practices dictated by their groups. The Catholic priest obeyed the requirement of absolute confessional confidentiality formulated in canon law; the Mormon bishop followed policies outlined in his denomination's manual for officials of the church; and the elders of the Church of Christ followed their church's fundamental insistence on obedience to New Testament scripture. Thus, it may be tempting to explain that these practitioners were simply doing what a Catholic priest, a Mormon bishop, and a Church of Christ elder are supposed to do; each was obeying the basic role expectation of his church. Because each acted as his denomination requires, it might then be claimed that there can be no real moral question concerning these cases. They were not deviant practitioners, but practitioners acting in accord with the religiously established norms for their denominations. Since these norms are *religiously* established and are the norms for *religious* organizations, they are not subject to moral critique.

Such explanations are to be roundly rejected. As a central operating principle in the analysis here, it cannot be assumed that because a certain course of action is required of a religious professional by the denomination's doctrines, beliefs, or policies, it provides adequate justification for so acting, nor does it settle the relevant moral questions. Antecedent denominational role expectations are also to be rejected as justificatory, both in general and in the three specific cases at hand. On the contrary, although the religious professionals in the three cases acted entirely in accord with the requirements of their denominations, in each case substantial moral issues remain.

By beginning with considerations from professional ethics, it is possible to see how these and similar cases of religious confidentiality are more complex than they appear initially and why they cannot be easily answered by an appeal to denominational requirements. The issue of confidentiality has been extensively examined in secular professional contexts, and what secular professional ethics has to say about dilemmas of confidentiality reveals many features of similar problems in religious contexts. Of the groups involved in the three true cases mentioned here, Catholicism and Mormonism will be considered first, with further complications introduced by the practices of the Churches of Christ. This inquiry will raise formidable methodological problems, and this chapter, like those following, will thus have both normative and methodological concerns.

## *Confidentiality in the Secular Professions*

In the secular professions, most discussion assumes that a professional has prima facie obligations of confidentiality to the client; further argument focuses on the circumstances in which these obligations may or may not be overridden. Circumstances in which the professional's initial obligation of confidentiality to the client are overridden are variously said to include those necessary to

1. prevent harm to the client
2. prevent harm to the professional
3. prevent harm to third parties
4. rectify past harm to third parties
5. prevent harm to the profession
6. prevent harm to society
7. observe the law[3]

The permissibility of violations of confidentiality in these circumstances is variously disputed in all of the professions, however, and even though most professional organizations have adopted policies that stipulate specific practices regulating confidentiality for their members, the issue remains pressing. Furthermore, policies governing confidentiality have varied widely even within specific professions. Medicine, for instance, has adopted different policies at different times, from the extremely strong requirement formulated by the World Medical Association in 1949, which would permit disclosure in none of conditions 1–7 above:

> A doctor owes to his patient absolute secrecy on all which has been confided to him or which he knows because of the confidence entrusted to him.

to the extremely weak requirement adopted by the American Medical Association in 1971, which would permit disclosure in at least conditions 1, 2, 3, 6, and 7:

> A physician may not reveal the confidences entrusted to him in the course of medical attendance, or the deficiencies he may observe in the character of his patients, unless he is required to do so by law or unless it becomes necessary in order to protect the welfare of the individual or of the society.

These policies are usually said to be based on the Hippocratic Oath's requirement that

> Whatever, in connection with my professional practice, or not in connection with it, I see or hear, in the life of men, which ought not to be spoken abroad, I will not divulge, as reckoning that all such should be kept secret.

984. §1 Even if every danger of revelation is excluded, a confessor is absolutely forbidden to use knowledge acquired from confession when it might harm the penitent.

§2 One who is placed in authority can in no way use for external governance knowledge about sins which he has received in confession at any time.[5]

This policy is far stronger than that employed in any of the secular professions. In principle, at least, it admits no violations whatsoever, regardless of legal requirements, threatened harms, or other circumstances. Once given, the seal of confession is to remain inviolate—even after the penitent's death. The confessor may not reveal confessional information to protect a third party, even when that person would suffer grave physical, emotional, or spiritual harm, or even, as in the case of Jürgen Bartsch, the West German butcher's apprentice, to prevent someone else's death. The confessor may not reveal information to rectify past injustices or injuries, even when other persons are being punished for the confessant's crimes. Nor may the confessor reveal the information to anyone even if that person has the best interests of the penitent at heart (for instance, a concerned physician, psychotherapist, or family member), no matter how great the benefits to the penitent may be and no matter how great the harms avoided—even if he could save the penitent from death.

Nor may the priest reveal confessional material in order to observe the law. Rather, the priest who is legally compelled to testify in a court of law is instructed to assert, even under oath (on the Bible, to God), that he knows nothing of the matter confessed—though, as we shall see, under U.S. law such situations rarely arise. Further, the priest may not reveal confessed information to prevent harm to himself. If, for instance, he knows (to cite a problem often discussed by medieval casuists) that the wine in the communion chalice has been poisoned and that by not drinking it he would reveal that he has learned it to be poisoned from confession, he must put the cup to his lips and die. He must not break confidentiality to preserve the church from scandal or to prevent other serious threats to the church. Finally, he must not reveal confessed material even if so doing would prevent grave wrongs to society as a whole. Penalties may be imposed on the penitent, but if so, it must be possible for the penitent to satisfy them privately or anonymously; it is prohibited to impose penalties from which other persons could infer anything about the fact or content of the penitent's confession. Although today's less conservative writers might not describe the absoluteness of confessional confidentiality so starkly, one theologian of the 1940s insisted: "Even though a priest, by violating the seal [of confession], could prevent the outbreak of a prolonged, devastating, world-wide war, he would, nevertheless, still be bound to absolute secrecy."[6] Not even the pope can release a confessor from his obligation to maintain the confidentiality of the confessional, according to these interpreters of canon law, and there are *no* consequences so grave that the seal may be broken.[7] The announced penalty for a priest who does break the seal of confession is automatic excommunication from the church. Although in rare cases the priest may refuse to grant absolution, he may *never* reveal the confession once the seal of confidentiality has been given.

Thus, the Catholic position favors one extreme of a variety of possible responses to the moral dilemmas of confidentiality. In practice, some priests skirt this absolute requirement in various ways—for instance, by leaking anonymous warnings to the police or by advising potential victims in ways that will protect them where serious harm or death is at stake. Alternatively, while many priests hearing confessions urge the confessant to bring the matter up again outside the confessional (the priest is prohibited from mentioning a matter raised in confession to the confessant outside the confessional, though the confessant may reintroduce the topic), since—as the priest but not always the confessant knows—requirements of confidentiality outside the confessional are not as strong. Nevertheless, deviations from canon law on confessional confidentiality are apparently infrequent and the church's teaching is virtually universally accepted and defended as absolute.

## *Mormon Practice*

The Mormon church, in contrast, incorporates in its practices what appear to be thoroughgoing violations of confidentiality. For Mormons, confession per se is not a scheduled ritual practice. It does not take place in special locations or in structures such as confessional booths. It is not accompanied by the recitation of specific formulas or the performance of ritual motions or gestures. Nor is confession anonymous, since the identity of the confessant is not protected from the confessor. Nevertheless, private confession does occur in two principal forms in Mormon practice.

The first is an informal consequence of the very high level of social intervention by religious officials. The Mormon bishop (which office in the religious hierarchy, while not a full-time profession, is roughly comparable to that of the local parish priest in Catholicism and is likewise restricted to males) is expected to assume an active role in the spiritual guidance of church members in his area. Discussion of personal matters of belief or behavior may be initiated by the member, but may also be initiated by the bishop. The bishop is explicitly permitted to initiate counseling during periods when members are "subject to temptation," such as courtship, divorce, and marital difficulties.[8] Mormonism also has a system of "home teachers" who call periodically at members' homes and who, although functioning primarily to promote the economic wellbeing and security of members, may also discuss matters of behavior and belief. In these situations of active intervention in domestic life by religious officials, sensitive material may include not only explicit statements or confessions made by the individual, but also whatever is observed by the bishop or home teacher about the individual's circumstances, habits, and way of life.

The second, more formal variety of confession occurs in the interview a member must have with his or her bishop in order to receive a "temple recommend" or permit to enter the temple. This interview requires the applicant to respond to a set of questions, including questions about adherence to doctrinally mandated abstinences (avoidance of alcohol, tobacco, addictive drugs, and stimulants), questions about religious beliefs, and questions about sexual relationships and practices. The member is expected to renew the temple recommend annually; a recommend must be obtained for permission to enter the temple to attend or participate in special rites such as weddings and baptisms.

When a member of the church confesses certain sins, either in informal interaction with the bishop, in the temple recommend interview, or when evidence of sin comes to light from other sources, the bishop decides whether to impose formal church discipline. This is done by convening a church court, now called a "disciplinary council." The case of a male member in full standing is presented to as many as sixteen persons (twelve members plus the stake president, his two counselors, and a secretary); a woman is tried before a bishop's council of three. One copy of the court report is stored in the confidential files of the ward or stake and a second is transmitted to central church headquarters.

The Mormon church is not the only one which maintains an internal court system for disciplining members. As will be discussed in chapter 4, many mainstream churches (including the Episcopal, Presbyterian, United Methodist, and Roman Catholic churches) have a system of internal church courts, either standing courts or courts constituted on an ad hoc basis. In most, a trial by church court can be held to examine either deviancy in belief or behavior that violates the standards of the church. Nevertheless, although many mainstream groups do have internal courts, certain distinctive features of the Mormon court system raise particularly compelling moral questions. These center on the issue of confidentiality.

In Mormonism, as in Catholicism, the group's scriptural texts contain no explicit statements about confidentiality in voluntary confession. The principal exception is the requirement in Doctrine and Covenants 42:89–93 that "if any shall offend in secret, he or she shall be rebuked in secret." The *General Handbook of Instructions,* a periodically updated manual which regulates the functions of bishops, stake presidents, and other church officials (popularly known as the "Bishop's Handbook"), asserts that strict confidentiality is required: "Bishops, stake presidents, and counselors . . . have a solemn duty to keep confidential all information members give to them in confessions and interviews. . . . Information received in a member's confession cannot be used as evidence in a disciplinary council without the member's permission" (p. 10-2). Members of the disciplinary council may discuss the matter only among themselves or with specific church officials. It is regarded as a gross breach of confidentiality for them to discuss it carelessly with others.

In Mormonism, confidential material may be divulged, whether to an internal church court, to civil authorities, or to others involved, if the individual consents to the disclosure. In some cases, the individual readily gives permission, particularly if he or she believes it is necessary for salvation. However, the costs for the individual of divulging confessional information may be high. While lesser penalties may be imposed if the infraction took place some time ago or if there is evidence of complete reformation and repentance (as determined by the council), in some infractions the likelihood of excommunication is great. Discipline is also a function of social status and visibility: excommunication is indicated for "Church leaders or prominent members whose transgressions seriously damage the reputation or significantly dilute the moral influence of the Church" (*General Handbook,* p. 10-5), and a disciplinary council must be held if the member's transgression is both serious and "widely known" (p. 10-4).

Within a tightly knit religious group like the Mormons—and others such as the Collinsville Church of Christ—release of confessional information may affect not only the individual's membership status, but may also profoundly affect a member's economic and social status. Particularly in population areas that have a high concentration of Mormons, excommunication may mean stigma for oneself and one's family, disruption of personal relationships, and the loss of one's job, since other members of the religious community may refuse to associate either socially or economically with an excommunicated person. These effects may be particularly pronounced if the individual has been prominent in the church or in public life. Of course, some excommunicated members who continue to attend church receive considerable emotional and social support; nevertheless, the consequences of an infraction can be harsh (particularly for infractions like homosexuality) and the confessant may be quite reluctant to grant permission for the disclosure of such information, if he or she is willing to confess at all.

The fact that Mormonism claims to protect confidentiality in confession, however, does not relieve the bishop or stake president who comes to know of a member's transgression of the opportunity or obligation to convene a disciplinary council. For most infractions, the bishop or stake president may impose formal discipline at his discretion. He examines the initial evidence, the amount of time elapsed since the infraction, and other matters and considers whether a proceeding is warranted. However, when there is evidence of particular infractions—murder, incest, being a "predator" (that is, "having tendencies that are a serious threat to other persons") or committing a serious transgression while holding a prominent church position—a disciplinary council *must* be convened, whether or not the individual admits the transgression or consents to attend the proceedings. In other serious transgressions, including adultery, fornication, homosexual relations, rape, child abuse, spouse abuse, theft, fraud, embezzlement, sale of illegal drugs, abortion (except in rape, incest, jeopardized maternal health, or severe fetal defect), and transsexual operations, although the bishop or stake president is not required to call a court, he may do so at his—not the member's—discretion. Initiating disciplinary proceedings against Clair Harward, the AIDS victim who confessed his homosexuality to his bishop, was in no way an exception in Mormon practice; it has been the church's officially stated procedure for dealing with homosexuality, at least where homosexual activity is not terminated.[9]

Furthermore, the obligation of confidentiality not only does not prohibit the bishop or stake president from convening a council against the wishes of the member, it directs him to gather evidence about the transgression from other sources (though prohibiting electronic surveillance devices, hidden cameras, and the like) and to urge the member to agree to release the evidence. As the Bishop's Handbook requires, the bishop or stake president should "attempt to persuade" the member to release the confession for use in the disciplinary council; to do so, he should "emphasize" to the member "that refusal reflects a lack of contrition and repentance, preventing justice and mercy from operating fully for the good of the transgressor." If the infraction violates the law, the bishop is to "urge" the transgressor to report it to governmental authorities; if it is adultery, to confess it to his or her spouse, and if it is fornication by a young, unmarried person, to inform his or her parents (p. 10-2).

In this tradition, the details of official procedures for dealing with serious sins are not explicitly stated to the general membership. The Bishop's Handbook provides the official statement of procedures to be followed, but is distributed to officials only and is not available to the general membership, except that a member's own bishop is permitted to discuss specific requirements. Rank-and-file members nevertheless discover, through their own experience or that of friends, the details of the policies in force; most Mormons are aware that serious sins are addressed in a court. Many, however, do not realize that disclosure of information gathered about them will occur with or without their consent and that voluntary confession does not always end the matter. Although reliable empirical data are difficult to obtain, bishops and stake presidents often acknowledge that the member generally brings expectations of confidentiality to the initial confession, which begins as a private admission of disturbing personal matters, made to a spiritual counselor one trusts.

Disclosure of information may involve a still more extensive violation of expectations of confidentiality. Grounds for disciplinary action that concern sexual sins (usually fornication, adultery, and homosexual relations) involve activities with a partner or partners. The bishop may ask the confessant for the identity of the partner(s), as Clair Harward's bishop did; failure to reply is interpreted as evidence of inadequate repentance. However, if the partner is identified and is a member of the church, the bishop is permitted or required, depending in part on the precise nature of the infraction and the status of the individuals involved, to report it to the bishop of the partner. The Bishop's Handbook stipulates that when "members of different wards commit transgressions with each other, and when one has disclosed to his bishop the identity of the other transgressor, the bishop to whom the disclosure was made should consult with the bishop of the other member" (p. 10-2). Once this information has been communicated, the bishop of the partner may confront him or her with evidence of complicity in the sinful acts and, if he deems it appropriate, convene another disciplinary council. The second disclosure may also be made with or without the consent of either the initial confessant or of the partner, and the disciplinary proceeding may also result in disfellowship or excommunication for the partner. There was nothing irregular in the bishop's use of Clair Harward's confession to bring charges against the roommate as well.

Adherents sometimes claim that reporting confessions within a closed hierarchy is not a violation of confidentiality. However, although church officers are required to keep the proceedings of a disciplinary action confidential, in a close religious community the fact that proceedings are being held is often a matter of widespread knowledge. If the council results in disfellowship or excommunication, the action is announced to the ward priesthood executive committee (for males) or to the ward Relief Society president (for females). If the grounds for excommunication are "preaching false doctrine," "predatory tendencies," polygamy, or other activities considered a threat to others, the action may be generally announced and members thereby warned (*General Handbook,* p. 10-8). Even if the specific grounds for excommunication are not announced, they are relatively easy to infer within a highly integrated community. The result is generally that the substance of one's confession, if not its precise details, does not remain confidential, whether one consents to its disclosure or not. As a former Mormon recounted the events following his trial for adultery,

> The next step was the worst: announcement to the Priesthood Meeting. The wording now used is " . . . has been excommunicated for action unbecoming a Christian." Immediately all one's neighbors know, and the Church defends itself against the charge that this breaches confidentiality by pointing to the vague wording. Actually I would have preferred a more direct announcement, if an announcement had to be made at all. Speculation becomes rampant, in the face of this type of announcement, as to what the sin actually was. Are you a homosexual? Was it child molesting? Did you steal Church funds? So one is then forced to clarify things with befuddled neighbors and friends.[10]

The two sharply contrasting confidentiality policies of the Catholic and Mormon churches illustrate extremes among groups practicing private confession to a religious official. It is in the most serious cases that the differences between Catholic and Mormon practice are most conspicuous: if the person seeking spiritual advice confesses a murder, for instance, as the butcher's apprentice did, or a sexual practice regarded as sinful, as Clair Harward did, the Catholic priest is required to keep it secret, while the Mormon bishop is required to bring the information (though not the confession itself) before a church court. Yet even in milder cases where the differences in practice are not conspicuous, the rationales underlying the policies of the two groups are quite different.

## Clergy-Penitent Privilege in the Law

Inspection of the law, if taken to reflect moral principles, provides little resolution of the issues. In the United States, clergy-penitent privilege is preserved in varying degrees in nearly all states.[11] This legal principle grants ministers of religion immunity from being compelled to testify in a court of law on matters communicated to them in confession. However, clergy privilege has not been recognized in England at least since the time of the Restoration, and some U.S. states—for instance, West Virginia—do not recognize it at all. The Federal Rules of Evidence defer to state statutes on the matter.

In some states that do recognize clergy privilege, all communications from confessant to clergy are protected. However, some courts distinguish between communications that are penitential in character or which seek spiritual advice or absolution and those that merely convey information, protecting only the former. Some states also protect any observations or inferences the cleric may make about the individual's beliefs, behavior, mental state, or character. In some states, the communication must be a "confession"; in addition, in others it is privileged only if the communication has been made in the course of discipline enjoined by the rule of practice of the clergy's denomination. Further, in some states, the penitent must also be of the same denomination. At least one state has suggested that such statutes would apply only to confessions made by Catholics to a Catholic priest, since Protestant denominations and non-Christian groups do not as a rule make confession a sacrament. However, in many states voluntary confession not required by church discipline has also been held to qualify for the privilege. In some states, the protection is the right of the clergy; in others, it is granted only if the confessant claims the privilege.

In practice, many clergy believe themselves to be protected under the landmark 1931 Minnesota case *In re Swenson*. In this case, a Lutheran minister had been visited in the parsonage by the husband in a divorce case who wished to talk with the pastor in private; in a lawsuit, the wife later attempted to compel the pastor to disclose what the husband had said to the pastor. The court upheld the pastor's refusal to testify. However, in some cases courts have held that confessions are not protected if not made in the discharge of a religious *duty* (*Knight v. Lee*); if the person hearing the confession is not a minister (in one case, the confessor was an elder and deacon rather than a pastor); or if the cleric was not acting in a professional capacity as, for instance, when a priest acts as a notary in drawing a deed.

Statutes enacted since 1958 have tended to broaden the privilege to cover more than penitential confession and to eliminate the requirement that confession be required of the individual by the discipline of the church in order for it to be privileged. Nevertheless, the status of communications in situations such as pastoral marriage counseling is often unclear. Recently enacted statutes requiring professionals and others to report child abuse raise still further questions about the status of the clergy-penitent privilege. Some states—for instance, New Hampshire—have a mandatory reporting requirement for ministers, priests, rabbis, Christian Science practitioners, and others to report child abuse, and grant no privilege; some states have conflicting laws, as Utah did until its legislature remedied the situation, one granting clergy-penitent privilege and another requiring all professionals with knowledge of child abuse to report it; and at least one state—Texas—does not recognize privilege in child abuse cases for communications between clergy and penitents but does so for attorneys and their clients.

Legal theorists continue to dispute the desirability of laws granting clergy privilege. Since, as one commentator put it, granting clergy privilege involves the suppression of evidence, while the rules of evidence are designed to promote the successful development of truth with a view to attaining a just result, the judicial process is thwarted to the extent that evidence of this nature is made inadmissible; yet the benefits to society in protecting opportunities for confidential spiritual advice well outweigh this loss.[12] On the other hand, it is often argued that if the statutes were made too broad, they would protect not only genuine ministers of religion but self-ordained and "mail-order" clerics, profiteers from groups with only marginal religious status, and other opportunists seeking immunity. Consequently, this view holds, jurisdictions should not broaden the privilege very far. In any case, state laws that grant or restrict clergy privilege raise compelling constitutional questions under the free exercise and establishment clauses. Even if the law were uniform, unambiguous, and constitutionally sound, it would not resolve the ethical issues. For the most part, the law has simply respected the declared policies of major religious groups; constitutional protections would simply reflect these policies.

Recently, focus on clergy privilege has been eclipsed by issues involving the disclosure of material in church discipline. The issue is not whether there shall be protection for clergy who do not wish to reveal a church member's confession, but whether there shall be protection for clergy who *do* reveal it. This is the issue in *Guinn v. Collinsville Church of Christ,* which we shall consider later in this chapter. The law is unsettled on this issue, which raises interesting new dilemmas beyond those of clergy privilege. But neither the law's traditional treatment of clergy privilege nor its initial decisions in the issue of church discipline do much to answer the questions that concern us here—what *ought* to be the policies of religious groups with respect to confessional confidentiality and what justifications, if any, would be sufficient for violations of confidentiality in an institutional religious setting?

Even if the law provides little guidance, ethical analysis can frame the question: When, if ever, may the religious professional violate confidentiality by revealing the confessed matter or any information about it, by identifying the person confessing or any partners in the act confessed; or by engaging in any activity that might reasonably be interpreted to indicate the nature or source of the confession? This is a *moral* question, not a legal one. Above all, it is not a purely theological question. It is one that can and should be addressed in much the same way as questions concerning confidentiality in the secular professions are addressed.

## *Methodological Considerations*

It may be objected that such a question cannot be entertained since practices concerning confession are doctrinally grounded and therefore inaccessible to ethical critique. For Catholics, the inviolability of the seal of confession is dictated by the code of canon law, part of the fundamental discipline of the church; confession itself is a sacrament, a core dogma of the faith. The Collinsville Church of Christ bases its practices on a literal interpretation of New Testament scripture; for this group, the Bible is the ultimate authority. Although the Mormon Bishop's Handbook is not available to the general membership, it is nevertheless a record of church-adopted, doctrinally based procedure; it serves to state the church's official policy in matters where issues of confidentiality might arise. Yet although all three views are matters of doctrine or of official regulation, this fact cannot give them privileged status in an examination of the ethical issues of confidentiality in religious confession.

This objection introduces the first of the serious methodological problems that scrutiny of religious practice using the apparatus of applied professional ethics raises: the status of doctrinal or doctrine-based assertions in moral argumentation. If such assertions enter the argument as premises, then the issue is antecedently decided. If they are excluded from the argument, only truncated conceptions of religious practice remain. The problem here is to discover a way of treating doctrinal assertions that neither trivializes the problem nor begs the question altogether. Nevertheless, there is a way to handle these assertions by considering them in their varied historical contexts: the issue of confessional confidentiality provides a particularly illuminating context in which to see how this strategy works.

Let us begin by examining confession-related items of doctrine with reference to the institutional structures and practices from which they originate or within which they have developed. In tracing the history of doctrinal assertions concerning confession and confidentiality, we find in Roman Catholicism a continuing developmental process from the earliest period of Christian history to the church's present position. We will also find a parallel (although shorter) developmental process in Mormonism, although it leads to a radically different conclusion. The two histories provide a basis for assigning particular doctrinal assertions a specific status in moral argumentation; they will also provide the outlines of a method for determining the appropriate status of doctrinal claims about any religious matter within any religious group.

The biblical texts James 5:16, Matthew 16:19, and John 20:23 are commonly cited as the scriptural bases for the practice of confession in Christianity. However, the precise nature of this mandate is far from clear; it is by no means evident precisely what practice or practices are required by the injunction to confess. James, the most straightforward of these texts, simply directs, "Therefore confess your sins to one another," but does not specify whether it shall be done privately or openly, singly or in groups, nor does it say how explicit the confession shall be, or what the hearer or hearers shall do with the information received.

Once the initial doctrinal mandate which a tradition recognizes is identified, however vague or indeterminate its expression may be, it is then possible to examine the historical ways in which it has been interpreted within a given religious group. Relatively little is certain about the actual practice of confession in the earliest days of the Christian church. While it has long been believed that the earliest forms of Christian confession were public and that the individual recited his or her sins before the assembled church community, some scholars now hold that the act of confession may have been predominantly private. Nevertheless, the acts of satisfaction—the evidences of one's status as a penitent—were clearly public: the individual wore a special penitential robe (the *cilicium*), stood among the ranks of public penitents in a restricted area of the church, and did not participate in the sacrament. From these facts, of course, others could infer something of the nature and gravity of the sins committed. During the period of penance, strict continence was required; the penitent could not marry, nor participate in military service, nor engage in most forms of commercial activity.

The period of penance lasted as long as several years (or longer, during the era of Tertullian and Cyprian), and an individual was permitted to do penance only once. If the infraction was repeated, the person was excluded from the church.[13]

To what degree the details of personal confessions were also made public is not clear. There is evidence—as, for instance, a letter written by Pope Leo I in 459—that some penitents were compelled to read an explicit list of personal sins in public; Leo rejects this practice as an abuse.[14] Some sources claim that Leo instituted private confession initially for priests and deacons in order to protect the church from the scandal that would otherwise arise from public knowledge of cleric misbehavior, and that the practice of private confession was later extended to the laity. More probably, it was the Celtic monks of the sixth century who introduced the new mode of penance, incorporating both secret confession to the priest and reconciliation without public penance, defamation, or legal consequences: one's sins became a private matter and were not for public display.[15] Some of the more fanciful accounts, often from later antipapist sources, claim that with the establishment of private auricular confession, personal abuses of penitents by priests became rampant, particularly the abuse of female penitents. One claims that the confessional booth was introduced (in Spain) to prevent such abuses: it prevented the confessor and penitent from direct vision and, more importantly, from touching.[16] Whatever the details of its origin, however, the booth also provided, for the first time, virtual anonymity for the penitent (though he or she could still be seen entering and leaving the booth) and complete privacy for the act of confession. With this, the possibility of full confidentiality first emerged, and with it the possibility of violating confidentiality. This, of course, gave rise to the ethical issues of whether confidentiality ought ever to be violated and, if so, for what reasons. By the time of the Council of Trent (1551), the issue had been settled in the eyes of the church: canons 983 and 984 assured complete confidentiality in all matters of confession and thus in effect rejected the claim that there ever could be sufficient reason for violating confidentiality. The church's position on this issue has remained unchanged since that time.

Mormon practices, too, display an evolving historical development, although their period of development is comparatively short.[17] During the lifetime of the church's founder, Joseph Smith, there was no institution of private confession; all confessions were public, made to the entire group. The bishop did not develop a pastoral and counseling function, in which private confession might occur, until after the group's exodus from Illinois in 1846 and arrival in Utah in 1847. During the nineteenth century, testimony meetings held the first Sunday of every month constituted the primary vehicle for public confession. Private confession generally took place in an adversary setting following investigation of a complaint or rumor about a member; confession followed confrontation with the evidence. During some periods of Mormon history, public confession was mandated by the church (for instance, on the occasion of the dedication of the Salt Lake Temple in April 1893), but by the early twentieth century public confession was being discouraged. Mormonism, according to some scholars, was becoming less insular and increasingly aware of its public image, and thus sought to avoid practices that might invite public review or criticism. Although monthly testimony meetings are still a major part of Mormon practice, members are now discouraged from giving explicit or general confessions of deviant beliefs or behavior on these occasions; personal confession is typically made privately to one's bishop.

Not all religious groups that treat James, Matthew, and John as scriptural have developed private confessional practices. In some groups, direct public confession is encouraged or required and is not preceded by any form of private confession. Here no guarantees of confidentiality are given nor are expectations of confidentiality raised: confession is expected to be made in front of the entire assembly. Other denominations, including much of mainline Protestantism, hold that confession can be made only directly by the confessant to the deity. These groups recognize no institutional or ritual practice of confession at all, and their closest approach is in private pastoral counseling. In some groups, confession is purely formal: it involves reciting a general acknowledgment of sin, but includes no specific description. Some groups, especially some of the cults and new religions, practice what is probably best described as forced confession, where issues of confidentiality are entirely beside the point. While the circumstances are sometimes private, no guarantees of confidentiality are given or understood. But of those groups that have developed private confessional practices, all have faced the same ethical dilemma: what ought the religious professional do when revelation of the confessed material, obtained in private under expectations of confidentiality, would have substantial consequences for the confessant or for other persons or institutions? Catholicism and Mormonism, the two initial specimen groups here, both take the same biblical texts as scriptural but have developed radically different answers to the moral problem that adherence to the mandate in those texts raises.

Surveying the developmental history of confessional practices, however fragmentary the specific details, permits us to articulate a general methodological principle governing the study of ethical issues in religious practice. Once we see that a practice precedes the doctrinal solution that is put forth to resolve the ethical problem the practice itself raises, we are able to differentiate those doctrines or recognized policies that develop in response to an institutional practice from those that antecedently mandate that practice. The problem of confidentiality is not associated with religious confession per se, nor is it a direct consequence of the fundamental scriptural mandate to confess. Rather, the problem of confidentiality arises only with the development of auricular confessional practices in which confession is made individually, in a private setting, without public evidence of penitent status. It is compounded when confession is made to a religious professional, rather than simply to another member of the group. In Catholicism, the problem does not arise with much force until the time of Leo I; in Mormonism, it does not develop until after the group's migration to Utah. In both, the problem of confidentiality does not arise until well after confession as a practice is already well established; it is with the reinterpretation of confession as *private* that the problem emerges. Indeed, the issue of confidentiality does not present itself with full force until after confession and satisfaction have become both wholly private and wholly professionalized, where confession is made in private to an officer of the church. Hence, doctrinal assertions governing confidentiality in confession must be regarded quite differently from doctrinal assertions mandating confession itself. The assertions requiring the priest to observe absolute confidentiality, as in Catholicism, or permitting the bishop to disclose—even requiring him to report—certain kinds of confessions, as in Mormonism, represent *conclusions* or answers to the moral problem that the practice of private confession creates, not premises in the moral argument concerning it.

This account may provide a general mechanism for treating doctrinal and quasi-doctrinal claims concerning a wide variety of religious practices. The essential point is that the logical status of a doctrinal assertion in moral argumentation is not invariant; it is relative to the practice with which it is associated and to the problem it serves to resolve. Unlike matters of fact and assertions of moral principle and rule, doctrinal assertions cannot all be accorded the same status in moral argumentation; while some may function as premises, others cannot properly be understood in this way.

To determine what status a given doctrinal claim should be accorded, we must examine not only the basic texts, teachings, and pronouncements of the group, but the history of the development of those doctrines. First, we can identify those articles of doctrine that originally mandate or prohibit certain types of actions. These may be called basic or "0-level" doctrines to suggest that they incorporate the fundamental general imperatives of the faith. These fundamental general mandates—including such imperatives of traditional Christianity as chastity, baptism, confession, monogamous marriage, charity, evangelism, and so on—are often, though not always, located in scriptural commandments. Of course, most scriptural passages do not yield fundamental general mandates or 0-level doctrines in this sense; they do not contain *basic* directives. Furthermore, many fundamental general imperatives are derived from sources other than scripture. Sometimes such mandates are pronounced by prophets or sages within a tradition; sometimes they are articulated by later theologians or scholars examining the roots of a tradition; and sometimes they are nowhere stated explicitly, but must be inferred from peripheral, established doctrines, much as the U.S. Supreme Court has located the constitutional right of privacy not in any specific text but in the "penumbra" of the Bill of

Rights. (In the next chapter, we will examine an 0-level mandate that is not stated explicitly in scripture but that is clearly fundamental to the Christian tradition.) Identifying 0-level imperatives, however, is not a matter of whim or convenience; it is a matter of discerning what is fundamental to a given religious tradition—what it takes as basic, nonnegotiable, and essential to its character and purpose. The 0-level doctrines are fundamental in that they are core precepts from which subsequent teachings flow and upon which they are based, and in that omission of these precepts would significantly alter the tradition. Of course, the sort of ethical analysis pursued here can err by misidentifying the 0-level imperatives acknowledged by a given religious group; however, it can also succeed in pointing out imperatives that the group recognizes in only an inchoate way.

When a religious group recognizes a fundamental mandate of this sort, requiring or forbidding a certain kind of action, it then typically develops an institutional mechanism for eliciting and regulating such actions. In doing so, it specifies how the fundamental general mandate is to be put into practice. This mechanism for putting 0-level mandates into practice is encoded in what may be called first-order doctrine. The practices specified in first-order doctrine are typically identificatory for the members of the group; to refrain from participating in them would typically mark an individual as a deficient or schismatic member. The practices may develop and evolve over time, as the institutional practice of confession has in the Catholic and Mormon churches, or it may be adopted in a relatively sudden way—as, for instance, when a church leader institutes a ruling. (Examples of the latter, often said to be based on visions or revelations, might include Mother Ann's prohibition of sexual activity to the Shakers, Joseph Smith's introduction of polygamy to the Mormons, or Sun Myung Moon's mass performance of arranged marriages in his Unification Church.) In either case, nevertheless, it is the institutional mechanism itself, the practice, that brings with it characteristic moral problems, particularly when the practice is conducted and enforced by the officials of the group. It is *these* dilemmas that demand resolution. For instance, the doctrinally mandated institution of marriage, whether practiced in group, polygamous, or monogamous forms, gives rise to moral issues involving contracts and promise keeping, which are accentuated as religious officials admit or withhold marriage rites or extract specific marriage promises. Similarly, admission to monastic orders gives rise to issues of informed consent, while the practice of baptism raises further issues in commitment and, if it involves infant baptism, second-party consent. The practice of discipline, in forms such as penance or excommunication, gives rise to issues concerning the nature and purpose of punishment generally. Even the practice of charity poses problems—for instance, the risk of paternalism and manipulation, especially where affiliation with the group may be a precondition for aid.

As doctrinally mandated institutional practices such as these develop and characteristic moral issues appear, religious groups develop answers or solutions to them. These solutions are, in turn, typically codified in doctrine or other dogmatic policy or church law. For instance, as an answer to the problems of promise keeping and contract making in monogamous marriage, some groups have come to view the commitment as irrevocably binding, regardless of changing circumstances or the desires of the parties involved, and doctrinal policies prohibiting divorce and/or remarriage have emerged. Other groups, reaching a different solution to the same underlying problem, do not view the commitment as irrevocable; while observing the same institution of monogamous marriage, these groups permit it to be dissolved. Similarly, facing the potential for coercive manipulation posed by the doctrinal imperative of giving charity, at least in circumstances in which the recipients are in severe need, some groups respond by repudiating simultaneous proselytism or by working to ensure that receipt of charity is not conditional upon embracing the faith. Other groups do not. Other groups resolve the issue in yet a different way and extend charity only to members or prospective members of their own group.

In all of these cases, what is of particular ethical interest to us are the policies serving as answers or conclusions that have been developed to resolve institutionally generated moral dilemmas. These policies may be called second-order doctrines to emphasize their different logical status; they are neither the primary requirements of the religious tradition nor the initial institutional directives, but serve instead to provide strategies for resolving the problems that those primary requirements and directives raise. But since they develop in order to resolve moral dilemmas, we cannot give them privileged status in the moral argument, regardless of the status the religious tradition itself assigns them. To do so would be to beg the question the practice in question raises, not to reach a solution to it. Rather, as ethicists, we must consider whether these second-order doctrines can provide adequate answers to the problems with which they are associated and attempt to show why or why not. It cannot be held, therefore—at least morally speaking—that the Catholic priest ought never violate the confidentiality of the confession because canons 983 and 984 forbid him to do so. Rather, since the ethical problem both historically and logically precedes the development of doctrinal answers to it, the applied professional ethicist concerned with the practice of religion must address the moral issue of confidentiality directly, without question-begging doctrinal appeal.

Of course, a religious tradition's 0-level doctrinal imperatives could also be subjected to ethical critique; but to do so would be to question the religious tradition altogether, not to address the systemic moral problems it generates. This point is crucial to the project here. One could question the foundations and legitimacy of religion altogether, as one may question the foundations and legitimacy of such fields as psychiatry or law, but that would exceed too soon the limits of the normative examination of institutional practice and policies that is so productive and informative in contemporary professional ethics and raise prematurely the question of its foundations. Work in legal ethics, for example, does not begin with a global challenge to the advocacy system, but rather examines the dilemmas that functioning within such a system pose for the practitioner. Work in business ethics does not *begin* by denouncing capitalist economies (though its conclusions sometimes lead in that direction), but by looking at the moral problems that arise within and are characteristic of capitalist business practice. In examining organized religion with the insights and apparatus of applied professional ethics, then, we must rule direct ethical assessment of 0-level imperatives initially out of bounds, not because such assessment cannot ultimately be done but in order to begin where applied professional ethics has the strongest hold.

With this, we resolve the procedural issue of whether questions concerning the moral status of doctrinally governed religious practices can be entertained. Religious practices are differentially accessible to ethical critique. The basic, 0-level foundational mandates of a religious tradition are to be regarded as initially immune to ethical scrutiny, while increasingly higher levels—first-order doctrines that specify practices typically identificatory of a group, second-order doctrines and policies that serve to resolve the ethical issues, and "excuses" (still to be examined) for residual moral problems—are to be seen as increasingly vulnerable candidates for ethical critique. Hence, even if a group takes all of its teachings to have the same force, its higher-order pronouncements cannot be granted the same unassailable status as the 0-level imperatives and cannot be given privileged status in moral argumentation. On the contrary, it is the higher-order doctrines that can be examined directly with the secular apparatus of professional ethics.

Consequently, we may address the issue before us directly, without appeal to doctrine: when, if ever, may or should the religious professional reveal information learned in confidential, confessional situations? In varying ways, the secular professions all recognize circumstances in which confidentiality is to be violated; none of them maintains a prohibition of confidence breaking that is absolute and without exception. But neither does there prevail in any of the secular professions a policy that encourages routine disclosure, without prior warning, of personal information obtained in privacy. Both Catholicism and Mormonism differ radically from the position generally accepted (though not without dispute) in the secular professions, though they do differ in opposite ways. We should, then, ask whether there is anything distinctive about *religious* confession that would justify such radical departures from the policies concerning confidentiality that are familiar in the secular professions.

To do this, we can begin by reconstructing a general argument for each of the two extreme positions. These are hypothetical sketches, philosophers' reconstructions, sensitive to the features noticed by professional ethicists; they are not orthodox church-sanctioned views. Precisely because of this, they may allow us to see what is at issue, and why.

## *The Catholic Position Favoring Secrecy*

Traditional Catholic analysis recognizes a fourfold classification of secrets, each of which is said to generate a different degree of obligation to secrecy:

1. *The Natural Secret*. The natural secret involves any nonpublic knowledge about a person the disclosure of which would cause pain, offense, or loss to that person. According to Catholic doctrine, the obligation to honor such a secret "arises from the nature of things" and thus derives immediately from natural law.[18]

2. *The Promised Secret*. The promised secret, which may also be a natural secret, is one arising from a specific promise made by the hearer of the secret not to reveal it. In such cases, the promise is typically made after the secret matter has been revealed.

3. *The Entrusted Secret*. In the entrusted secret, the hearer's promise not to reveal the secret is given antecedently, whether expressly or implicitly. The promise of secrecy may be requested and given formally or it may be implied in the relationship between the two parties concerned. In the latter case, it is usually identified with the professional or *official* secret arising from secular role expectations, as that between attorney and client or between physician and patient.

4. *The Confessional Secret*. The confessional secret is a variation of the entrusted secret endowed, however, with the sacramental "seal": an explicit promise by the priest that the matter will not be conveyed. The seal can be given only in formal confession and does not apply in cases where the individual consults a priest for advice *extra tribunal*.

For the first three types of secret, according to Catholic teaching, the obligation to preserve secrecy is not absolute. Each may be violated if the advantage gained from the revelation outweighs the loss sustained, all factors being taken into account. The obligation to preserve professional secrets is the strongest, yet even here a secret may be revealed to prevent a disproportionately grave injury to the common good, to an innocent third party, to the hearer of the secret, or to the person whose secret it is. Thus, under Catholic teaching, a secular professional whose patient or client confesses plans to murder someone might well be permitted to reveal it. However, the same confession, made to a priest in a sacramental situation and endowed with the seal of confession, may *never* be revealed.

Two general objections, both implicit in much of what has been said, may be brought against Catholicism's policy of absolute confessional secrecy.[19] First, although Catholic doctrine recognizes that ordinary secrets may be violated in some circumstances and thus acknowledges that there may be compelling reasons for doing so, confessional secrets may portend the same serious harm as natural, promised, or entrusted secrets and may have the same disastrous effect on innocent third parties. If these reasons are compelling for overriding ordinary secrets, it is not clear why they are not equally compelling in confessional situations. For instance, the penitent may confess a plan to assault, rob, cheat, or kill. He or she may confess to having committed a crime or moral atrocity for which the victim has not been recompensed, or for which an innocent person has been convicted, criticized, stigmatized, or even executed. Cases of preventable murder draw perhaps the greatest criticism of a policy of inviolable secrecy. For instance, the case of Jürgen Bartsch, whose priest knew but did not reveal who was killing the boys, provoked widespread public outrage—including demands that the priest be defrocked at once. (Under canon law, the priest would have been defrocked if he had told, not if he had not told.) Where keeping confidentiality will result in serious harm, the challenge to the Catholic position is most severe.

Second, the Catholic policy favoring secrecy may seem to compromise the moral integrity of the confessor and the church. To keep confessed material secret when there are compelling reasons for revealing it brings upon both the confessor and the church a moral taint, perhaps tantamount to complicity in the crime itself. To fail to act to prevent a serious wrong—as Bartsch's priest failed to prevent three additional murders—is to fail to make the morally, if not legally, required response and thus to compromise or destroy one's own moral integrity. Similarly, to forbid a priest to reveal the information that would overturn an erroneous conviction, for instance, and end an innocent person's undeserved years in jail for a crime he or she did not commit, is to make that priest a moral accomplice to the unjust jailing.

Against these two objections favoring the disclosure of confessional material, three arguments central to the Catholic position can be formulated. These arguments, though stated here in a philosophic rather than dogmatic way, form the basis for Catholicism's insistence that confessional secrets are a class apart from natural, promised, and entrusted secrets and are not subject to breaches of confidentiality in any circumstances at all. Although all of these arguments have both deontological and utilitarian features, though in differing proportions, none trades on theological assumptions, and we are thus within the proper scope of applied ethics.

The first argument is a largely deontological argument about keeping promises. It points out that by its very nature, confession is a confession of something shameful, regretted, disturbing, troubling, dangerous, or in other ways painful to the confessant and which he or she believes might increase the pain if revealed. Believing this, the confessant is willing to reveal the matter to another person only under conditions that ensure the secret will be kept. That the secret, if exposed to the light of day, might prove objectively trivial is not the point; the confessant believes that telling the secret will increase his or her torment and therefore does not want it revealed. A central feature of the confessional relation, then, is the promise—tacit or explicit—believed by the confessant to be extended by the confessor, under protection of which the confessant first becomes willing to reveal the secret of his or her sins at all. It is this promise that compels respect for the privacy of confession.

The second argument is a related view favoring confidentiality in confession, partly founded in prudential considerations for the confessant, but also in benefits to be gained. Only under a policy of absolute confidentiality, it is argued, will it be possible for the confessing individual to be complete, forthright, and fully honest in the confession; otherwise, according to an argument recognized at least as early as Thomas Aquinas, confession would be "insurmountably difficult to employ."[20] Trust in the absolute secrecy guaranteed by the priest and by the religious institution within which the priest functions is what makes complete, real confession possible: the unburdening of the darkest, most shameful facts of one's past and one's future intentions. Strict, exceptionless confidentiality is the precondition of genuine, unfettered confession, where considerations of prudence and self-protection need play no role. But this yields a benefit: it makes true inspection of conscience possible. As a Protestant pastor commented on the Bartsch case, "We can only be thankful that we still have one place left in the world where a man can speak freely and not fear retribution."[21] This view sees confession as making repentance possible and, hence, of benefit to the confessant. Since genuine, completely frank confession is good for the confessant and since only complete confidentiality can elicit it, complete confidentiality must be guaranteed.

Third, it is argued in a primarily consequentialist view, because a policy of secrecy permits the confessant to reveal his thoughts, hopes, dreams, motivations, values, hates, and fears completely, it allows the priest an unparalleled opportunity to mold the penitent's conscience. Because the priest has access to moments of the confessant's life and experience where issues of values and behavior are most pressing, the priest can shape and install values, forming and educating the conscience much more effectively than is possible with external teaching or preaching. In confession, the priest is as close as possible to the moral experience of the confessant; consequently, his efforts to reform the confessant's conscience are of greatest efficacy. Confession is a mechanism of crucially important moral teaching and reform. In its truest forms, confession is not simply an obligatory, mechanical recitation of sins, but a true self-inspection of conscience and of one's moral character. As such, it provides an unparalleled opportunity for genuine repentance and reform.

These three arguments also provide the basis for counterobjections to the two principal objections against the Catholic policy of absolute confidentiality. These objections can also be examined in wholly philosophic terms, without relying on theological assumptions.

First, it is true that a policy of secrecy will sometimes mean that harm to persons that could be prevented—assault, theft, murder—will be permitted to occur. However, it is argued, cases in which the priest can actually prevent such harm are much less frequent than one might suppose. For one thing, regardless of the act the confessant may be contemplating, the priest may not be able to predict accurately whether the contemplated or feared act will actually occur. Of course, because of the very secrecy of the confessional there can be no reliable empirical data to substantiate this claim. Yet there is no reason to suppose that religious professionals will be better at making accurate predictions of future dangerous behavior than psychiatrists or psychologists, especially without specific training in the psychological sciences. But even trained professionals in these sciences have notoriously poor success at accurately predicting future crimes. Were priests to inform secular authorities, family members, physicians, or potential victims about projected violence, the number of faulty disclosures of confidential information might very sizably outnumber the accurate ones. If the argument is that the priest ought to prevent future harm, there are few guarantees that he could do so with success.

This first reply, however, is not wholly successful. To acknowledge that the priest who believes the confessant will commit a harm may err in his prediction is not to absolve him of moral responsibility for doing what he can to prevent it, particularly in those cases where the likelihood of harm may be very high. This may be particularly true where the infraction is repetitive or where the confessant has already engaged in such behavior in the past, such as frequent cruelty to a spouse, consistent fraud or tax evasion, or repeated child abuse. Problems of accuracy are also much less pressing where the infraction is a past one. Problems of accurate prediction do not disappear completely, of course, for it may be imaginary or fabricated crimes that are confessed, especially by people with emotional disturbances; the confessor may find it difficult to distinguish these from transgressions actually committed. Nevertheless, in some cases, although the harming act is past, the victim remains harmed or an innocent third party continues to be punished for a crime he or she did not commit. Here, the confessor may be quite accurate in his ability to prevent or rectify harm.

A second argument favoring absolute secrecy of the confessional points out that absolute secrecy gives the priest not only an unparalleled opportunity to mold the conscience, but therewith an unparalleled opportunity to prevent harm. If the confessional is genuinely secret and the confessant need not fear betrayal by the priest, he or she is free to confess his or her deeds and any awful plans in full; but this gives the priest access to these facts and plans and, in so doing, provides the priest with an opportunity to dissuade the confessant from acting on those plans. This is an opportunity the priest would not otherwise have. Were confidentiality violable only in cases of proposed grave harm, it is in precisely those cases that confession would not be made. It is true that a policy of absolute secrecy would prohibit a priest from preventing some serious crimes—like the three additional murders by the butcher's apprentice—but while these cases are grievous, they are comparatively infrequent. They are clearly outweighed, on this consequentialist argument, by the many many cases in which the priest persuades the penitent that the deeds contemplated are wrong. Because the confessional, if it is absolutely secret, gives the priest an opportunity to shape the moral conscience of the penitent and thus to prevent serious future wrongs, its very secrecy works to protect potential victims.

Although this second reply comes much closer to answering the major arguments against the Catholic view, it is not entirely successful. It, too, trades on the consequentialist claim that secrecy in the confessional works to prevent harm, but there can be no empirical evidence to establish—or refute—this claim, beyond the impressions of the priests involved. This is an objection in principle, not an accidental lack: if the confessional is genuinely secret, confirming data can never be obtained. Thus, consequentialist arguments of this sort do not succeed, and the original question remains: whatever general policies may or may not be effective, ought not the priest prevent what he believes will be a serious harm to another person?

## The Mormon Position Favoring Nonconfidentiality

For Mormons, one's actions and beliefs in this world directly influence one's status in the next. Although in Mormon belief all persons are resurrected, admission to differing levels of afterlife kingdoms is a function not only of divine grace but of one's present obedience to sacred law. Deviation in belief or in behavior, if unrepented, entails that one will attain a lesser status in the afterlife; if the deviation is severe enough, one is, in effect, condemned to "outer darkness" or hell. By and large, good standing in the church reflects the righteousness of one's personal life and should intimate one's expectations for the hereafter.

Consequently, to engage in sinful thought or behavior is to invite upon oneself the most severe harm: loss of a superior degree of eternal life. (These claims and background metaphysical assumptions are matters of the fundamental doctrine of this group; no assumptions should be made here as to their truth or falsity.) Insofar as the church official with pastoral functions, particularly the bishop, is committed to promoting the spiritual welfare of the members within his care, he is expected to support them in their avoidance of sin and to help them recognize and repent of sin they have incurred. This duty is reflected in his obligation to help members in good standing in the church remain so and to help those whose status is in jeopardy correct their beliefs or behavior so that they may regain their standing in the church. "The first purpose of Church discipline," the Bishop's Handbook reminds officials, "is to save the soul of the transgressor" (*General Handbook,* p. 10-1).

As a result, the Mormon argument favoring nonconfidentiality continues, the bishop must use every opportunity to encourage members to avoid sin. Teaching, counseling, and the setting of examples may be sufficient; but for the member who will not recognize or acknowledge his or her sins, the bishop must confront the member directly with them. As the Handbook insists, "God does not overlook sin, and his servants cannot ignore serious transgressions if they have knowledge or evidence of them" (p. 10-1). Admonishment by the bishop may be adequate to help the member control his or her behavior, but if the deviation is severe or the member is recalcitrant, admonishment may be both ineffective and inadequate, and the transgressor must face a higher, more substantial confrontation. For this purpose, it may be necessary for the bishop to hold a disciplinary council. The individual guilty of serious sin can regain good standing only by submitting to this procedure, sustaining possible disfellowship or excommunication, and being rebaptized. Consequently, in the Mormon view, it is for the sake of the individual who transgresses that the bishop must reveal the information—with or without consent—to higher church authorities and to the members of a council in order to assist this individual in making appropriate spiritual amends. The individual who is repentant may be willing to consent to disclosure as part of the penance for transgression, but the welfare of the recalcitrant, unrepentant individual must be kept in mind as well.

Furthermore, the Mormon rationale for violating confidentiality continues, the same argument applies to other persons associated with the confessant in a practice viewed as sinful. Other persons who are confidantes, accomplices, or partners in unacceptable criminal, sexual, or other activities are for the same reasons also in jeopardy. Indeed, since they have not voluntarily confessed to their own bishops, they are in jeopardy to a greater degree. Thus these persons, too, in order to repent, avoid sin, and regain good standing, must be confronted with their errors. It is for this reason that the bishop of the initial confessant is expected to inform the bishop of the partner or partners, so that all the parties to the acts may be confronted, subjected to discipline, and ultimately have their good standing restored.

Third, such discipline is viewed as necessary for the "cleansing of the church," since it is held to remove unsavory, subversive, or dangerous influences from the community as a whole. In this way the bishop exercises his responsibilities not only toward those whose standing is under immediate threat, but also those who may be threatened in the future. This is viewed as a particularly strong obligation where an unacceptable activity threatens to become widespread—as, for instance, in doctrinal criticism or objections to church practice or policy (traditionally called "murmuring"), heretical spreading of deviant beliefs, or participation in sociosexual practices such as viewing pornography or practicing homosexuality, adultery, or polygamous marriage—all activities that, it is often believed, will encourage other morally vulnerable individuals to engage in similar behavior.

If we look for the central feature of the Mormon view, we find that in spite of assertions in the Bishop's Handbook that confidentiality is guaranteed (and these assertions have been added only in recent years),[22] the group's official practices presuppose that absolute respect for confidentiality is a morally *irresponsible* policy, since it would ignore the welfare of the transgressing member, of other persons associated with or affected by that member, and would fail to protect the moral integrity of the community. Considerations of an individual's interests in confidentiality must give way to considerations concerning others and the church as a whole.

In this way, the Mormon view is radically different from that of Catholicism. Catholicism, the Mormon view might hold, underestimates the prevalence and nature of harm to third parties: sinners may perpetrate not only major criminal harm, but more frequent and subtle—though equally immoral—transgressions, especially sexual sins. Second, the Mormon view might add, Catholicism has failed to recognize the responsibility of the religious professional to *all* the members of the faith, not just to specific, current clients; the religious professional can neither prefer the interests of the immediate client to those of others affected by him or her, nor prefer the interests of any individual to those of the overall community.

But the differences between Catholicism and Mormonism may be still more substantial. Catholicism requires violation of a fundamental moral principle when it forbids the confessor from preventing serious harm. But although Mormon practice appears to honor this principle, it violates others. First, it requires that implied promises of confidentiality, however they arise, must in some cases be broken. Second, it involves deception: since distribution of the Bishop's Handbook is restricted and there is no other public disclosure of church policies that permit or require that confessional or other information be transmitted to other bishops or to a disciplinary council, this may lead members to believe that information about them will be treated as confidential when in fact it will not. Paradoxically, the possibility of deception has increased as the church has given greater weight to assertions of confidentiality in recent years. Third, it involves coercion, both in requiring persuasion of the member to relinquish claims to confidentiality and in using confessed information to oblige partners, confidants, or accomplices to confess. Both the confessing member and the partner, when confronted with evidence of their sins, are thereby effectively forced to admit them even when a voluntary confession would not have been forthcoming. Thus, both traditions, Catholic and Mormon, require in their different ways the violation of basic moral rules.

## *Excuses*

Both traditions claim that although fundamental moral principles must be violated in the practice of confession, they are violations in good cause. However, though each tradition may seem to make its case persuasively, neither adequately answers the moral challenge that the practice of private confession puts to it.

In Catholicism, despite the relative strength of the argument that absolute secrecy in the confessional may serve to protect third parties from harm, the question remains: Ought not the priest intervene to prevent a severe, foreseeable harm when he cannot dissuade the confessant from his plan? To this question, Catholicism has developed two further answers.

First, it holds, the seal of confession—the promise of absolute secrecy—cannot be given if the confession is imperfect, that is, if the confession is simulated, not contrite, or insincere, not made sacramentally and in order to seek absolution but, for instance, to deceive, ridicule, or seduce the confessor. In such cases, the rules governing natural or entrusted secrets apply, since no seal has been given, and if there is a proportionately grave reason to do so, confidentiality may be broken. Unless a confession is contrite, the confessant is not genuinely penitent; he or she declines to make a firm promise of amendment, refuses to rectify the wrongs committed or persists in the intention to initiate or repeat an evil act. This covers most of the cases in which severe harm is threatened and thus tempers the uncompromising severity of the second-order position on confessional confidentiality that Catholicism has adopted. Nevertheless, it does not fully eliminate the moral problem, for once the seal has been given, it must—regardless of the consequences—be kept.

As a second defense, Catholic doctrine supplies a more basic, general answer. Even when he could do so easily and without risk, the priest who has knowledge of a person's intentions from confession is forbidden from intervening to prevent serious harm; this might seem to make the priest responsible in part for the harm he, in effect, allows the person to do. But Catholic teaching also asserts that the priest holds confessional knowledge in a different way from ordinary knowledge upon which he might act. Confessional knowledge is held "in God" or "as God" and is not *known* in the ordinary sense at all.[23] Consequently, the priest is believed not to be morally complicit in any crime, even though he may appear to allow it to occur. Furthermore, should the priest be compelled to testify in a court of law concerning a confessant's revelations (though, since clergy privilege is recognized in most jurisdictions, this is unlikely to happen in the United States), he is required under canons 983 and 984 not to reveal these matters. Under Catholic teaching, he must therefore deny—even under oath, on the Bible— any knowledge of them.[24] This may seem to involve both deliberate falsehood—lying—and violation of the law. But under this teaching, the priest cannot be blamed for lying or violating the law; he is giving a truthful account of the fact that he knows nothing of the matter in the ordinary way. With this doctrine of knowing "in God," Catholicism moves to answer the last remaining objection to its policy of absolute confessional secrecy.

This defense, however, we may recognize as itself another among the higher-order doctrines that have developed to resolve the ethical issues of a doctrinally mandated practice; it, too, seems to announce itself as an "answer." Similarly, it, too, is an evolved response to the disturbing moral questions the practice of private confession raises. However, it differs in an important way: It does not simply dictate a policy requiring a specific course of action designed to resolve the moral dilemma generated by a first-order doctrine, as second-order doctrines do, but serves to *excuse* the residual objections that remain even after the adoption of these specific, action-dictating second-order doctrines.

Of course, excuses as well as acts are of interest to the applied ethicist. Insofar as the priest is capable of repeating the confession and understanding its meaning, he *does* know it (that is, he knows what the confessant has said, not that the confession is true) and cannot so easily elude moral criticism. (Of course, some priests claim that they do not remember what confessants say to them; this is a psychological comment, not a moral excuse. In any case, a confession of planned harm, such as the butcher's assistant's murders, would surely be retained.) To claim that the priest cannot prevent a harm or testify truthfully because he does not know the confessed information attempts to excuse him from moral expectations that may be very strong, and the applied ethicist will want to consider whether such an excuse is adequate. Like second-order doctrines that function as dilemma-resolving, action-guiding answers, third-order doctrines that function as excuses also cannot be accorded status among the premises in the general moral argument concerning confidentiality, and it does not settle the issue to say that the priest cannot act because he does not know. He *does* know, and the moral question still persists: Should he act?

To be sure, Mormon teachings, doctrines, scriptures, internal policies, and public statements do not describe the church's practices in disclosing confessional material as promise breaking, coercion, or deceit, although informal interviews lead me to believe that many bishops and church members privately feel them to be so. Nor do the primary scriptural texts or statements reveal anything that might count as a doctrinal excuse for such practices. Nevertheless, recent Mormonism appears to be developing a third-order teaching designed to answer the ethical discomfort felt by many about the church's policies of confidentiality. First articulated in the supplement to the Bishop's Handbook for 1979, this teaching is that trial by a church court (changed to "disciplinary council" in 1989) is redemptive in character in that it "allows" or helps the transgressor to repent more fully than would otherwise be the case.[25] "Church courts are courts of love and redemption," said the 1985 Handbook (p. 8-1). "Without formal Church discipline," says the 1989 revision, "some transgressors may never experience the change of behavior and the change of heart necessary to qualify them for redemption" (p. 10-1). It is important not to confuse this recent teaching with the traditional first-order doctrine that confession, remorse, and repentance are redemptive; the traditional teaching is common to both Mormonism and Catholicism and is originally derived directly from primary biblical texts. Quite different from this, contemporary Mormonism's new assertion is that the *disciplinary* process is itself necessary, serving not merely to chastise individuals but to save their souls. This new assertion does appear to have developed in answer to the residual ethical problems of adopting a policy that permits nonconsenting disclosure, deception, and coercion. Under this new teaching, the bishop who reports a confession cannot be accused of harming the confessant or any partner(s) because the disciplinary council elicited by his disclosure is a benefit to them, not a harm.

As an excuse, this doctrine functions as an analogue of the Catholic teaching that the priest has knowledge of confessed material only "in God." In the Catholic version, the priest is not blamable for lying or for ignoring harm that might result from confessional secrecy because he does not know the confessional secrets in any usable way. In the Mormon version, the bishop is not blamable for promise breaking, deceit, or coercion, since, as it turns out, he is bringing the confessant benefits rather than harm. Both of these excuses seem to rest on theological claims—the Catholic one on the notion of "knowing in God," the Mormon one on the notion of a council's serving to "save the soul" of the transgressor. But when we see how these claims function within a structure of 0-level and higher-order claims, the excuses become easily accessible to ethical critique. Is either excuse adequate? Insofar as they both attempt to cloak, rather than resolve, the residual moral problems that confidentiality practices generate within their respective traditions, the answer must be no.

## *Fundamentalist Doctrine: The Collinsville Church of Christ and the Case of Marian Guinn*

The analysis of Catholic and Mormon practices concerning confidentiality of confessed material has been pursued in some detail not merely to display the differences between quite different religious groups, but to develop a methodology for treating doctrinal claims in ethical inquiry. This has involved developing a typology of such claims. It distinguishes fundamental or 0-level imperatives or mandates; first-order imperatives, which provide directives for putting 0-level imperatives into practice; second-order claims which attempt to resolve the moral dilemmas introduced by first-order imperatives; and third-order claims, which serve as excuses for residual moral problems. But this typology is open to a substantial objection: it cannot state how the 0-level imperatives are to be identified or how they can be distinguished from upper-level doctrinal claims. After all, these fundamental imperatives may occur in scripture but need not; they may be delivered as direct pronouncements of sect leaders or have a long history within a tradition; they may or may not be explicitly stated. A given doctrinal claim may function as 0-level in one religious group but as first-order in another, or not at all; two different traditions may root similar practices in different 0-level claims. For a variety of reasons, a religious tradition's 0-level imperatives may be difficult to identify. Yet an examination of the ethical features of the practices of religious groups depends, it would seem, on accurately identifying and comparing the 0-level imperatives on which they are based.

This problem confronts us directly in considering yet another group. In Catholic and Mormon practices, the specific 0-level mandate on confession for both groups could be identified at James 5:16, Matthew 16:19, and John 20:23—essentially stated as the command to "confess your sins." This common basis makes it easy to see different ways the two groups put this single, fundamental imperative into practice, the different moral problems that arise in each, and the excuses made by each group for residual moral problems it was unable to resolve. However, if it is to be useful, this account must be able to accommodate still other religious groups as well. This chapter opened with not just two but three true tales about confidentiality, and it is the third that provides a substantial and informative challenge to the procedures developed here. To see what this challenge is, consider the case of Marian Guinn.

In February 1974, Marian Guinn, recently divorced and supporting her four small children on welfare, moved to Collinsville, Oklahoma.[26] Guinn and her children lived for about six weeks with Guinn's sister and brother-in-law, members of the Collinsville Church of Christ, and began attending the church. Guinn, originally a Baptist, received some basic teachings and saw a few filmstrips about the Collinsville church and after a few weeks became a member. During the following years, she studied first for a certificate of high school equivalency and then for a nursing degree; members of the church assisted her extensively during this time. The church helped her purchase an automobile; it set up an account for gasoline; members contributed food and clothing for the children; and they provided babysitting while she studied for the equivalency exam. The church threw a party for her when she completed the exam and again when she graduated from Tulsa Junior College. However, after she received her degree, she accepted a job in nearby Tulsa as a registered nurse and was required to work on Sundays. This, among other things, caused her to stop attending the church on a regular basis.

During this period, Guinn had become friends with Pat Sharp, the town pharmacist and former mayor of Collinsville. During the winter of 1979 their friendship developed into something more intimate. Sharp had been divorced the previous summer, and Sharp's former wife accused Guinn of being partly to blame for the breakup of the marriage. In the summer of 1980, one of the elders of the church heard a rumor that Guinn was having an affair with Sharp and that Guinn had been the cause of Sharp's divorce. Since Churches of Christ elders believe that they are "obligated by their religion to approach members regarding spiritual problems and to discuss those problems with the affected parties" and that they are "responsible for the souls of the congregation,"[27] as well as for the reputation of the church, they approached Guinn. Two of the elders, Ted Moody and Ron Witten, first confronted Guinn in a laundromat, telling her it was "mandatory" that she go with them immediately to the church. She replied, "I told them I was in the middle of the laundry and my four children were there, and I didn't want to leave them alone. They said again it could not wait, and it was imperative that we talk right then."[28] Leaving the children behind, she went with the elders to the church, where the third elder, Allan Cash, met them. According to her testimony at the subsequent trial, the three elders "said that anything I said would be held in confidence," and that after confronting her with the evidence—

that she had been seen in Pat Sharp's car, that his car had been parked on her property one evening, and that she had been seen behind the counter in his drugstore—they prayed with her and informed her that she must break off the relationship. "It would be better for your spiritual goodness," they told her. They refused, however, to tell her the source of the rumor. After confronting her twice more during the following summer with the claim that she was violating scripture and the demand that she publicly repent of her sins, they warned her that if she did not, they would be obliged to tell her sins to the church. In a letter of September 21, 1981, they wrote to her (quoted verbatim):

> Dear Sister Marian,
>
> It is with tremendous concern for your soul and the welfare of the Lords church that we exhort you to consider the impact of the results of the course you have elected to pursue. We have and will continue to follow the instructions set forth in the scriptures in dealing with matters of church discipline. The Lord set forth the procedure in Matt 18:15–17, We have confronted you personally as verses 15 & 16 requires, however to date, you have not responded, so you leave us no alternative but to "tell it to the church." (v-17)
>
> . . . It is the prayerful desire of the entire body of Christ that you correct this serious matter and avert the "withdrawing of fellowship" of the saints.[29]

Matthew 18:15–17, on which the elders based their warning that they would disclose the matter to the church, reads as follows:

> If another member of the church sins against you, go and point out the fault when the two of you are alone. If the member listens to you, you have regained that one. But if you are not listened to, take one or two others along with you, so that every word may be confirmed by the evidence of two or three witnesses. If the member refuses to listen to them, tell it to the church; and if the offender refuses to listen even to the church, let such a one be to you as a Gentile and a tax collector.[30]

Marian Guinn did not deny that she had had an affair with Pat Sharp, though she later testified that they had had sexual relations only "three or four" times, none of them after the second time the elders accosted her. Three days after the church's warning letter to her, she wrote in reply:

> I don't want my name mentioned before the church except to tell them that I withdraw my membership immediately!
>
> Anything I told you was told in confidence & was not meant for anyone else to hear. You have no [more] right to get up & say anything against me in church /than someone at work getting up before nursing staff saying anything that would embarrass me & my family. . . .
>
> I withdraw my membership. I was raised Baptist & will always be— & do not accept your doctrine. I never have & never will. I do not believe God appointed you men (elders) as judges on earth.[31]

The elders replied by informing Guinn that she could not withdraw her membership from the church, since there was no precedent for it in the New Testament. According to the beliefs of the church, they told her, she would always be a member. The following Sunday, September 27, 1981, the elders read a letter to the congregation asking them to pray for Guinn and to contact her so that she would have a "penitent heart," informing the congregation that if she did not respond by the next Sunday, another letter would be read detailing the scriptures she had violated.

Guinn did not respond. On the following Sunday, October 4, virtually the entire congregation was in church—some 110–115 people in a town numbering about 2,200, more than 5 percent of the town's population. The second letter was read, quoting in detail scriptural passages prohibiting fornication: Ephesians 5:1–3, I Corinthians 5:9, I Thessalonians 4:1–4, and Hebrews 10:25–26 and 13:17. Copies of the letter were mailed to four other Churches of Christ in the immediate area. The congregation then withdrew fellowship from Guinn.

As more than one observer remarked, that Guinn responded by filing suit was much in the American tradition. Her initial action, filed October 26, 1981, claimed damages for defamation, but because the charges of fornication were true, she amended the petition to state two invasion-of-privacy claims and a claim for intentional infliction of emotional distress. She argued that the matters revealed in the church's public discipline and dismissal of her were "highly offensive and of no legitimate interest" to those informed.[32] "What I do or do not do is between God and myself," she told the court, and she asserted that the elders had no right to "mess with someone else's life." Her attorney, Thomas Dee Frasier, told the court in closing arguments: "I demand the right, on behalf of Marian Guinn, to lead her life the way she chooses," and by way of comment added, "He was a single man. She was a single lady. And this is America!" The trial court jury awarded damages to Guinn on all three claims: $205,000 actual damages and $185,000 punitive damages, a total of $390,000.[33]

The elders appealed and the case went on to the Oklahoma Supreme Court. The court, taking Guinn's right to resign from the church as central (despite the church's doctrinal claim that this was not possible),[34] remanded the case to the trial court, directing it to award damages to Guinn only for invasion of privacy or intentional infliction of emotional distress which occurred *after* she notified the church of her withdrawal. In effect, this decision held that although a religious group could not discipline a member who had withdrawn, it could—under First Amendment protection—discipline a current member as it wished.

In *Church Discipline and the Courts,* Lynn Buzzard and Thomas Brandon list a number of similar cases following *Guinn.*[35] These include a $5 million suit by John R. Kelley against the Christian Community Church in California for disclosing "confidential, intimate, and embarrassing details of his sexual and marital life" learned in connection with family counseling; a $3 million suit by Jan Brown against the Fairview Church of Christ in Garden Grove, California, for publicly denouncing her divorce as "sinful behavior"; a slander suit by James Shive against the First Baptist Church of Pagosa Springs for accusing him before the congregation of being a "heretic, deceiver, fornicator, coveter, idolater, liar, [and] disorderly"; and a suit in connection with the public revelation of a confidential confession of marital infidelity against the Evangelical Orthodox Church of Santa Cruz by a former bishop of the church. Since all of these cases appear to involve violations of confidentiality, they seem to raise issues similar to those in *Guinn*. Yet it is important not to leap to such conclusions, for rigorous ethical analysis requires sensitive attention to the specific facts of each case and to the practices of the religious group within which they occur; only then is it possible to understand the methodological issues they raise. Indeed, some groups—like the Churches of Christ—are so loosely organized and exhibit enough variety in their practices that analysis can be made only at the most local level. The Collinsville Church of Christ in which the *Guinn* case arose is an autonomous body, part of a loose federation of Churches of Christ but without a national organization or central governing authority, and while its biblically based practices are strongly similar to those of other Churches of Christ, they may not be uniform in the smallest—but often most important—details. An analysis of *Guinn* will show why.

The defense in *Guinn,* representing the position of the Collinsville Church of Christ and its elders, insists that the elders were simply following the scriptural commandment in Matthew 18. This commandment requires the person against whom another member of the church has sinned to follow a four-step procedure:

1. The person must first go to the one who commits the sin and discuss it in private.
2. If the one who commits the sin does not relent, the person should take one or two other persons with him or her as witnesses in order to establish the facts.
3. If the one who commits the sin still does not relent, the person should report the matter to the church.
4. If the one who commits the sin persists in refusing to relent, the person should treat him or her "as a Gentile and a tax collector," that is, as alien or estranged from the religious community.

It would seem that the Collinsville elders, taking this biblical passage as a fundamental imperative, in general followed these steps. When they heard the rumor about Marian Guinn's affair with Pat Sharp, they summoned her and counseled her in private. They repeated this private confrontation twice more and Guinn did not relent. Only after so pursuing steps 1 and 2 did they move to step 3 and report the matter to the church—that is, the congregation; and only after the matter was reported to the congregation was step 4 taken and Guinn disfellowshipped. Since the elders were following scripture, which they take to incorporate a fundamental imperative here, it would seem that ethical objection has little weight. After all, our methodology for applying the insights of secular professional ethics to religious practice prohibits assigning a truthvalue to basic doctrinal claims or subjecting them to direct ethical analysis, and hence cannot say that the claims in Matthew 18 are either true or false or that the procedure stipulated there is moral or immoral. Since this appears to be a basic imperative and the elders were following the procedure it dictates, the analysis, it seems, must end here.

This objection might be countered by claiming that the scriptural passage that the elders followed functioned not as an 0-level imperative but as an upper-level doctrinal assertion deriving from a different underlying 0-level imperative; many biblical passages function in this way. In such cases, the upper-level assertion would therefore be more accessible to ethical critique. On this claim, Matthew 18:15–17, stipulating the four-step procedure, could be viewed as a way of putting into practice the more fundamental imperative in James 5:16 to confess. As an upper-level imperative rather than basic mandate, the four-step procedure and its application in the case of Marian Guinn would then be open to critique. Thus, for instance, the extraordinary violation of Guinn's privacy—no light matter in a small town—could be subjected to criticism under the norms of ordinary morality and professional ethics—especially those of nonmaleficence and autonomy. The elders did Guinn harm and they failed to respect her wishes. It would be appropriate in particular to consider, as indeed her lawyers did, the considerable emotional distress Guinn suffered from repeated confrontations with the elders and from negative publicity, the distress to her children, the damage to her reputation, and so on, versus any putative gains to Guinn or the community from having the matter revealed. As with the practices of the Catholic and Mormon churches, the practices of the Collinsville Church of Christ could in this way be examined without reference to theological assumptions. No doubt it would turn out that there are grounds for calling these practices by the ethically condemnatory term Guinn's lawyer used, *extortion*—especially the elders' threat to tell the church if she did not meet their demand to publicly confess. But this analysis would be possible only if it could be reliably established that the passage at Matthew 18 functions in the practices of this group as an upper-level imperative, not a basic, 0-level mandate.

Clearly, however, it does not. The Collinsville Church of Christ did not treat Matthew 18 as a derivative expression of a more basic, general imperative. For this fundamentalist church, Matthew 18 is the fundamental imperative itself; obedience to the passage needs no rationale or further justification and cannot be defined by any other imperative. It simply *is* the divine law. Thus, the relativist problem looms large here. Normative considerations of confidentiality issues in differing religious groups would seem impossible if the practices under discussion are not all derived from the same underlying commandment. While it was possible to compare the ethical features of Catholic and Mormon practice, there would be simply nothing we could say about the practices of the Churches of Christ.

This would be correct if Matthew 18 functioned in the Collinsville church as 0-level doctrine *and* could be obeyed without further development of higher-order practices. Under the methodology employed here, ethical criticism could not then be pursued. But a case like Marian Guinn's invites a perceptive look at just those features our typology encourages us to notice: developed doctrines, evolving institutional structures and practices, and the diverse ways that have emerged within different groups for putting a fundamental imperative into practice where the imperative itself does not supply concrete details. In short, such a case invites us to question the possibility of practices *directly* dictated by 0-level imperatives.

Certain features of the Marian Guinn case must be noticed. For one thing, it begins when the elders hear a rumor in the small town of Collinsville. The saga of Marian Guinn does not begin with her confession to the elders; it begins with rumor, rumor to which the elders respond by extracting a confession from Guinn. It is not clear who the source of the rumor was, though it is clear that Sharp's former wife's accusation that Guinn had broken up their marriage played a considerable role. Did Sharp's former wife directly approach the elders with her complaint? Did others relay the rumor from Sharp's wife to the elders? Did Faye Jarnigan, one of the church members who recited the rumor to the elders, invent it herself; if not, who was her source? Did it come from the people who observed Guinn riding in Sharp's car, observed Sharp's car parked at Guinn's house late in the evening, or saw Guinn behind the counter at Sharp's drugstore—and brought this information to the elders?

These questions might seem to be the stuff of gossip columns or romance novels, but they are, in fact, central to the ethical issue. It is with these questions that the first subtle evidence of a relevant institutional structure within this church is found. The church is adapted, so to speak, to listen to rumor; it can accommodate rumor and is structurally disposed to do so. Although any official within any organization might hear a rumor and react to it, certain features of this church give structural support to hearing rumor. The elders listen to rumor when it is presented to them; they make themselves available and accessible for this purpose. In contrast, in the Catholic church the priest is *prohibited* from acting on rumor or any third-party reports and may respond in the confessional only to the penitent's own confession of sin; he may not confront the penitent in the confessional with accusations heard elsewhere. To observe these differences between two religious traditions is not to identify one or the other as morally suspect, but to point out differences in institutional structure and resultant practice that confirm that these are not matters dictated solely by 0-level doctrine but by higher-order imperatives that, because they are developed, not basic, are more accessible to moral critique. Developed Catholic practice, in effect, blocks the church's officers from listening to rumor; developed Churches of Christ practice, like that of Mormonism, permits it.

Additional details of the Marian Guinn story may seem equally minor, but prove equally telling. When the elders heard the rumor, they summoned Guinn from the laundromat, forcing her to leave her four small children there, and made her go immediately to the church building so that they could remonstrate with her. Later they summoned her to the church a second time, although a power outage forced them to converse with her in a car in the church parking lot. They confirmed Guinn's confession by asking Pat Sharp directly, in a late-night telephone conversation, whether he had had sexual relations with her. They wrote her a letter on church stationery outlining the church's doctrinal position; they warned her in detail what action the church would take in announcing the matter in Sunday services and that it would disfellowship her. But in doing these things, the elders, as elders, acted *on behalf of the church*. In adhering to the biblical passage, the church had at the same time assigned *itself* a role in the discipline of sin that is not articulated in the original four-step procedure of the biblical text. Thus, we must see the church's actions as reflecting a policy developed in order to put into practice the four steps required by Matthew 18. This is not to say that this policy is wrong, but only that it is not an 0-level practice, immune to immediate ethical critique, but a first-order practice, which—as with virtually all first-order practices— generates its own moral problems.

Like fundamentalist, Bible-based groups elsewhere, the Collinsville church and its elders, as well as supporters in other denominations,[36] fail to recognize what is involved in the position they take. They sincerely believe that they are scrupulously following the biblical commandment; this is what marks them as fundamentalist groups. But they fail to see two crucial things: first, that the biblical passage is indeterminate in certain important respects, thus forcing them to develop more specific practices in order to implement it; and second, that the institutional structures and practices that have developed within the church for putting the commandment into practice constitute just one alternative among various possible ways of doing so. Insofar as a church follows one alternative rather than another, it is open to ethical assessment for preferring the route it does.

The alternative adopted by the Collinsville Church of Christ raises several other moral issues as well. These include issues concerning the intimidating role of officialdom, the binding nature of official promises of confidentiality, and the gender-related threat posed by three older men accosting a younger woman alone. While there is not time to explore them in detail here, it is on specific moral issues such as these that a full evaluation of the practice must eventually center.

After all, a church presented with the same situation as *Guinn* could have developed quite different policies while still adhering to Matthew 18. For example, it could have refused to listen to rumor altogether, and insisted that there must be *proven* evidence of sin. It could have required that a church member confronted with sin visit the errant individual first alone, then again with two or three other individuals *not* in the role of church officials, and then bring the matter before the congregation as a private individual. This would be an alternative to the substantial institutional role adopted by the church. The church could also have insisted that if it was Sharp's former wife who was harmed by the affair, it be she rather than others to accost Guinn. This is not to say that there would not also be moral problems at the second-order level with these alternatives or any others; alternative practices might raise even greater ethical issues than those associated with the practice actually followed. But they would be different specific ethical issues: if the church were to require the former Mrs. Sharp to accost Guinn, there would be no gender-related threat, for example, but perhaps a more pressing issue concerning objectivity in assessing Guinn's alleged sin. In adopting one practice over another, a church must be held accountable for all of the moral issues that that practice raises, even when no alternative is free from moral problems altogether.

Interpreted most literally, Matthew 18 appears to require that whomever was affected by Guinn's sin should have gone directly and privately to her, not started the rumor or informed the church. Asked why a fundamentalist church would not adopt policies encouraging this behavior rather than bringing rumors to the church, a preacher in a Church of Christ in another city explained that although Matthew 18 does seem to require someone who is confronted with sin to go to the individual in person and alone, he or she "might not feel qualified to handle it" and for this reason would bring the matter to the attention of the church.[37] But it is the *church* that honors such excuses and makes it possible for someone to have the church function as a surrogate; to this extent, the church develops a practice that is thereby open to ethical critique.

Still other questions arise in the *Guinn* case. Were the elders' reasons for refusing to honor Guinn's resignation from the Collinsville Church of Christ, made in her letter of reply to their warning, adequate? (That the Oklahoma Supreme Court did not accept them does not decide the issue.) Of what relevance is it that Guinn's confession was not volunteered but extracted from her by the elders? Were Guinn and others aware that the church adhered to a doctrine of public discipline? If not, should this have been part of her training before admission to the church—perhaps, like her other training, presented in a filmstrip? Why did the church not discipline a male church member, whom Guinn claims "practically raped" her, in the same way it disciplined her—at least not until two other women also reported his sexual advances? (The man's situation was different, claimed elder Ted Moody. "His was a private matter, while her situation was of a public nature" because of the rumors.) Scrutiny of these questions and the practices associated with them would lead to similar conclusions: that they, too, involve developed, not 0-level, doctrines. It is not the fact of telling Guinn's acts to the church that is morally problematic (though it was the basis of her legal claims of invasion of privacy and intentional infliction of emotional distress), since telling the church is clearly mandated by the 0-level imperative this group accepts. What is morally problematic is the body of supporting practices that have developed within the church to put the imperative into practice.

As the *Guinn* case shows, the claim that a church or its officials are acting wholly in accord with the dictates of scripture and hence are immune to ethical critique—a claim broadly characteristic of fundamentalist churches—cannot be accepted without scrutiny. This is not to say that it is impossible for a group to act in direct accord with the dictates of 0-level imperatives, but that—given the indeterminate nature of most such imperatives—even a fundamentalist group striving for fidelity to scriptural command is forced to develop ways of putting them into practice. Ironically, Ted Moody, one of the elders, said that although they believe that they had "acted properly and scripturally as shepherds trying to rescue and discipline a strayed lamb" (even Guinn conceded that she thought the elders were "acting out of love"), they are also now "rethinking some of the methods they used."[38] If this rethinking is broad enough to question not just the church's heavy-handed methods, such as confronting people in laundromats or on their front lawns, but to reexamine the whole body of practices that constitute the church's role in responding to private, confessional material, it would be precisely the moral evaluation our procedure recommends. The same rethinking would, of course, be equally appropriate for those developed practices concerning confidentiality and confession in the Catholic and Mormon churches, as well as all other religious groups in which this issue can arise. None, I think, will prove entirely immune.

# CHAPTER 2

# High-Risk Religion

*Informed Consent in Faith Healing, Serpent*

*Handling, and Refusing Medical Treatment*

In some of the more colorful groups on the American religious spectrum, the religious faith of believers involves a willingness to take substantial physical risks—risks to health, physical functioning, and even the risk of death. In several of these groups, the risks a believer takes are indirect, as in refusing blood transfusions or medical treatment; in others, the risks are direct and immediate, as in drinking strychnine or handling poisonous snakes. We may think of these practices as extraordinary tests of religious commitment. We may take willingness to risk death as a demonstration of the extraordinary value religious goals can have for believers. In fact, willingness to risk death for religious reasons is often extolled as the highest test of faith. But this willingness also raises a set of disturbing moral issues concerning the ways in which religious groups bring it about that their adherents are willing to take such risks. In what follows, I want to take a closer look at the influence of religious groups on their adherents' choices, focusing on high-risk decision making that can result in death. In addressing these issues, I do not wish to suggest that a religious believer's willingness to risk death may not be sincere and devout; rather, I want only to cast a morally inquiring eye on the way in which religious institutions engender these sincere, devout beliefs.

## Risk Budgets and Styles

To pose the problem more precisely, we can conceptualize it as it might be addressed in the field of professional ethics. Drawing on issues concerning the formation and manipulation of choice, especially in medicine, we can approach this problem under the general rubric of *informed consent*. This conceptualization permits us to begin with the first prong of our pincer apparatus, involving the application of norms from professional ethics to practices within organized religion.

In everyday life, risks that a person voluntarily and knowingly takes can be described as the result of a prudential calculation, however rudimentary that calculation may be in practice, in which he or she elects a course of action hoping it will produce a gain or avoid a loss, though at the same time recognizing that it may either concurrently or alternatively result in a (further) loss. This prudential calculation involves a survey of the range of possible outcomes of the action proposed, an assessment of the likelihood of the various possible outcomes (the decision is made *under risk* if the probabilities are known, *under uncertainty* if they are not), and an assessment of the relative desirability or undesirability of each of the possible outcomes. Typically, avoidance risk taking weighs two or more projected negative outcomes against each other; gain-oriented, positive risk taking may weigh various positive outcomes against each other, or a positive outcome against both the cost of failing to achieve it and the cost of failing to take the risk. Whatever the specific context of the risk decision, the decision maker properly makes the calculation by multiplying the value of each possible outcome times the probability that it will occur, if known, or the best approximation to it, and then choosing the course of action promising the highest expected utility. That this calculation may be made in a completely intuitive, nonquantitative way does not obscure its nature: conscious decision making under risk or under uncertainty always involves acting so as to produce some preferred outcome despite recognition that this action may instead produce a different, undesired result.

Each individual, Charles Fried has pointed out, has a distinctive *risk budget*—the degree and severity of risk he or she is willing to accept in order to avoid certain losses or to achieve certain gains.[1] The risk budget is a function, of course, of the possible courses of action the individual foresees, the probabilities he or she assigns to the various possible outcomes, and the utilities he or she attaches to each of these, influenced by any characteristic errors the person may make in performing the prudential calculation that indicates what course of action promises the greatest expected utility. But while the risk budgets of ordinary individuals in a culture appear to be fairly uniform with respect to the background risks of everyday life (for example, in drinking the water in a given locality or in using electricity in one's home), there is considerable divergence in the willingness of individuals to accept specific higher foreground risks—for instance, in financial dealings or in high-risk sports like hang gliding or mountain climbing. This is just to say that some members of a culture take risks that other members of the culture won't.

Furthermore, each individual has a distinctive *risk style:* the degree of deliberation or abandon he or she exercises in making a prudential calculation under risk or uncertainty. Some people assess perceived risks with meticulous, painstaking care, regardless of whether the risks are mild or severe and the amount of information they have about the probabilities of various possible outcomes; others take both big and little risks in a comparatively cavalier way. Different individuals also process relevant information in very different ways. For instance, some are naturally optimistic, focusing primarily on the benefits to be gained; others are comparatively pessimistic, attending to possible losses—even when their estimates of the probabilities of the outcomes are the same. In processing information, some individuals may be more prone to characteristic errors of reasoning in risk assessment than others. Like risk budgets, the risk styles of persons within a culture are relatively uniform with respect to background risks, but may vary considerably among individuals with respect to certain more conspicuous risks. Some people make their choices about risks in ways that other people would regard as foolish.

The problem presented by the practices of certain religious groups arises with an observation about risk budgets and styles. The members of a culture ordinarily exhibit broad commonalities in both risk budgets and styles with respect to background risks; they also typically exhibit a range of idiosyncratic, individual risk budgets and styles with respect to certain conspicuous, higher-risk decisions. However, the risk budgets and styles of the members of certain religious groups display striking uniformities not so much with respect to background risks, but with respect to major, conspicuous, foreground risks—direct risks to health, physical functioning, and even risks to life. Furthermore, the kinds of risk characteristically taken by members of these groups often fall well outside the risk budgets and, in addition, violate the risk styles of most other members of society—even outside the quite broad range of individual variation in risk budget and style that members of the culture ordinarily display in their decisions. Put another way, the members of certain religious groups take risks other people do not and decide to do so in ways that other people would not, but they nevertheless do so in remarkably uniform ways. Nor are these trivial risks; some are potentially fatal ones.

These characteristic risk-taking patterns, each distinctive of a particular group, may seem to be just another element in the colorful spectrum of American religious diversity. But this diversity cloaks substantial moral issues about the ways in which religious groups influence and shape individual decision making among their members. It is not merely that these people take risks other people do not and decide to do so in ways other people would not; it is the very uniformity of these group-specific risk budgets and styles and the degree to which they fall outside the ordinary range of variation that invites scrutiny of the mechanisms by which they are produced. What we will find, I think, are systematic, doctrine-controlled violations of the principle of autonomy—that is, of that moral principle familiar in professional and ordinary ethics that requires both protection of an individual's capacity to choose and respect for the substance of that choice.

If there are violations of the principle of autonomy, they can be identified by locating the precise point at which they occur in the paradigmatic decision-making process, evident in varying forms in the four religious groups to be examined here. These are groups whose adherents regularly make choices that indirectly or directly expose them to risks of death. Are these choices *informed*? Do they involve *consent,* genuine consent that is voluntary and uncoerced? In answering these questions, raised in approaching the problem from the standpoint of professional ethics, it will become clear that some of the ways in which religious groups shape and control high-risk decision making are morally indefensible. However, this is not true of all of the ways in which high-risk decision making is influenced—even among the four groups isolated for discussion here—and it will be necessary to develop a general criterion for distinguishing morally indefensible practices controlling religious decision making from those that may be morally defensible. This criterion will serve in concert with the typology of doctrinal claims developed in the previous chapter to fix more precisely the range within which we can discern and address *ethical* issues generated within organized religion.

Three of the groups we shall examine participate in practices that impose varying degrees of indirect risk of death by refusal of medical treatment or some component of it—Christian Science, Jehovah's Witnesses, and the Faith Assembly. The practices of a fourth group impose, in addition, a direct threat of death—the various serpent-handling, strychnine-drinking pentecostal groups within the Holiness churches. Two of these, the Faith Assembly and the Holiness churches, are generally regarded as cults or fringe groups; the other two, Christian Science and the Jehovah's Witnesses, occupy intermediate positions between the fringe and the mainstream of American religious groups. That these are all generally Christian denominations, though differing considerably in their teachings, should not suggest that similar moral issues do not arise in other world religions, but only that the issues of high-risk decision making in religious commitment are particularly prominent in certain strands of the Christian tradition.

## Risk Taking in Four American Religious Groups

*Christian Science.* The First Church of Christ, Scientist, takes the refusal of conventional medical treatment in favor of Christian Science healing as central among its practices and as indicative of faith.[2] According to Christian Science belief, what we (mistakenly) call "disease" is produced by a "radically limited and distorted view of the true spiritual nature and capacities of men and women";[3] illness results from "human alienation from God,"[4] produced by fundamental misunderstanding. Disease is symptomatic not of physical disorder but of underlying spiritual inadequacy and a failure to understand one's true spiritual nature. When a faithful member of the church falls ill, he or she consults a Christian Science practitioner to seek treatment which consists "entirely of heartfelt yet disciplined prayer."[5] The practitioner, who is often consulted by telephone (sometimes long distance) and need not make a bedside visit, has no medical training in either diagnosis or treatment. The practitioner does not physically touch or examine the patient. Rather, the practitioner assists the ill person in prayer, the objective of which is to relieve physical symptoms by promoting the correct and reverent understanding of the true nature of disease—that in reality there is no such thing. Hence, prayer is believed to be incompatible with conventional medical treatment, since medical treatment presupposes the misleading assumption that there is such a thing as disease, that it is of physical origin, and that it can be treated by physical means. Properly, one cannot speak of *cure,* for there is no disease to be cured; rather, the relief of symptoms is a "demonstration" of the correctness of the principles upon which Christian Science is founded. Christian Scientists do generally use the services of dentists and oculists and sometimes have physicians perform what they call "mechanical" procedures not involving medication, such as setting broken bones, but other than this, no conventional medical procedures, either diagnostic or therapeutic, are used.[6] For services rendered in praying for and with the individual who is ill, the Christian Science practitioner receives a fee roughly comparable to the fees conventional physicians charge. This fee is reimbursable by many insurance companies (including some Blue Cross/Blue Shield plans) and by some state and federal Medicare and Medicaid programs.[7] There are about five thousand Christian Science practitioners who practice healing through prayer on a full-time basis.[8]

Frequently, the choice between Christian Science healing and conventional medical treatment does not constitute a subjectively recognized *risk* for the devout Scientist, since belief in the efficacy of Christian Science healing may be very strong. In such cases, the individual may be confident that Christian Science healing will provide relief from the condition that troubles him. Nevertheless, the choice to accept treatment from a Christian Science practitioner rather than an M.D., or not to accept treatment at all, resembles in structure any other prudential calculation under risk: various possible outcomes—cure, continuing illness, incapacitation, and death—are foreseen under specific valuations and under more or less quantifiable expectations about the likelihood of their occurrence. Christian Scientists are, of course, aware of the availability of conventional medicine; medical treatment is a possible choice, but one that, on prudential grounds, the believing Christian Scientist does not make. The believing Scientist not only thinks he or she is acting in accord with the dictates or expectations of the faith, but also that he or she will maximize the likelihood of achieving the outcome with the greatest expected utility—namely, a successful cure—by preferring Christian Science healing to conventional medicine. It is in this choice that the risk taking lies, though for the believing Christian Scientist, of course, it is seen as a good risk.

*Jehovah's Witnesses.* Jehovah's Witnesses refuse a single component of medical treatment, the transfusion of blood or blood derivatives into their bodies. They do so on the basis of a variety of scriptural passages, especially Genesis 9:4 ("Only, you shall not eat flesh with its life, that is, its blood"), Leviticus 17:12 ("Therefore I have said to the people of Israel: No person among you shall eat blood, nor shall any alien who resides among you eat blood"), Deuteronomy 12:23–25 ("Only be sure that you do not eat the blood; for the blood is the life"), and Acts 15:28–29 ("For it has seemed good to the Holy Spirit and to us to impose on you no further burden than these essentials: that you abstain from what has been sacrificed to idols and from blood and from what has been strangled and from fornication"); they believe that the scriptural prohibition of eating or drinking blood includes any form of taking the blood of another into one's own body, including by transfusion.[9] Although they will accept the infusion of nonblood solutions to expand blood volume, faithful Witnesses consent to surgery—even major surgery—only under the understanding that it be performed without additional blood.[10] They will not accept blood in emergency situations or accidents, and relatives are asked to refuse consent on behalf of those who are unconscious. Nor will they accept blood or blood derivatives in treatment for diseases of the blood, such as anemia or leukemia. In a series of cases, the courts have generally upheld the right of competent, adult Jehovah's Witnesses to refuse blood transfusions, even where the risk of death is high, provided that the patient has no obligations to dependents that cannot otherwise be met.[11] However, the courts have generally not permitted pregnant women to refuse transfusions, nor parents to refuse transfusions for their minor children.

For Jehovah's Witnesses, the situations in which these choices arise are comparatively rare, though when such situations do arise they may be extremely serious or life-threatening. Frequently, too, such decisions must be made in conditions of extreme urgency, as for accident victims, where exsanguination is an immediate, life-threatening risk. Despite the urgency, however, such choices also conform to the risk-taking paradigm: the two principal possible outcomes—survival with transfusion, versus death without transfusion—are foreseen under evaluations assigning great weight to obedience to church belief and the highest value to an expected salvific afterlife, versus a great but comparatively lesser value to continuing physical existence. As in all risk taking, that option believed to promise greater utility under the assigned valuation is the one that the prudent, rational Witness will choose.

*The Faith Assembly.* The Faith Assembly, a small fundamentalist group centered in northeastern Indiana, at its height prohibited its members from consulting doctors or from using any medical treatment at all, including vaccination and other preventive treatment, assistance in childbirth, emergency treatment, prostheses, eyeglasses, or hearing aids. This group was founded in the mid-1960s by Hobart Freeman, a former Southern Baptist minister who had been dismissed from the faculty at a fundamentalist theological seminary for failing to conform to its beliefs. Freeman started the church in his basement, moved it to a rural barn (the "Glory Barn") and, after a dispute with the owner, moved the church again to its present center near Goshen, Indiana. Freeman taught the members of the fledgling church to shun doctors and to rely on prayer and faith for healing—a teaching that stiffened into a rigorous antimedical policy enforced by the threat of expulsion from the group. Freeman also claimed that he would never die.

In the spring of 1983, two reporters from the *Fort Wayne News-Sentinel* investigated evidence of fifty-two deaths attributed to the group's prohibition of medical treatment.[12] The dead included twenty-eight babies whose mothers refused prenatal care, seven children with untreated illnesses and injuries, ten adults with untreated illnesses, and seven mothers who died of untreated complications of childbirth. The reporters also identified a living five-year-old child with a basketball-sized tumor of the abdomen whom they expected to become the fifty-third death. But they also found evidence that compliance with the group's policy of refusing medical treatment was by no means universally voluntary. They documented the existence of an underground network by which mothers were taking their children to physicians in neighboring cities to seek medical treatment without fear of exposure, punishment, or excommunication for themselves or the children. They also described in detail the case of Sally Burkitt, a twenty-seven-year-old woman who hemorrhaged following the unassisted delivery of her child: medical attention was denied her and she bled to death fifty-six hours after delivery—despite her explicit, repeated pleas for a doctor. ("We'll get the best doctor there is," her husband had promised, but what he meant was Jesus.[13]) By late 1985, at least ninety deaths had been attributed to the practices of the group; by 1988 the figure had reached one hundred. Hobart Freeman had been indicted in connection with the death of a fifteen-year-old girl, but in December of 1984 he himself had died—with advanced heart disease, gangrene in one foot, pneumonia, and possible diabetes, having refused all treatment. By 1988, eleven parents had been convicted in the deaths of their children, and without Freeman, the group had begun to relax its prohibition of medical care.

*The Holiness Churches.* Serpent handling is a practice found in many cultures, including those of certain southwest American Indian groups, but is particularly widespread in the Appalachian regions of the southeastern United States. It was apparently introduced in 1906 in Grasshopper Valley, Tennessee, by a man named George Went Hensley, who carried a rattlesnake in his hands down from a ridge where he had been bitten. Hensley evangelized throughout Appalachia; his legacy includes many of the small, independent Holiness churches found in the region. While not all Holiness churches practice serpent handling and while it is illegal under state law in Kentucky, Virginia, and Tennessee and under municipal ordinances in North Carolina, the practice is nevertheless found in rural areas in much of Appalachia.

Serpent handlers base their practices on a literal interpretation of Mark 16:17–18: "And these signs will accompany those who believe: by using my name they will cast out demons; they will speak in new tongues; they will pick up snakes in their hands, and if they drink any deadly thing, it will not hurt them; they will lay their hands on the sick, and they will recover."

At the Scrabble Creek Church of All Nations (about thirty-seven miles from Charleston, West Virginia), prayer meetings are held in a small, one-room building with benches or pews and an open area at the front. The meeting is attended by members of all ages, including infants and children, and sometimes by visitors as well. Meetings may last four to six hours, two or three times a week, and consist of hymn singing, preaching, foot washing, healing, and personal testifying of increasing emotional intensity. Participants dance, sing, shriek, shout, crouch or lie on the floor, and may exhibit glossolalia and motor automatisms including spasms, jerks, and seizures. At the climax of these meetings, live poisonous snakes (usually rattlers or copperheads from nearby mountains) are produced from a box or wicker basket and passed among those who wish to handle them. Some participants simply touch or hold the snakes; others coil the snakes around their arms, heads, or throats.[14] The purpose, participants say, is to "receive the Holy Ghost" or to "confirm the word of God" in Mark 16. Bites do occur, but although one source claims that George Hensley said of his forty-six years with the Dolley Pond Church that he had been bitten four hundred times until he was "speckled all over like a guinea hen,"[15] bites are not particularly frequent. Many members also refuse medical treatment if bitten, claiming that the bite provides a further test of God's will.

Many serpent handlers claim that they are "afraid of snakes like anybody else,"[16] but that they lose this fear when they are "anointed" to handle snakes and enter an ecstatic condition. Said Sister Eunice Ball of Newport, Tennessee, "When the anointing's on me, I'm not afraid of the serpents. Other times I'd run. I've taken up as many as six serpents at one time—five copperheads and a large rattler. I've not ever been bitten. There's something there that you know without a doubt that it won't harm you. My hands don't get stiff. I can move my hands, but the feeling's still there."[17] Serpent handlers variously believe that they will not be bitten or that if bitten they will not die, that recovery from snakebite is a miracle wrought by God, and that each snakebite death that does occur is a sign that the Lord "really had to show the scoffers how dangerous it is to obey His commandments."[18] Detractors' claims that the snakes have been de-venomed, drugged, or otherwise deliberately rendered harmless are clearly false, and naturalistic explanations such as that grasping snakes by their midsections produces cataplectic reactions in the snakes or that human body heat or motion disturbs their reflexes also seem inadequate.[19] Between 1910 and 1977, the total number of deaths attributed to religious serpent handling was about forty.[20] Fatalities are also reported from drinking strychnine (sometimes called a "salvation cocktail"), especially in serpent-handling groups in West Virginia.

## Religious Risk and Freedom of Religion

Of course, showing that risk-taking conduct occurs in various forms and degrees of potentially fatal risk among different religious groups is not to reach a normative conclusion. It cannot simply be assumed that risk taking is wrong, however extreme the consequences for the person taking the risk. Quite the contrary, it is plausible to defend risk-taking conduct in religion under the general principle of autonomy, regarding religious choice as one kind of choice an individual is entitled to make by virtue of his or her right of self-determination. Furthermore, since religious belief may be at the heart of an individual's identity and since action according to these beliefs may be central to the individual's maintaining this identity in the world, religious choice—even where it involves serious, potentially disabling or fatal risks—may seem particularly worthy of protection and respect. Of course, some religiously committed individuals may not perceive their behavior as involving risk, nor, for that matter, as involving any choice or decision at all. In fact, it may be those most firmly committed who see themselves as having no options, in that they feel bound to do whatever God or the specific religious group requires. Some may even believe that they cannot do otherwise not only in a normative sense but in a metaphysical sense as well: ultimately, they believe, God determines both what shall happen and how they shall act. Still others may recognize a single antecedent choice—for instance, the choice "for Jesus" or "for God"— but hold otherwise theodeterminist views. Nevertheless, many believers recognize the distinction between subjective and objective risk, and even if they feel their personal commitments oblige them to make certain choices rather than others, acknowledge that in many religiously relevant situations it would be possible to perform any one of several alternative actions, each of which would yield differently valued outcomes and incur different degrees of risk. The principle of autonomy defends all varieties of high-risk choice in religion where choice is voluntarily and knowingly made—that is, where the criteria of informed consent are met—even when the outcome may be death.

A principal objection to the view that autonomous risk-taking conduct in religion should be respected, the only objection with legal standing, appeals to the harm principle by citing the social costs of such behavior. Under this principle, risk-taking religious conduct may be morally condemned, as well as restricted or prohibited under law, where it imposes harm or substantial risk of harm to others. For instance, emotional and financial costs for immediate family members or the dependents may be severe if the risk that person takes turns out badly. Whether a parent dies because he or she has undergone surgery without blood, or was fatally bitten in a serpent-handling prayer meeting, or died after refusing medical treatment for a curable illness, the consequences for a dependent child are the same. Some legal cases appear to restrict religious risk taking on the ground of obligations to dependents, as in the Jehovah's Witnesses cases, but this remains a much-disputed issue.

Religious risk taking may also be restricted if the risk involves not only the individual who voluntarily assumes it but bystanders and dependents as well. For instance, in *Swann v. Pack,* a 1975 case, the Tennessee Supreme Court outlawed serpent handling on the ground that it constitutes a public nuisance. In this case, a prayer meeting of the Holiness Church of God in Jesus Name was described by the prosecution as involving the "handling of snakes in a crowded church sanctuary with virtually no safeguards, with children roaming around unattended, and with the handlers so enraptured and entranced that they were in a virtual state of hysteria,"[21] although the defense presented further evidence to show that the snake handling was performed on a stage in front of the audience and that the area was roped off with guards stationed at intervals to prevent any snakes from escaping. Although laws explicitly prohibiting serpent handling have been passed in only a handful of states, observers suggest that in many other states such practices would most likely be construed as constituting a public nuisance.

The costs society must absorb for those who are injured, incapacitated, or killed in religious risk taking may, of course, be considerable. However, a general analysis that focuses on the social consequences of religious practices must surely cut the other way: a great deal of the behavior encouraged by religious groups is strongly risk reductive, especially where nonviolent, continent ways of life are required, and results in social savings rather than costs. Methodists and Mormons do not drink; Seventh-day Adventists avoid food additives, stimulants, and meat; Quakers do not go to war. Catholics, like those in most Christian groups, are forbidden to commit suicide. The Amish generally shun modern conveniences, such as motor vehicles and electric power appliances and tools and thus risk fewer accidents. Most Christian-based groups discourage pre- and extramarital sexual activity and violent lifestyles, thus reducing the risk of injury, pregnancy, and sexually transmitted disease. Where these prohibitions are effective, they lower the risks to health and life considerably, and the social savings that result clearly vastly outweigh the social costs of increased risk taking by those who refuse medical treatment and the handful of snake handlers in rural Appalachia. Of course, an appeal to the harm principle introduces the extremely interesting further question of whether a religious group ought to encourage or require its members to consider the potential impact of their own risks on others before taking them, and just how the impact ought to weigh in their choices. The more fundamental issue, however, directly concerns the ways in which members of religious groups come to take such major risks in the first place.

In this examination of the ways in which four specimen groups—Christian Science, Jehovah's Witnesses, the Faith Assembly, and the Holiness churches—elicit risk-taking behavior, it has been assumed that their practices do, in fact, increase risks of ill health, disability, or death. Comprehensive, reliable figures for the actual rates of risk or the frequency of negative outcomes are not available for any of these groups, however, and for some of them information that might provide evidence of increased risk is either not collected or very closely guarded. Of course, there are some scattered data on which to base this assumption. As we have seen, by 1988 one hundred deaths had been attributed to the practices of the Faith Assembly in its two decades of existence. A joint study by the Indiana State Department of Health and the Center for Disease Control in Atlanta calculated that in Elkhart and Koscuisko counties, Indiana, where many Faith Assembly members live, mothers in the sect were one hundred times as likely to die from complications of pregnancy as other women in Indiana and that babies up to one year old were three times more likely to die.[22] About forty deaths had been reported by 1977 among snake-handling groups. The coroner of King County, Washington, did a retrospective analysis of deaths in the years 1949–51; he found eleven apparently preventable deaths among Christian Science children and calculated that 6 percent of all Christian Science deaths were preventable. This study, though simplistic in its methodology, also reported that among Christian Scientists, the death rate from cancer was double the national average. In King County, the average longevity of Christian Scientists was very slightly lower than the average longevity of the non-Scientist population.[23]

Case-by-case data on deaths of children in religious groups that reject conventional medical treatment are available from CHILD, Inc. in its extensive newsletter.[24] This group, founded by Rita and Doug Swan, former Christian Scientists whose young son died of meningitis after receiving only Christian Science healing, lobbies actively to have religious exemptions from requirements for medical care for children removed from state law. However, case data cannot provide reliable estimates of the increase (or perhaps decrease) of risk in these religious behaviors. Rigorous statistical analyses of morbidity and mortality patterns associated with treatment refusal or direct risk are not, in general, available for any of the groups considered here.

No complete figures are available, for instance, on the number of Jehovah's Witnesses who have died as a result of refusing blood transfusions, though certain individual cases can be documented from court or medical records. On the contrary, Jehovah's Witnesses often claim that surgery without blood or with only nonblood volume expanders may offer equal or better results than surgery with blood transfusions, partly because of the risks of disease transmission in transfusion and partly because of the greater surgical caution and skill employed by the surgeon who must operate without using blood.[25] Nevertheless, it is believed that many Witnesses have been denied surgical treatment by surgeons unwilling to assume the risks of operating without blood. For instance, although accurate figures are not available, it was rumored some years ago that one of the busiest trauma hospitals in Dade County, Florida, had a blanket policy of refusing to treat Witnesses.[26] As surgical techniques improve for operating without blood and as recognition for Witnesses' firmly established legal right to refuse blood becomes more widespread, however, the risks for Witnesses are declining, though they still remain higher than for persons receiving competently performed surgery with blood where needed. For a variety of reasons, the use of transfusion is no longer virtually automatic in major surgery even where religious belief is not an issue; some conjecture that this can be attributed to better surgical and laser techniques as well as to volume expanders developed partly in response to the dilemmas that surgery on Jehovah's Witnesses had presented.

Similarly, until very recently there has been no controlled study of the mortality of Christian Scientists compared with persons accepting conventional medical care. A 1989 report in the *Journal of the American Medical Association* comparing mortality data for the graduating classes from 1934 to 1983 at Principia College in Elsah, Illinois, a small liberal arts college for Christian Scientists, with a control population of graduating classes from the College of Liberal Arts and Sciences at the University of Kansas in Lawrence found that the death rate for Christian Science alumni was significantly higher—especially for women.[27] That their religious practices increase the risk of ill health or death would, of course, be disputed by many Christian Scientists—who sincerely believe that theirs is a tradition of consistent, effective healing—and perhaps by the Faith Assembly and Holiness churches as well. Nevertheless, there is no persuasive evidence to the contrary, and there is good reason to think that the risks are in fact substantially elevated in all these groups: they forgo blood transfusions, they avoid medical treatment known to be effective, and they handle poisonous snakes.

## Altering Risk Behavior

That the members of these four religious groups exhibit distinctive commonalities in risk budget and style that fall well outside the risk budgets and styles of most other persons in society is evident enough, but these commonalities do not all arise in the same way. If we examine the practices and policies of the four groups more closely, four quite different mechanisms are in evidence by which these commonalities are produced. Each involves autonomy-compromising interference with the paradigmatic decision-making structure at a different point. It is the varying nature of the interferences that renders the practices of each group subject to a different point of moral critique and that makes it possible to distinguish between those interferences that are morally defensible and those that are not. In the actual world of religious practice, of course, none of the mechanisms ascribed to each of these groups occurs in isolation, and each group has some of the features of the others—as do many other religious groups as well. Nevertheless, these mechanisms—artificially isolated here—are clearly most prominent in and distinctive of these groups.

*Coercion.* One way a religious group (or any group) can alter the risk-taking behavior of its members is by coercion. Within the Faith Assembly, although some members voluntarily accepted its policy of refusing medical treatment, others—according to the accounts of the two Fort Wayne reporters—did so only under threat of other sanctions. These included public humiliation, repudiation by spouses, friends, and other members of the group, and expulsion from the group altogether. Coercion operates by introducing a new outcome variable into the calculation that the risk taker makes. Not only must the risk taker weigh the probabilities and costs or benefits of possible negative or positive outcomes, but also the very large cost that will be imposed if he or she refuses to take the risk. Coercion thus suppresses the possibility of the initial choice. The force of the coercive measure is a function of the perceived costs to be imposed and the likelihood that the measure will actually be imposed, weighed against the costs and benefits of the risk itself. However, such sanctions are typically viewed as virtually certain to be imposed—especially those that involve not only institutional discipline but humiliation and rejection within the group. A number of religious groups, especially among the cults and new religions, are said to use coercion in securing compliance with fasting, socialization, work regimens, expressions of loyalty and group commitment, and the contribution of one's financial and other resources to the group: the Oakland Family of the Unification Church, or Moonies, and the International Society for Krishna Consciousness, or Hare Krishna, are often cited in this regard. The People's Temple at Jonestown provided no doubt the most horrifying example. Within the Faith Assembly, the sanctions were comparatively mild, but still strong enough to produce compliance in many cases where the risks apparently would not have been voluntarily sustained.

*Altering Risk Styles.* A second way a religious group can alter the risk-taking conduct of its members is by altering their risk styles. For instance, a group may work to make its members consider certain choices more carefully than they ordinarily might, often to the individual's ultimate advantage. This may be the effect of much of the pastoral marriage counseling that many mainstream and other religious groups provide, since counseling usually encourages the individual not to leave a marriage impetuously or in temporary anger, but only after sustained reflection, thought, and prayer. However, some religiously induced changes in risk style appear to work in the other direction, toward less considered, less cautious styles of taking risks; it is these that present deeper moral issues.

Among serpent-handling groups, for instance, individual choices to touch or hold a snake appear not to be coerced; there is no sanction, either official or informal, during the prayer meeting or afterward for declining to handle snakes. Nor are snakes thrust upon people; those who choose to handle them must come forward to do so. Many members of Holiness churches where serpents are handled attend prayer meetings on a regular basis but never touch snakes. In fact, the teachings and traditions of this group explicitly encourage members to handle snakes only when they feel called or moved—"anointed"—to do so, and urge them not to do so otherwise. Persons are not blamed or chastised for failing to become anointed or for not handling snakes. Thus, serpent handling in the Holiness churches appears to be free of the kind of coercion characteristic of the Faith Assembly's refusal of medical treatment.

However, serpent-handling meetings involve active participation by many of the members. Services consist not only in singing and preaching, but in moving about the room, touching, shouting, and shrieking; this very high level of activity is sustained over several hours. These factors tend to produce an extremely heightened level of emotionality, which in turn invites the trembling, tactile hallucinations, glossolalia, and physical convulsions that members believe are the identifying signs of being anointed to handle snakes. But, according to the teachings and practices of the group, it is in precisely this (abnormal) condition that an individual's choice to handle serpents on this specific occasion must be made. One cannot decide in advance to handle snakes; one must wait to be "called." Reverend Robert Grooms describes his first anointing, which occurred at the Holiness Church of God in Jesus Name, Carson Springs, Tennessee, in 1970, in the following way: "It was like a bucket of water pouring over me. I was tingling all over. I was so anointed with the power that I was just shouting. . . . It's sort of like feeling the heat from a light bulb. It's tremendous. It came over me in such a fantastic way. I felt it through my whole body. I just went plumb out in under the power. But I knew exactly what it was for. God was telling me to take up the serpent."[28] This is the condition that the prosecution in *Swann v. Pack* called "so enraptured and entranced" that worshippers can be described as in a "virtual state of hysteria." It is in this agitated condition, then, that the risk of sudden death is undertaken.

While it is easy to point out the moral deficiencies of coercive alterations of risk budgets or styles, alterations brought about by producing heightened emotionality may be somewhat harder to assess. Under the principle of autonomy, recognized by both ordinary morality and professional ethics, self-harming choices ought not to be honored where emotion is heightened, at least not if it is so heightened as to impair the capacity for autonomous choice. Instead, paternalistic intervention may be necessary to protect autonomy where the individual's decision-making capacity is impaired. Nevertheless, we do in practice respect many sorts of risk-taking decisions made in emotionally heightened conditions, for instance, those made in love, in patriotic fervor, in moments of altruistic self-sacrifice, in daredevil sports adventures, in emergency rescues, and so on. Thus, we have rather ambivalent antecedent standards concerning impairment in risk-taking choices. It is not properly the actual risk involved in serpent handling that should arouse moral suspicion (especially since the risk of death from snakebite may not be greater than in certain dangerous sports, such as hang gliding), but rather the way in which the group engenders a highly charged emotional climate and then requires that risk-taking choices be made in this impaired condition.

Of course, the antecedent choice to attend a serpent-handling prayer meeting is not made under the same emotionally charged conditions, and thus is not subject to the same ethical reservations. However, participants claim that they do not know in advance whether they will in fact be anointed to handle snakes at a particular meeting; they do not decide in advance to handle snakes, but rather they simply decide to attend the meeting. Of course, to decide to attend the meeting is to decide to expose oneself to the risk of deciding to take the risk, but it is not a decision made while confronting the snakes or in the volatile surroundings of the prayer meeting. The specific decision to handle snakes is not made during earlier, calmer, or presumably more rational moments—namely, those moments in which a serpent handler might say "I'm afraid of snakes like anybody else"—but only at the meeting under the extraordinary conditions that occur there.

*Altering Risk Budgets.* Even when the risk taker's prudential calculation is neither skewed by the imposition of coercively large costs for failing to take the risk nor made in an emotionally heightened condition, there are still two further ways this calculation can be distorted. Like any other group, a religious group can influence the individual's estimate of the probability of the various outcomes he or she foresees, or it can change the evaluations assigned by the individual to these outcomes, or both. In both cases, the effect of the influence is not to coerce choice or to impair its quality by altering risk style, but to alter the individual's risk budget.

*Altering assessments of probabilities.* A person reasonably conversant with the circumstances of the world knows certain facts: that malnourishment impairs health, that rattlesnakes are poisonous, that acute appendicitis can be fatal, and so on. These commonplaces are as familiar to the religious person as to the nonreligious; they are part of the common stock of background information shared within a culture. Hence, the religious risk taker—at least when the risks are understood to be common, physical ones—will have a fair amount of background knowledge about the risks he or she takes. A snake handler knows that rattlesnake bites can be fatal; that is what makes snake handling important and why it serves as a test of faith.[29] Similarly, Faith Assembly members know that hemorrhage in childbirth can be fatal; that is why it is a test of commitment to the church's beliefs to refuse treatment and why Sally Burkitt pleaded for a doctor instead. Of course, in many cases religious risk takers will not know the precise degree of risk involved—as most of us do not know the precise risk from hemorrhage in childbirth or from untreated rattlesnake bites—but we all share a general conception of the relative dangers of these threats. It is against this background conception of general estimates of danger that religious risk taking occurs.

Yet it is possible to change an individual's estimate of the likelihood that various possible outcomes will occur. Given an array of evaluated possible outcomes, this may involve making specific positively valued outcomes seem more likely, or making specific negatively valued ones seem less likely, or both, so that a recalculation of the risk would result in a different choice.

Take, for instance, the case of the Christian Scientist with acute appendicitis who seeks relief. Like other members of contemporary society, he or she will have some background understanding of the likelihood that untreated appendicitis could result in death. Although this is by no means a scientifically rigorous conception, the person can say, for instance, that the likelihood of death is greater in untreated appendicitis than in, for example, untreated influenza. However, the teachings of the individual's church persuade him or her that although this background information is accepted by nonbelievers and correctly describes the probabilities confronting them, the probabilities are quite different for persons who understand the nonphysical nature of illness, the power of Christian Science healing, and the true nature of prayer. The believer holds that achieving a correct understanding of illness as resulting from defective mental attitudes will free him or her from illness—even when the risks would otherwise be very high—and that the way to achieve this correct understanding is in prayer. Thus, the Christian Scientist will hold, the risk of death from acute appendicitis treated only with Christian Science prayer is, in fact, much lower than the shared cultural conception would insist—in fact, that it is actually lower not only than the risk from untreated appendicitis but lower than the risk in appendicitis treated with conventional medicine. Prayer, in this view, is the most effective treatment of all. This shared perception of risk explains why Christian Scientists exhibit similar, though unusual, risk budgets in medical choices of this sort; but it also invites us to ask how this shared perception of risk is attained.

How does the believing Christian Scientist reach this still lower estimate of the probability of death? Let us look at the kind of evidence with which the believer is supplied and upon which he or she bases prudential calculations of risk.

Support for claims of the efficacy of Christian Science healing, following the pattern of assertions made in *Science and Health with Key to the Scriptures* and other writings of Mary Baker Eddy, is provided largely by the testimonials of those who recount the ways in which they have been healed from disease or injury. These testimonials are typically quite detailed and fervently sincere in tone; they are direct, first-hand accounts of what is often an extremely powerful, faith-confirming experience. For example, a woman living in the Mojave Desert area of California writes: "On a warm afternoon last May while coming into our house through the laundry room (which is part of the garage), I felt a sharp pain in my right foot. Looking down, I saw what appeared to be a rattlesnake, disappearing under the washing machine."[30] She goes on to recount her fear, the assistance of the Christian Science practitioner in praying for her recovery, the development and eventual subsiding of a discolored, numb swelling on her foot, and the confirming effects this experience had upon her faith.

This testimonial is typical of the handful published in each issue of the *Christian Science Journal,* a monthly periodical widely circulated among Christian Scientists and, like the weekly *Christian Science Sentinel,* a primary source of information about the church. The *Journal* asserts that "the statements made in these testimonies with regard to healings have been carefully verified,"[31] and that it retains on file the originals of testimonials together with the three written verifications or vouchers required for publication. Since 1900, some 53,900 testimonials of healing have been published in the periodicals of the church; they are said to be "the most important body of evidence concerning Christian Science healing."[32]

According to a First Church of Christ, Scientist, authority defending healing in a recent issue of the *New England Journal of Medicine,* a careful examination of testimonials published in Christian Science periodicals between 1971 and 1981 shows "647 testimonies concerning illnesses that had been medically diagnosed, in some cases both before and after a healing . . . [including] leukemia and other neoplasias, both malignant and benign; diptheria; gallstones; pernicious anemia; club feet; spinal meningitis; and bone fracture, among numerous others."[33] This figure includes 137 pediatric cases. Healing in such cases might seem to constitute an impressive record. But the record is wholly anecdotal in form, appealing simply to isolated cases without reference either to general patterns or trends or to comparisons based on control groups. The effect of this kind of information—independently of whether the claims are actually true—is to exacerbate one of the most common, frequent errors in decision-making under risk.

Many kinds of error are possible in risk-taking choice. Objective errors include misidentification of the range of possible outcomes and assignment of faulty probabilities to possible outcomes (often as the product of subjective factors such as unwarranted optimism or pessimism), misidentification of the values one assigns to possible outcomes, inconsistent weightings of possible outcomes, self-deception, and so on. But there is a common, documentable error characteristic of rational choice, frequently discussed with reference to informed consent in medical situations. This is the tendency to overrely on case information and to underrely on base-rate information.[34] Ordinary patients in ordinary medical contexts do this: they tend to base decisions on anecdotal accounts, supplied by physicians, friends, personal experience, or other sources, and to downplay or ignore information about the rates of incidence of specific conditions, side effects, self-limiting conditions, spontaneous recovery, and so on. But while ordinary medical patients do this rather naturally, Christian Scientists in situations of medical risk are in effect encouraged to do so, since they are supplied with information that makes miscalculation inevitable. What are *not* available from the Christian Science church or from its publications are data that might counteract this tendency or that could contribute to establishing reliable base-rate information: How often, given a specific medical condition, does Christian Science healing appear to be effective? This is a much easier question to answer than "How often is Christian Science healing actually effective?"—but even for the easier question about apparent results no data are available.

Clearly, 647 documented cases over a ten-year period is sparse evidence, in view of the number of Scientists and the frequency within the general population of the diseases involved. There might, of course, be many undiagnosed, undocumented cases or a lower incidence of the conditions among the Christian Science population, but these conjectures do little to provide the Christian Scientist with a reliable sense of the frequency with which Christian Science healing, once attempted, is effective. Testimonials of failures are, of course, not published in the church's periodicals. Furthermore, the lack of negative information is compounded by false positives—cases in which Christian Science healing is credited with the cure of a condition that was self-limiting or would have resolved spontaneously anyway—as when the cold that vanishes after troubling a person for two weeks is taken as proof that Christian Science really works.[35] Even the account by the woman bitten by the rattlesnake under her washing machine should be seen in light of the fact that rattlesnake bites, especially at distant sites on a limb (the woman was bitten on the foot), are comparatively seldom fatal; but this information was not provided. Yet it is only with adequate base-rate information, making it possible to calculate overall frequencies of success and failure in non-self-limiting conditions with given forms of treatment, that a person can rationally compare conventional medical treatment with Christian Science healing of the same condition, and make a choice in an informed way.[36]

To assert that Christian Science healing cannot be chosen on a rational basis is, of course, not to assume that Christian Science healing is in fact less effective than conventional medical therapy (a point possibly conceded by some critics of the group, given substantial rates of iatrogenic illness in conventional treatment and the fact that a very large proportion—variously estimated at 75 or 80 percent—of the "illnesses" initially seen by physicians are either self-limiting or psychogenic in origin), but only to point out that the basis on which a Christian Scientist makes a choice in seeking relief from symptoms is not rationally defensible. Christian Science healing might, in fact, be more effective than conventional medicine, but even the Christian Scientist would have no way of knowing this. Yet the church does claim to supply persuasive, empirical *evidence* for the efficacy of healing; this is part of the point of *Science and Health with Key to the Scriptures* and part of the point of providing testimonials at all.

Nicholas Rescher takes the crucial distinction in risk assessment to be that between *realistic* and *unrealistic* appraisal.[37] But despite the fact that the individual Christian Scientist's choice to rely on Christian Science healing is not rationally defensible, it cannot be said to be unrealistic in a general sense. This is because the individual Scientist has not exaggerated, underestimated, misinterpreted, or otherwise misapprehended or distorted the available evidence. Given the evidence he or she has, the tools provided for assessing it, and the surrounding claim of a trusted institution that the evidence is compelling, he or she makes a subjectively realistic assessment; the fault is not the Scientist's, given that he or she is both a believer and a member of the church. In fact, the Christian Scientist characteristically believes that such a choice is a good, sound decision based on a large body of compelling evidence—evidence that, though ignored by non-Scientists, is rationally persuasive. As one Scientist wrote,

> My own family has relied on Christian Science for generations. I have never considered prayer a gamble. Please understand: I'm not speaking of some crude kind of "faith healing" that implores God to heal and says it was His will if nothing happens. I'm speaking of responsible spiritual healing practiced now over a century by many perfectly normal citizens and caring parents.
>
> I'm concerned about not being taken seriously—that nobody in the media . . . is really taking into account that these healings have been happening over many years. Not just in my family, not just my friends. I'm speaking of the massive, long-term experience in a whole denomination.[38]

If this believer's assessment of risk is objectively unrealistic, any moral complaint must be directed not primarily against the believer, nor against church teachers and officials, since after all they too share the same set of assumptions as members of the church. Rather, blame should be directed primarily against the institutional perpetration of the claim that the evidence is valid, and the complaint should point out how the encouragement of belief in the efficacy of healing rather than objective confirmation of it compromises the possibility of autonomous choice. Of course, there is fault on both sides: the medical establishment has been as uninterested in examining alleged Christian Science healings (being generally content to assert that they must either be spontaneous recoveries—perhaps associated with the placebo effect—or have been inaccurately diagnosed in the first place) as Christian Science has been to provide well-documented evidence, in particular evidence scrutinized under contrary hypotheses.

But there is a further complexity to the risks Christian Scientists take in choosing healing over conventional medical treatment. Not all healing is successful; some people remain incapacitated, some are sent to Christian Science sanitariums or nursing homes, and some die. Christian Science teaching explains this at least in part as the result of a failure on the part of the patient to understand fully his or her own nature as a spiritual being or to pray adequately for release from incorrect attitudes; the devout Scientist believes that the risk of death from disease correctly understood and adequately prayed for is nil. But what the Scientist, devout or otherwise, is not encouraged to assess in making risk-taking choices is how likely it is that he or she will correctly understand and adequately pray for release from the condition. This crucially relevant factor in a prudential risk calculation under these religious assumptions is simply not brought into question or discussed, nor is any evidence bearing on it, anecdotal or otherwise, provided. How often does the explanation of a patient's failure to recover appeal to the claim that the patient failed to pray appropriately or had the wrong attitude? This information, too, is of great relevance in risk-taking choices, yet is nowhere forthcoming.

Furthermore (although there is some lack of agreement on this issue)[39] Christian Science generally holds that healing through prayer is incompatible with conventional medical treatment, since prayer consists in achieving an understanding of the nature of disease that contradicts the causal, physicalist assumptions of medicine. Stories abound of people being denied continuation of the services of a Christian Science practitioner if they also enter the care of a physician. Patients who enter Christian Science sanitariums receive care only from nurses who are members of the church and from church practitioners; the nurses are prohibited from doing anything "material" to evaluate or relieve disease and suffering.[40] Thus, although conventional physicians are quick to recognize the psychotherapeutic value of ordinary prayer by the patient, whatever advantages might accrue to the ordinary patient from a combination of medical treatment and religiously supported hope are not available to the Christian Scientist. Rather, the Scientist is forced to make a choice between therapies without knowing whether the chance of survival with both kinds of therapy is better or worse than with only one or the other. Christian Science periodicals do not print testimonials from persons who see doctors as well as healers, any more than they do from persons who see doctors alone.

The institutional practice of altering persons' risk budgets by providing only anecdotal information unaccompanied by base-rate data, as Christian Science does, and by ignoring the incidence of failed cases and of any special conditions that must obtain for the supposed course of action to be effective, fails to satisfy the third basic initial criterion for autonomous choice: not only must it be voluntary and rationally unimpaired, it must be adequately informed. It is true that anecdotal information of the kind provided in Christian Science periodicals can be extremely effective in stirring faith and may be of great significance in a person's life. It may well produce a sizable placebo effect. And it is possible that Christian Science healing is actually efficacious, even in cases of non-self-limiting, serious illness. But insofar as merely anecdotal information is put forward as the evidence for claims of efficacy in healing and as a basis for refusing conventional medical treatment, it is clearly an inadequate basis upon which to encourage people to take such substantial risks. Neither their reliance on religious healing nor their refusal of conventional medical treatment meets the conditions for "informed consent." Hence, if we are to assess the practices of this church in the same way we would assess those of medicine or other secular professions that encourage people to take life-threatening risks without granting them the right to give informed consent, we would be tempted to say that they involve manipulation, callousness, or deceit.

The analysis given here of evidentiary claims concerning the efficacy of nonmedical healing applies not only to Christian Science, but to any religious group that appeals to alternative varieties of healing, whether the healing involves denominational practitioners, faith healers, or the assumed direct influence of a divine being. The Faith Assembly, for instance, regards Jesus as the sole physician, but, at least if the scant evidence available concerning this group is correct, relies on much the same persuasive structures (where it does not directly coerce) as does Christian Science to produce acceptance of its claim. So do individual faith healers of various sorts, groups such as the Church of the First Born and the Faith Tabernacle Congregation, and many of the contemporary "televangelist" preachers. One might also want to inquire into the way in which beliefs about the efficacy of healing are furthered at such institutions as the Roman Catholic shrine at Lourdes, as well as into the practices of groups which accept faith healing but do not reject conventional medical treatment, such as the Assemblies of God and certain charismatic subgroups of Catholicism and Anglicanism. Thus, while Christian Science may provide the most conspicuous example of a certain sort of religious intervention in high-risk decision making, it will have many features in common with other groups, and ethical censure, if it is appropriate at all, ought hardly be reserved for this group alone.

*Altering evaluations of outcomes.* In addition to altering assessments of probabilities, risk budgets can be altered by changing the evaluations that the risk taker assigns to various possible outcomes. Since the prudential calculation the risk taker makes is the product of assessments of the probabilities of the various outcomes times the value he or she assigns to them, changing evaluations will alter risk behavior as effectively as altering estimates of probabilities.

The Jehovah's Witnesses, who refuse blood transfusions although they accept other components of medical treatment, accept a risk of death that is as serious as that taken by serpent handlers, Christian Scientists, and members of the Faith Assembly. However, the prudential calculation that the Jehovah's Witness makes has quite different ingredients. Whereas the Christian Scientist seeks a cure for his or her illness (although the Scientist does not call it a "cure" nor recognize the condition as an "illness") and makes a decision whether to accept conventional medical treatment or to rely on Christian Science healing based on a calculation concerning the efficacy of the two forms of treatment, however ill-informed, the Jehovah's Witness, in contrast, does not seek a cure at all. To be sure, the Witness hopes to get well, and hopes not to die. But the primary commitment is to honor a prohibition that he or she believes to be divinely mandated, *whatever* the costs in health or life, in order to ensure eventual salvation. Of course, the Jehovah's Witness will be party to the culturally shared background information concerning the likelihood of death in whatever medical condition he or she is suffering, whether it is acute appendicitis or intestinal hemorrhage, but the church makes no attempt to alter the individual's assessment of these probabilities. What the church does instead is supply him or her with a reevaluation of outcome states.

The Jehovah's Witness suffering an intestinal hemorrhage, for instance, will have at least a general awareness (sometimes intensified by an unsympathetic surgeon) that the chance of surviving with both surgery and blood transfusion are good, but that the chances of surviving with surgery alone, without blood, are markedly reduced, though they are not so low as the chances of surviving without any treatment at all. The church does not disguise these facts, nor does it encourage the Witness to base his or her choice on anecdotal information in the absence of base-rate data. But there is something new in the picture here, not much evident in the Christian Scientist's choice between medicine and healing as the better risk for staying alive: the Jehovah's Witness sees the choice as one for maximizing the chances of eternal life rather than temporal existence. Clearly, the Witness does not want to die; otherwise, he or she would not consent to surgery at all. But the believing Witness wants something else still more, obeying the divine command because he or she believes that failure to do so might end all hope of salvation. Thus, although the believer's prudential calculation is in structure just like the calculations made by the serpent handler, the Christian Scientist, and the member of the Faith Assembly, its scope includes a wider set of possible outcomes. This range of outcomes believed possible is expanded by the teachings of the church, which supplies not only the claim that there is such a condition as salvation, but a set of conditions for attaining it; it also identifies in its doctrines a particular act, accepting blood, that would preclude reaching this state.

To expand the range of possible outcomes a person foresees in this way has two associated consequences: it forces that person to reassess the disvalue he or she has assigned to the possible loss or adverse consequences previously expected, and it forces the person to reassess the value of the previously expected probable benefit or gain. Reassessment typically takes the form of diminution of the extreme values assigned to the previous best and worst outcomes, though they remain possibilities within the schema, and distinctively religious outcomes are substituted that now assume the most extreme values. These altered value rankings are so strongly bipolar and so extreme that one, salvation, acquires complete priority over the other, damnation, and over all intermediate outcome states as well. Life and death become trifles in the face of these new outcomes so that they come to play a subsidiary role, if any, in risk-taking choices.

It is this double substitution in the value rankings of outcomes that is characteristic of religious recommitment and conversion, and it is the adoption and maintenance of these value rankings that is central to much religious education and—as we shall see in the next chapter—to convert seeking. (It is also this feature of reevaluation that distinguishes this type of risk-budget alteration from simple coercion, discussed earlier. There, additional sanctions were added to the individual's perceived range of outcomes, but this did not produce reevaluation of the initial possible outcomes foreseen.) A reevaluation of outcomes of this sort would have evident effects on the risk-taking calculation: virtually any risk that might secure salvation would be worth it, whether it cost one's life or anything else, provided only that failure in the risk would not preclude future chances of achieving salvation after all. Similarly, one could venture *no* risk of damnation, no matter how attractive the intermediate gain.

To be sure, this starkly bipolar conception of an afterlife is too rigid and primitive for the many more liberal, contemporary forms of religious faith; heaven and hell in a hereafter are not the outcomes envisioned by every religious consciousness. Many religious groups (or at least the more liberal elements within them), especially among main-stream Protestants and some Catholics, have been discarding traditional notions of the afterlife. But this does not diminish the capacity of the more liberal religious groups to alter their members' evaluations of outcome states in risk-taking situations. For some modern groups, "heaven" and "hell" are taken to apply to conditions of this world and there is no life after death; heaven and hell label states of human consciousness, but are equally strongly to be sought or avoided. These states are not to be confused with pleasure and pain or happiness and unhappiness. Borrowing Catholic terminology, they might best be called "beatitude" and "sin," though this conception is by no means confined to Catholicism. They are distinctively *religious* conditions, though they may on occasion coincide with positive and negative hedonic states.

The more contemporary interpretations of traditional afterlife notions exhibit a second way in which religious groups can alter evaluations of outcomes in risk-taking calculations; they can divert the individual's assignment of maximal value from secular states of happiness, pleasure, or utility, generally defined, to the distinctively religious condition of this-world beatitude. This change might seem to be merely terminological, if an individual is simply to switch risk-taking strategies from maximizing utility in the secular sense to achieving this-world beatitude: it is still the state the individual most strongly prefers. But while secular states of pleasure or happiness are by and large identifiable both by the agent and, though less reliably, by external observers, it is the religious group, drawing on the theological tradition behind it, that stipulates what counts as beatitude. It is also the religious group that defines the conditions for identifying it. Thus, the religious group both promotes achieving the state and urges the believer to be willing to risk all to gain it, and yet at the same time identifies what that state is and provides instructions ("discipline") concerning how to attain it. For some strains of Catholicism, for instance, this-world beatitude seems to be identified with "the beauty of suffering": what one should want most is to be like Christ and to feel the full measure of Christ's sacrifice. In other strains of the same tradition, it is identified with humility, with mystic transport, or with complete self-sacrificing charity. In still other traditions, particularly those influenced by eastern religions, the maximally valued state (often called "enlightenment") is stipulated as egolessness, detachment, or perhaps complete obedience to a "master." The range of this-world conditions that are identified as maximally valued possible outcomes may vary widely from group to group, but in each case it is the religious group that identifies the condition and assigns both its preeminent status in the believer's value schema and its capacity to reevaluate or eclipse ordinary value rankings. It is in this way that a religious group alters the risk budgets and hence the risk behavior of its members, first by stipulating what sorts of outcomes they should be willing to risk serious harm or death to attain and then by urging them to take the risk.

Looking back at the three forms of intervention in high-risk decision making previously described, it is easy to see where moral analysis gains a foothold. The Faith Assembly methods involved clear-cut coercion, at least on some occasions. The Holiness churches avoid coercion but foster a kind of circumstantial manipulation resulting in impairment of decision-making capacities. Inasmuch as Christian Science practices involve providing only partial, misleading information wholly inadequate for the sort of choice to be made, they involve manipulation, callousness, or deception. Coercion, manipulation, deliberate impairment, callousness, and deception are familiar themes in moral analysis. But risk encouragement by a reevaluation of outcomes, as occurs among the Jehovah's Witnesses, may prove a difficult matter to assess by ordinary moral analysis. There are two principal reasons for this difficulty. First, since encouraging risk taking in this way does not seem to involve coercion, deception, or impairment of the individual's reasoning processes—at least not to the same conspicuous degree as in the three other groups examined here—it does not appear to violate the conditions of autonomous choice. Second, the reevaluation of values is a familiar, accepted strategy for behavioral change and is characteristic of many other enterprises: education, psychotherapy, moral training, discipline, criminal justice, and so on. In each of these areas, reevaluation proceeds by persuading the individual that the old goals, aims, fears, objectives, and so on, were unsophisticated, immoral, or foolish, and by encouraging him or her to accept new, better, healthier ones. The new goals then assume preeminent status; as the older ones are completely eclipsed or recede into triviality, the reevaluation is achieved.

Although reevaluation may make use of a variety of specific techniques, moral objections to deliberate alteration of an individual's valuation of outcomes, where it does not involve coercion, deception, or impairment of reasoning processes, typically attach not to the fact or methods of reevaluation but to the altered valuation itself. Regardless of its methods, we object when an institution—a school, for example—attempts to turn a humanitarian into a bigot, but are much less likely to object when a similar institution using similar methods seeks to reverse the process. By and large, we take the reevaluation to be a salutary one when it assigns greater importance to rationally defensible value rankings such as happiness over unhappiness, pleasure over pain, beauty over ugliness, health over illness, compassion over cruelty, and so forth, both for the agent and for those affected by the agent's actions. However, in a religious context like that of the Jehovah's Witnesses, the reevaluation can move outside the range of rationally defensible value rankings to assign preeminent status to distinctively religious conditions.

It is this that makes it difficult to evaluate some forms of risk taking in religion and to assess the means by which some religious groups elicit such behavior. The altering of risk budgets by reevaluation of outcomes that characterizes Jehovah's Witness practice should, presumably, be evaluated by assessing the actual moral value of those outcomes that are assigned the highest rank in the individual's new evaluative scheme. Of course, it is not possible to supply morally objective, non-faith-based assessments of these outcomes, nor for that matter objective, non-faith-based evidence for the reality or attainability of such outcomes. The Jehovah's Witness may be quite willing to risk death by refusing blood transfusions in order to attain salvation, but he or she has only faith-based "evidence" that there is such a thing as salvation or that keeping the commandment to avoid blood will be instrumental in attaining it. Similarly, the traditional Catholic who seeks beatitude in suffering has only faith-based evidence, supplied by the doctrines or teachings of the church, to assure him or her of the intrinsic superiority of this condition over pleasure, happiness, or other secular states. Nonbelievers will be skeptical of both claims and hence quite ready to say that these (erroneously) expected outcomes do not warrant the risks made in their names. Consequently, the skeptics will further argue, the institutional church that promotes risk taking to achieve these outcomes has no warrant for controlling the behavior of its adherents in this way. It may be one thing to hold or even teach such beliefs; it is quite another, the skeptics will add, to encourage or require persons to make high-risk personal decisions based on these beliefs, especially when it may cost them their lives. Where religious risk taking is elicited by a reevaluation of outcome states in a way that deviates from rationally defensible rankings of outcomes, there is no way to defend such practices but little way to denounce them either, since they are to be evaluated on the basis of religious outcome values that cannot be assumed either true or false. Thus risk encouragement by reevaluation cannot be attacked in the direct way that risk encouragement can be attacked when it proceeds by coercion, impairment, or deception, but it cannot be granted a clean bill of ethical health either.

It is now possible to see why it is often difficult, in the religious situations covered here, to distinguish between decisions under risk and those under uncertainty. In many or most of these decision situations, the individual has very little, if any, knowledge of the actual probability of the outcomes he or she can foresee; objectively, decision is made under uncertainty. But in most cases a believer's religious group supplies both a general conception of the likelihood of various outcomes and a conception of what the range of possible outcomes is, though these conceptions are likely to be conveyed by trading on hopes, conveying promises, supplying assurances, discounting counterevidence, and so on. Significantly, the religious group typically supplies the believer with a conception that the probabilities are very strongly favorable ("Since Jesus loves you, mere serpents cannot harm you"), though he or she has little or no objective evidence that this is so. Thus the individual *believes* he or she knows the probability of possible outcomes; subjectively speaking, the choice appears to be a decision under risk, though to an external view, it is a decision made under uncertainty of the most complete sort.

## The Doctrinal Status of Risk Taking

To show that risk-taking religious conduct occurs in various forms and with various amounts of risk in various religious groups is not yet to reach a normative conclusion. It cannot simply be assumed that the making of decisions in which one risks death is wrong, nor can it be assumed that there is something wrong with the mechanisms that religious groups employ to influence people in making these decisions—however extreme the risks, however manipulative the manner of encouraging them, and however severe the consequences for both the risk taker and for others. These are the features that an examination of religious practices using professional ethics exposes; yet to identify features is not to establish that they are morally intolerable, since such conduct is governed not only by moral considerations, but also by the doctrines, teachings, and authoritative pronouncements of the specific religious groups.

In examining the issue of confidentiality in confession in chapter 1 a typology was developed to distinguish various levels of doctrinal assertions with respect to the ethical dilemmas involved. The typology recognizes four distinct levels or orders of doctrinal assertions: 0-order or base-level doctrines, the fundamental imperatives of a group (often, though not always, stated in scriptural texts); first-order doctrines or teachings, which stipulate ways of putting basic imperatives into practice but which characteristically generate new moral problems in doing so; second-order doctrines or teachings, which establish a position that attempts to resolve the ethical problems presented by first-order doctrines; and third-order doctrines or teachings, which function as excuses for residual moral problems. This four-level typology provides a basis for distinguishing the more fundamental religious imperatives of a group from dictates that, though they may have achieved similar doctrinal status, exhibit later historical or theoretical development within a tradition and are best viewed as "answers" to and "excuses" for the moral problems posed by the fundamental imperatives and the ways they are put into practice. Because of their derivative status, whatever doctrinal position they may enjoy, they are to be treated as initially more vulnerable to ethical review than the basic imperatives of the tradition within which they arise.

In surveying the huge variety of risk-taking practices evident among various Christian and Christian-influenced groups, this typology serves to differentiate between those risk-taking dictates that are more vulnerable and those that are less vulnerable to ethical criticism. Of course, since the risk-taking practices described here do not form a coherent, unified, single tradition but occur in a spectrum of denominations and sects with differing histories, application of this typology will not be completely tidy or uniform. Nevertheless, it is possible to identify doctrines, directives, teachings, and other authoritative pronouncements at all four levels.

This identification is most difficult at the 0-order, base level, since most Christian groups do not point to a single, explicit statement of a risk-taking command in their scriptural texts in the same way that they point, for instance, to scriptural commandments to confess. Although suggestive biblical passages do exist, they do not yield a clear, fundamental imperative. Nevertheless, even in the absence of explicit biblical texts that clearly mandate the taking of risks, it is fair to characterize Christianity, with its history of heroism, persecution, and voluntary martyrdom, as a religion of personal commitment and sacrifice: it is a religion in which one must be fully committed and "risk one's all" for God. (This feature of Christianity is particularly evident when compared to Hinduism, Buddhism, and other eastern religious traditions.) Of course, Christianity also offers comforts, including assurances of divine benevolence and of eventual personal salvation, but these comforts are available only to those who are willing to risk themselves for the faith. Christianity, at least in its earlier forms, is not simply a religion of gradual, confident, relatively automatic self-development and unfolding, but a religion in which one's future is always at stake: one is dared, so to speak, to put one's faith in God, even when doing so will invite hardship, sacrifice, penalty, or death.

If this central challenge to risk oneself in religious commitment constitutes the fundamental, albeit penumbral imperative underlying religious risk taking—that is, the making of high-risk decisions by opting to take the risk—the emergence of first-order doctrines stipulating *how* the risk is to be taken can be expected. Here there are two divergent developments that become increasingly distinct in later, post-Reformation periods of Christian history. In some groups, teachings emerge that interpret risk as a matter of faith or belief and do not promote physical risk to health or life at all. It is coming to *believe* certain things that, in these traditions, constitutes the risk one must take for God. Risk lies in the "leap of faith," not in the danger of bodily harm. The tendency to treat the risks of religious commitment as wholly mental, emotional, or spiritual is characteristic of the Protestant tradition and of some recent contemplative, eastern-influenced Christian groups as well. Catholicism, with its traditional emphasis on fasting, mortifications of the flesh, celibacy, pilgrimage, crusade, and martyrdom, has not always interpreted the risks of religious commitment in a wholly mentalized way. Contemporary mainstream Catholicism—except perhaps for its monastic communities, political activist groups, penitential communities, and organizations such as Opus Dei—may now much more closely resemble Protestant practice. At the other extreme, the groups considered here understand the risks that religious commitment poses as primarily physical, though the distinction is not sharp and psychological risks may be intertwined with them. No doubt, many of the members of groups that construe risk as largely mental would say that they are prepared to risk their lives and physical selves should the occasion demand it; but they do not belong to groups that have adopted high-risk behavior *as a practice* of the group. It is this latter feature that is central to the groups considered here. Thus the crucial distinction at this first level of doctrinal development concerns institutionalized risk-taking practices, which determine how the fundamental imperative is to be honored, and specifically whether these practices are institutionalized primarily as mental or as physical risks.

These schematic claims may seem to raise again the "relativism" issue discussed in chapter 1: How can 0-level imperatives be identified reliably? Even if the historical account given here of the general relationship between the fundamental Christian imperative to risk one's all and derivative, upper-order practices interpreting these as mental or physical risks seems intuitively accurate, the groups discussed in this chapter will not seem to fit this model very well. However, there is a reason for this: these groups are not representative of the full scope of practices associated with the fundamental imperative, but only a small part of it. To display the full spectrum of risk-taking practices character-istic of Christianity, we would need to include groups ranging from mainline Protestantism, where risk is typically understood to be largely mental, if any risk is undertaken at all, to those groups whose practices involve such complete submission to physical harm that it barely seems meaningful to speak of "risk." Such groups might include some that are no longer extant, such as the second- and third-century North African Donatists, who deliberately courted martyrdom at the hands of the Romans, or the Donatist subgroup called the Circumcellions, who in addition practiced religiously motivated suicide. Groups en-gaging in high-risk penitential practices might also be included, like the Spanish-American group found in the high plateaus of the Sangre de Cristo mountains in northern New Mexico and southern Colorado, the Brothers of Jesus of Nazareth, better known as the Penitentes. The Penitentes' practices involve reenactment of Jesus' passion and crucifix-ion; they are performed by flagellating oneself, enduring severe scourging with cactus whips, and dragging huge wooden crosses up a hill. Although the practice of using nails to fix the penitent to the cross was last observed in 1908,[41] these penances still sometimes result in fatalities. However, these more extreme groups are not the focus here. In this chapter, unlike the previous one, a range of groups chosen to represent the broadest variety of possibilities for expression of a funda-mental imperative well distributed across a spectrum is not addressed. Focus, rather, is on a few groups that exhibit similarities and differ-ences within a much tighter range. Even within these limits, it is still possible to differentiate upper-order, developed practices within a group from its basic 0-level doctrines.

For example, in the serpent-handling groups it is Mark 16 that serves as an 0-level imperative—a basic, nonnegotiable, fundamental commandment, functioning in approximately the same way that Mat-thew 18 did in the Collinsville Church of Christ's disciplining of Mar-ian Guinn. Similarly, the serpent-handling groups observe a highly specific imperative, one that if honored at all in other groups would be viewed as derivative from a more general mandate. But while the serpent-handling groups take Mark 16 as basic, this passage stipulates nothing about how serpents are to be handled. It does not say how, where, when, or with whom serpents are to be handled, or even whether serpent handling is to be initiated at all, rather than performed only in response to confrontation with a snake. The Holiness churches have developed practices that settle these questions: serpents are to be handled on a specific occasion—the prayer meeting; in a specific location—the church; in the presence of other individuals—the congregation; and in ways that pose very substantial risks—picking them up, coiling them around one's arms, trunk, or neck, and doing so without protective equipment or surgical devenomization of the snakes. The how, where, when, and with whom questions that Mark 16 does not answer are made determinate in these practices; they are first-order practices, developed to put the basic imperative into practice. Of course, the biblical imperative to handle serpents could have been put into practice in various forms. For instance, it could have been taken to require handling snakes alone, in the woods, without music, singing, praying, or other background noise. It could have been taken not to encourage handling snakes, but only to require not avoiding them when they are encountered. The minister of a West Virginia Full Gospel church that does not practice serpent handling explained that he interpreted the phrase "they shall take up serpents," as it occurs in the King James translation of the Bible—the one most serpent handlers would be familiar with—as instructing people to "remove" snakes where they find them.[42] To put the biblical commandment concerning serpents into practice by handling serpents *at religious services* is already a developed, upper-order practice and hence one open to ethical critique. Of course, this developed, first-order practice of handling serpents at religious services poses obvious moral problems, among them those of voluntariness and of danger to participants and observers. To "answer" these moral problems, second-order doctrines and practices emerge: those recognizing the distinctive condition of anointment and holding that it is prerequisite to handling snakes; those discouraging criticism of church members who do not handle snakes, those precluding offering snakes to visitors or to children, and so on. These are all ways of minimizing the physical and emotional damage the practice itself can create; but these doctrines, too, are open to ethical review.

Similarly, for Jehovah's Witnesses, the 0-level imperatives the group observes can be identified by inspecting the texts it regards as fundamental: Genesis 9:4 and similar passages prohibiting the drinking of blood. The group's developed practices are those that involve interpreting these biblical passages as applying to blood transfusions (after all, transfusions are not explicitly mentioned in the Bible) and the structures of religious education and reinforcement that promote this interpretive teaching. Here, obviously, it may be difficult to distinguish the development of a practice from the development of an interpretation; but as in all groups, the development of a practice occurs simultaneously with the emergence of a doctrinal interpretation. The distinctive nature of the Jehovah's Witness interpretation and practice based on Genesis 9:4 and other texts can be more clearly seen by contrasting it with that of Judaism, where the same texts prohibiting the eating or drinking of blood are differently interpreted as dietary laws and have developed together with an extensive code of kosher slaughtering, food preparation, and food serving.

Within the practices examined here, some risks eventuate badly: some persons who take these physical risks suffer serious damage to their health; some die. The typological model employed here predicts the emergence of a further level of doctrinal, quasi-doctrinal, or authoritative claim, identified as third-order doctrine, that provides "excuses" for the residual moral problems the practices in question generate. For instance, when a Christian Scientist practicing his or her beliefs by relying on healing refuses conventional medical treatment and dies, some account consistent with both the basic doctrinal imperative and with the first- and second-order teachings is needed to explain or justify the negative outcome. Similarly, since serpent handlers act to honor the assertion in Mark 16 that "they will pick up snakes in their hands, and if they drink any deadly thing, it will not hurt them," the group's continued acceptance of the basic religious imperative depends in part on providing a doctrinally acceptable account of how snakebites and snakebite fatalities can occur—that is, an excuse for the negative outcome resulting from the risks a person takes in relying on the scriptural assurance that no harm will come from handling snakes.

These third-order teachings or excuses for failed risks are usually easy to identify, though they are not always encoded in official doctrine. When a Christian Scientist who refuses medical treatment and relies on prayer worsens or dies, the most frequent explanation, as observed earlier, is that he or she failed to pray adequately and hence failed to achieve the proper understanding of the nature of disease. Similarly, the Faith Assembly member who dies after refusing treatment is said to have lacked faith in Jesus' power to heal—an accusation so prevalent in this group that Hobart Freeman extended it even to those who use automobile seat belts. The serpent handler who is bitten is sometimes said to have failed to be sure he or she was genuinely anointed before taking up the snakes. For instance, in an informative cautionary tale circulated among serpent handlers, the story is told of a woman who *planned* to display her powers to handle snakes at a prayer meeting the following Sunday. She kept a snake in a jar for this very purpose. When she took out the snake at the announced time she was bitten and died—clearly, so the tale holds, because she had failed to wait for the appropriate anointing by God. A variant form of excuse appeals to higher purposes. For instance, not long before receiving a bite on the toe, Reverend Clyde Ricker of Hot Springs, North Carolina, offered this account: "I'd say that if I get bit, and I swell up, that's not a sign that I denied the faith, or that I wasn't anointed. . . God was just using me to prove to somebody that the serpents have teeth, and to show what snakes can do to you."[43]

Not only is it easy to identify these third-order teachings or excuses for the negative outcomes that a group's risk-taking practices have brought about, but it is easy to see a common feature of many of them. They explain the negative outcome as a result of a failure on the part of the individual harmed. This is true in the Faith Assembly, the Holiness church, and Christian Science. Even Clyde Ricker's prescient attempt to explain the bite on his toe as "God using me to prove that serpents have teeth" is preceded by an attempt to defuse the usual institutional explanations—that he denied the faith or was not anointed. Thus, in examining the excuses various groups encode in their doctrines, we can begin by considering whether excuses that lay the blame for unsuccessful risk taking at the feet of the risk taker are themselves morally defensible, or whether a defensible excuse must be of some other form.

In contrast, the Jehovah's Witnesses appear to offer no excuse when a Witness refuses transfusion and dies. Notice, however, that under the reevaluation that is characteristic of Jehovah's Witness practice, there is nothing to excuse. The faithful Witness who dies because he or she refuses blood—according to the teachings of the group—nevertheless achieves salvation, even if it means the loss of life. Achieving salvation is, under the reevaluation, the maximally valued outcome the choice could yield, whereas losing one's life under the reevaluation assumes much lesser importance. Consequently, for the devout, the death need not be excused.

## The Moral Evaluation of Risk Taking in Religion

In looking at the practices of our four specimen groups, it has been tempting to draw the immediate conclusion that these practices cannot be morally defended—and, furthermore, that they should be denounced on moral grounds. We have already established that the developed practices and teachings of religious groups, as distinct from the fundamental imperatives, are vulnerable to ethical critique, and when we now look at these practices, we see that they involve clear abuses of identifiable, uncontroversial moral principle. In examining issues in confidentiality in chapter 1, we found practices that variously involved lying, nonconsenting disclosure, manipulation, and the permitting of serious, preventable harms. In looking at issues in risk taking in this chapter, we find coercion, impairment of rational capacities, manipulation, callousness, and deception. No doubt we could look further and find more. But to identify these apparent moral abuses is not to establish that they are abuses in religious contexts; we have only seen them this way because we instinctively appeal to principles familiar in secular life. Yet even though we have established that certain religious doctrines and practices are open to ethical evaluation, we cannot simply assume that the principles presupposed by this catalogue of apparent abuses are applicable here.

Of the moral principles these apparent abuses seem to violate, that of autonomy is central. This principle is highlighted by the strategy of using the apparatus of professional ethics to examine issues of religious risk taking—in particular the concept of informed consent. The principle of autonomy, received in both its Kantian form and in the utilitarian version defended by John Stuart Mill, is not itself contested in either ordinary or professional ethics, though there certainly are continuing, vigorous debates about how it should be interpreted, about the degree to which individuals are capable of genuine autonomy, and about when, if ever, the principle may be overridden. This principle has been central in contemporary professional ethics. Here, too, disagreement virtually exclusively concerns the conditions under which paternalistic or harm-based exceptions to the principle are legitimate; there are no real challenges to the principle of autonomy itself.

Throughout our examination of the practices of various religious groups, both in confession and in high-risk decision making, we have seen repeated violations of autonomy. Though they are often explicated within professional ethics in more elaborate ways, the conditions for autonomous choice involve three criteria: (1) the decision must be uncoerced, (2) it must be rationally unimpaired, and (3) it must be adequately informed.

As we have seen, these are precisely the conditions that the practices of these groups violate. The Faith Assembly, at least on some occasions, coerces its members into refusing medical treatment. The Holiness serpent-handling groups encourage making potentially fatal decisions about handling snakes under extreme emotional impairment, calling that condition an anointment for taking the risk. Christian Science provides selective, anecdotal information only, without base or failure rates, in a way that is inevitably deceptive in influencing a high-risk choice. Nor is it apparent that these interferences in autonomous choice can be excused on the ground of limiting risks to third parties or for compelling paternalist reasons. Consequently, since these practices are vulnerable to ethical critique and the infractions of the principle of autonomy are so clear, it would seem that moral conclusions could readily be drawn.

But I do not think this is so. Since our apparatus for evaluating religious practice is not yet complete, the principle of autonomy cannot be directly employed. Upper-level doctrines and practices are *candidates* for critique; but we have yet to establish on what basis the critique can be made. To condemn practices for violating conditions of autonomous choice involves an unwarranted leap in ethical evaluation, even though these criteria are well established in both professional and ordinary ethics. It is a leap we can make—and then only in limited ways—only after our initial typology is supplemented with the appropriate critical principle.

The principle to which we shall appeal, the fiduciary principle, is a distinct moral principle not reducible either to that of autonomy or to those of nonmaleficence and beneficence. Most explicitly articulated in law, it is vaguely recognized in various forms in all of the secular professions. The fiduciary principle serves to identify the obligations of the professional vis-à-vis the client in professional contexts and, except for a few distinctive interpersonal relationships, it is usually thought to be limited to professional contexts.

To employ a principle adopted from professional ethics to examine organized religion is not to presuppose that religious functionaries are all professionals in the fullest sense. Clergy of the mainstream denominations have traditionally been regarded in this way, though cult leaders, evangelists, faith healers, gurus, and the like have not. But while the fiduciary principle has been developed in professional contexts, its scope is broader and provides a crucial distinction in assessing religious practice.

The fiduciary principle, which applies to all aspects of professional-client interaction, regulates practice by stipulating that it must be possible for the client to *trust* the professional in the course of the interaction, even though the professional's own interests may conflict with those of the client. Put another way, the fiduciary principle prohibits the professional from taking advantage of the client—that is, violating the client's rights or harming his or her interests—in the course of the professional relationship, though of course the professional's superior status, power, and knowledge would make it easy to do so. For example, the lawyer has fiduciary duties to the client; this means that the lawyer must use his or her professional skills to advance the client's interests or, at least, not to harm them. Similarly, the trustee, as fiduciary to the beneficiary of a trust fund, must refrain from usurping the beneficiary's interests in the fund, just as the director of a corporation must refrain from promoting his or her own interests at the expense of the corporation. The fiduciary principle may seem similar to the more general principle of nonmaleficence, but it has a specific application to the professional-client relationship and to the characteristic imbalance of power this relationship exhibits. It is broader in scope than the comparatively narrow principle of autonomy; it requires the professional not only to respect the client's autonomous choices and to protect the client's capacity to make them, but also to ensure (and this does not rule out paternalistic intervention) that the client's interests are served. Thus, the principle is a complex one, with conditions often in tension between autonomist and paternalist demands, and not reducible to the simpler principles often cited in professional and ordinary moral discourse. To say, as Charles Fried does, that the fiduciary "owes a duty of strict and unreserved loyalty to his client"[44] is correct, and makes it clear that the professional's primary obligation is to the client, rather than to the professional's own interests, to the institution, or to others who might be involved, but leaves open the question of how the sometimes conflicting requirements of this complex principle are to be satisfied.

Inasmuch as the fiduciary principle has autonomist components, the three conditions for the protection of autonomous choice identified above—noncoercion, freedom from rational impairment, and adequate informedness—can all be derived from it, though in some circumstances they may be in tension with paternalist components of the principle. In professional areas such as medicine and law, these three conditions protect the client from the professional in very specific ways. The client, it is assumed, consults the professional in order to advance his or her aims and interests; the protection needed is protection from possible dishonesty, manipulation, or greed on the part of the professional. For instance, when the patient consults the doctor for help in curing an illness, he or she occupies an unequal, vulnerable position in the relationship (the patient, after all, is both sick and untrained in medicine) and must rely on the physician's obligations as fiduciary to keep from being made worse off—specifically from being made worse off with respect to health. The legal client consults an attorney for help in protecting his or her rights and similarly relies on the attorney's fiduciary obligation to a client. Since the attorney is far more skilled in the law than the client, the attorney could easily jeopardize those rights. Professionals are also often in a position to jeopardize other interests of the client (both doctors and lawyers, for instance, can easily threaten a patient's or client's emotional, social, or financial well-being), but it is with respect to the specific interest or set of interests about which the client has consulted the professional that the fiduciary principle most directly applies.

Like other professionals, the religious professional, whether minister, priest, rabbi, pastor, evangelist, faith healer, or guru, is in a position to make individuals within the group either better or worse off. He or she can affect their emotional, social, financial, or other peripheral interests. The religious professional can also affect either positively or negatively the specific aim or interest for which they seek help in the first place; it is this fact that initially supports the appeal to the fiduciary principle made here. What the fiduciary principle requires is that the priest or the preacher not treat those who come as prey, even in the most subtle ways, or use them either for self-interested ends or other institutional goals, but instead remain worthy of trust.

To construe the relation between the religious professional and member of the religious group in this way invites us to identify precisely what it is that the religious believer comes to the religious professional for, that is, what interests he or she hopes to serve in approaching the religious professional. Although this may be very difficult to do for a specific case, we can venture certain general observations. Consider, for instance, the reasons why the Christian Scientist or a member of the Faith Assembly has contact with the leaders of his or her group, as contrasted with the reasons why, for example, a member of a serpent-handling group might do so. The Christian Scientist calls a practitioner when he or she is ill and does so for help in restoring health. Similarly, the member of the Faith Assembly rejects medicine and relies on Jesus in order to get well, but he or she also acts to retain membership and avoid humiliation by the group. The serpent handler, on the other hand, attends a prayer meeting and handles serpents in order to satisfy the injunction he or she believes Mark 16 states; there is less evidence here of some particular external objective. Then again, the Jehovah's Witness appears to refuse blood in order to satisfy the biblical commandment, much as the serpent handler does, but does so in order not to jeopardize his or her chances of salvation.

Of course, identifying reasons why people engage in religion is a murky business at best; a full psychological explanation of such behaviors is far more complex than can be treated here. Nevertheless, it is evident that strikingly different degrees of rational prudence, in the pursuit of self-interest, are exhibited by the members of various groups. The Christian Scientist seeks to get well, just as any ordinary patient seeing any ordinary doctor does; in doing so, the Scientist acts to promote one of his or her interests—health. The Scientist does not call the condition "illness" nor recognize its symptoms as those of "disease," nor does he or she understand the end-state sought to be a "cure," but rather a "demonstration" of the truth of the principles of Christian Science. Indeed, the Scientist rejects the entire causal metaphysics of medicine. Nevertheless, he or she accepts, and the church promotes, a variety of external similarities, many dating from the earliest period of the church,[45] which reinforce the claim that what the believer seeks is what any ordinary patient does: help in regaining health. For instance, the Christian Scientist calls the practitioner only when he or she has discomforting symptoms (whether or not viewed as symptoms of disease). The practitioner can be found by looking in the Yellow Pages; an appointment is made; the practitioner's services are paid for at rates roughly comparable to those of a physician; and, in some states (Massachusetts, for instance) Blue Cross will pay the bill. To put it another way, Christian Science functions as an alternative health-care system, though it denies medicine's metaphysics and makes no use of medical techniques; we can easily identify the professional institution to which Christian Science promotes itself as an alternative.

Not all risk-taking practices function as alternatives to secular professional institutions. The serpent handler, for example, does not so clearly seek to advance his or her interests by risking health or life but instead acts simply to obey an injunction he or she believes is what the

Lord demands. There do not seem to be external similarities promoted by the group that would reinforce the claim that in handling snakes the believer attempts to further the same aims and interests that clients of other professionals do. Serpent handling is not an *alternative* anything; it is simply a practice of the group.

Noting these differences should allow us to see why the fiduciary principle, while vaguely asserted in the secular professions, is not discussed much there, and why—in contrast—it is of particular interest in the religious sphere. The fiduciary principle prohibits the professional from violating moral principles in such a way as to undermine those aims or interests for which a client seeks protection or advancement in using the professional's services. In medicine and law, as in other secular professions, this covers the entire range of cases: patients and legal clients use the services of doctors and lawyers in order to protect and advance their own aims or interests, or those of organizations and causes with which they identify, and generally not for any other reason. They come to lawyers and doctors to protect their rights, broadly construed, or to get well. Since virtually all of the activities in which the professional engages with the client are initiated in response to such purposes on the part of the client, there is nothing distinctive in these areas of professional practice that the fiduciary principle might isolate and identify as protected under this principle. Of course, some clients do not voluntarily consult professionals, but are delivered to them, such as the unconscious emergency patient or the impoverished defendant in the criminal justice system, but even in these circumstances the fiduciary principle applies by extension. On some occasions a client might consult a professional for purposes that do not appear to serve his or her self-interests, as, for example, when a person consults a doctor to donate a kidney to someone else, but even here the patient does so with the aim of protecting his or her interests as well as those of the recipient, and does not ask the doctor to remove the kidney without regard for his or her own health. Even if the fiduciary principle is not particularly conspicuous in the secular professions, largely because it covers virtually all available cases, it will nevertheless play a central role in sorting out those cases in religion to which ordinary moral norms apply and those to which they do not.

The fiduciary principle functions in critiquing religious practice by identifying under what conditions upper-level practices and doctrines may be reviewed with the moral principles available in professional and ordinary ethics—such principles as autonomy, nonmaleficence, and beneficence; while the working typology developed in chapter 1 makes it possible to distinguish between fundamental, 0-level imperatives and upper-level, developed doctrines and practices, it does not specify whether all of the latter are actually open to critique. The fiduciary principle functions as a second general principle, supplementing the earlier typology, and further limits the application of moral norms to religious practices. The fiduciary principle does not in itself aid in sorting out conflicts and tensions between the demands of autonomy, nonmaleficence, and beneficence, either in general or in specific cases like those of Faith Assembly members or Marian Guinn; this is work for the applied professional ethicist concerned with organized religion, the "ecclesioethicist," to do. But the principle does tell us when the ecclesioethicist can get to work, by telling us under what conditions the basic moral principles can be applied to upper-level doctrines and practices. In religious contexts, the fiduciary principle asserts that *the developed practices, doctrines, methods, and teachings employed by religious professionals or their religious organizations must meet (secular) ethical criteria wherever the individual participates in these practices to advance his or her self-interests.* The fact that the religious professional is *religious* does not exempt him or her from treating clients in ways that are morally binding in the secular professions, as well as in ordinary morality, wherever the client approaches the religious professional for the same sorts of self-interest-serving purposes as he or she would approach a secular professional—even if the client is also a believer and adherent of the group. For example, if the Christian Scientist seeks help from a Christian Scientist practitioner *in order to get well,* then he or she is entitled to the same freedom from coercion, from impairment, and to the same adequate information to which an ordinary medical patient would be entitled in seeking to get well. In a word, the religious believer, like the medical patient, is entitled to the protections of informed consent; one's status as a believer does not abrogate this right. However, if a believer approaches a Christian Science practitioner not to get well, but in order to deepen his or her faith—as many devout Christian Scientists clearly do—then it is not so clear that these constraints apply. Many Christian Scientists conceive of healing not as an alternative medical system at all, but as a process of prayer that is part of the effort to achieve a certain spiritual condition—of which a side effect, though not the central purpose, may be the restoration of health.[46]

It may seem that the religious organization, or the religious professional within it, can have no such fiduciary obligation, inasmuch as neither the professional nor the organization has control over the reasons for which an individual approaches them. Of course, this is not so, for the way in which a religious organization, including its officials, is approached is very much a function of the way in which it announces or advertises itself. After all, announcing or advertising an organization is an interactive process between the organization and the individuals who approach it. The process is not much remarked upon in the secular professions since most secular professions announce themselves in uniform ways, but it is a process of tremendous variability in religion. Christian Science, for instance, announces and promotes itself as an alternative healing system by the very fact that it distributes testimonials that recount favorable recoveries using Christian Science healing (even though these testimonials are described primarily as serving to give thanks to God) and by asking Blue Cross to cover the services it renders. In response to the way in which Christian Science announces and promotes itself, prospective users of the church approach it in kind, seeking to receive these services in order to further their aims and interests in getting well. At the same time, that prospective users of Christian Science healing, both members and prospective converts, seek to further their aims and interests in getting well leads the church and its officials to promote the church's services in this way. Similarly, for example, the Church of Scientology promotes itself as providing help in achieving psychological stability and growth; in this sense, it attempts to function as an alternative psychotherapeutic profession. As in Christian Science, Scientology's public stance is interactive with the aims and purposes for which prospective users of its services approach the church: it announces itself as able to provide psychological help and personality development, and people who seek these things turn to it.

In the secular professions, when we talk about why a client seeks a professional, we are saying as much about the professional and the background organization as we are about the client. Thus, to phrase the fiduciary principle in terms of what the client seeks is also to identify specific professional and institutional postures. In religion, since the fiduciary principle underwrites the application of standard ethical principles—autonomy, nonmaleficence, beneficence, and justice—when adherents approach with self-interested aims, it thus also underwrites the application of these principles when the religious group and its officials announce themselves as available to help persons pursue their interests.

Of course, it may be that virtually all religious invitation contains some appeal to self-interest. Insofar as a group makes such an invitation, however, under the interpretation of the fiduciary principle advanced here, it is obligated to protect and promote the aims and self-interests to which the invitation is directed. The church that announces itself as able to satisfy certain interests of persons who are attracted to the church in this way opens itself to *secular* moral critique of the practices and doctrines it employs in satisfying those interests. Not all of the upper-order practices in a religious group will be susceptible to ethical critique under the fiduciary principle; but many of those that have been tradi-tionally protected by the notion of religious immunity will be clear targets for ethical examination and can be assessed using the secular moral criteria developed in ordinary and professional ethics. (Curiously, the distinction between upper-level practices that are vulnerable to ethical critique and those that are not is reflected, though somewhat crudely, in the growing area of clergy malpractice insurance; malpractice insurance is available in approximately those areas in which clergy do what other professionals do, especially counseling, but not for practices much less directly related to the satisfaction of individual self-interests, such as the performance of rites, the maintenance of beliefs, or the uphold-ing of orthodoxy.) The distinction is not always clear; most groups give off mixed signals and are approached for mixed reasons. Nevertheless, the theoretical importance of this distinction is considerable.

This chapter began with a discussion of the practices of four religious groups in encouraging their adherents to take risks. In that discussion, appeal was made to both general moral principles, such as autonomy, nonmaleficence, beneficence, and justice, and to their application in requirements such as informed consent. But while it was established in chapter 1 that upper-level practices such as these, which encourage risk, are candidates for moral critique, we did not see why critique is appropriate in these specific cases. Use of the fiduciary principle provides an answer. At least in the cases of the Christian Science, Jehovah's Witnesses, and the Holiness churches, there is good reason to think that individuals consult religious professionals to promote their own interests and that these groups promote characteristic practices under a corresponding appeal to self-interest of the members of the group. Christian Scientists choose prayer over medicine in order to get well; the church promotes prayer as a means of healing. The Jehovah's Witnesses refuse blood to avoid precluding salvation; this church and its officials promote the practice of refusing blood at least in part with this rationale. If it turns out that the serpent handler does not after all act only to obey the biblical commandment but simply seeks the heightened sensory or emotional experience provided by the dangerous thrill of handling snakes, then this, too, belongs under ordinary ethical scrutiny. After all, heightened sensory or emotional experience is available in ways that are less life-threatening.

The distinction drawn by the fiduciary principle also explains why it seems natural to examine confidentiality in religious confession with the secular apparatus of professional morality: confession is often seen chiefly as a mechanism that allows people to pursue self-interests in relieving guilt or enhancing their spiritual status and ultimate rewards. Confession is not primarily conceived as of something done for the sake of the religious group or for God but for one's own sake—to rectify one's conscience, repent of sin, and hence to advance one's prospects of salvation. If this is so, then the principles employed in secular discussions of confidentiality are also applicable here.

Applications of the fiduciary principle in organized religion are not likely to be easy in practice. The principle refers to the reasons for which people use religious services, as induced by the religious organization and vice versa, and these reasons may be multifarious and obscure. Nor can we assume that the reasons for which people consult religious professionals are anywhere nearly as uniform as the reasons for which they consult doctors or lawyers. Individuals go to church or see their ministers for an enormous variety of reasons, including relieving anxiety, coping with fear, preserving a marriage, restoring health, increasing security, dealing with grief, curbing aggressive or suicidal impulses, maintaining social standing, and so on. A very large part of what leads the religious believer to a religious professional involves the protection and advancement of interests like these; a very large part of the comforts that religious groups offer are directed toward the satisfaction of these interests. Self-interested religious behavior may be very difficult to distinguish from self-interested nonreligious behavior. However cumbersome applications of the principle might be in practice and, consequently, however poor a basis it might make for policy formation, it is an appropriate basis for distinguishing those religious activities and practices that are proper targets for ethical critique from those that are comparatively immune.

It is also a proper basis for scrutinizing the way that religious groups advertise themselves and their services, both in securing continuing commitment from their members and in attracting new ones. The televangelist groups and their leaders are particularly revealing targets for scrutiny. Oral Roberts, for example, makes a direct appeal to the financial interests of prospective contributors by promising immediate material reward. Roberts sends multicolored prayer sheets to his "prayer partners" to be mailed back (together with a contribution) with a list of needs for which he can pray: "The RED area is for your SPIRITUAL healing; the WHITE area is for your PHYSICAL healing; the GREEN area is for your FINANCIAL healing. Check the needs you have and RUSH them back to me."[47] Roberts is by no means the only media preacher who announces his brand of religion as likely to enhance a believer's interests in material comfort and financial success; but because they invite persons to approach them for the same sorts of reasons for which one might approach a secular financial counselor or investment firm, they are open to the same sort of ethical critique.

In general, religious operatives promising satisfaction of their audience's financial interests provide a ripe field for further inquiry.

However, not all individuals approach religious professionals or organizations to promote their own self-interests. Consider, for instance, the person who describes why he or she sees a minister or goes to church as wanting to "strengthen my faith." This seemingly central religious purpose bears close scrutiny, for it must be asked why the believer wants to strengthen this faith. If, for instance, it is evident that the believer seeks assistance in strengthening faith to "be sure to go to heaven," the motive sounds very much like the kind of self-interest that other forms of rational prudence display. Once it is assumed or believed that there is a heaven, then it is not so much a matter of *religion* to want to get there; it is a matter of rational prudence, particularly considering that the only available alternative under this belief system is hell. Consequently, even the apparently purely religious purpose of strengthening one's faith in consulting a religious professional or participating in religious practices falls under the fiduciary principle just articulated. Hence, the professional's methods of providing these services and the established church practices that support them are subject to the same working moral criteria as other areas of professional ethics, at least if we assume that the religious professional is in any way capable of either advancing or undermining the interests a person seeks to advance.

This conclusion does not mean, however, that the same local principles or rules of professional ethics apply in religion as they do in medicine or law, for while the fiduciary principle may provide a basic moral standard for all areas of professional practice—including organized religion—it may be that specific applications of the principles derived from it, as well as local rules such as confidentiality and truth telling, differ from one area of professional practice to another. Thus, for example, principles governing the protection of autonomy in decision making under risk may differ from psychiatry to medicine to sports coaching to religion, but they must all satisfy the general fiduciary requirement that the professional be loyal to and not take advantage of the client.

Although having one's faith strengthened in order to get to heaven may not be a distinctively religious purpose for consulting a religious professional, some purposes are. A person who initially expresses a desire for help in strengthening faith might explain that he or she seeks this help because God is supremely worthy of worship and therefore he or she wishes to worship God more fully—regardless of the impact this fuller worship might have on himself or herself. This kind of purpose in seeking assistance from a religious professional does not involve seeking to advance one's own interests, thereby putting them in a position vulnerable to the professional's influence. Consequently, it is not a purpose to which the usual strictures of professional morality under the fiduciary principle apply. For instance, some Christian Scientists, as perhaps some Faith Assembly members, Jehovah's Witnesses, and Holiness church members, may observe their church's teaching not to enhance their health or to secure salvation, but simply because—as they believe—it is the word of God. As yet, we have no basis for applying secular moral criteria in cases like these—regardless of the nature of these practices and doctrines that have developed or the group's methods in promoting this behavior. (This is not, of course, to say that they are justified.) However, these cases may be very few, and such people as rare as saints. If most religious behavior is actually the pursuit of self-interest under a special set of metaphysical assumptions, then the "professionals" who are the purveyors and caretakers of these assumptions in the form of religious doctrine, teachings, and practices are obligated—as in any fiduciary relationship—to protect these persons in that pursuit.

# CHAPTER 3

# Making Believe

## *Paternalism and the Ethics of Converting People*

A couple of summers ago, three bright young college students knocked at my door. They were on a scavenger hunt, they said. One wanted a paper clip; another needed a three-inch length of blue thread. There's a certain cooperative, contributory delight that occurs when you can find the silly things scavenger hunters want, and I also managed to find a turkey wishbone, a cigarette butt, and a European road map. However, by the time one of them asked for "a person who has been thinking about the meaning of life," I realized something was different. Sure enough, they were not on a scavenger hunt at all, at least not an ordinary one; they were missionaries from the Campus Crusade for Christ and they had come to talk about Jesus.

This is one modest example of religious convert seeking, a practice also called, in its various forms, evangelism, missionizing, and proselytism. The Campus Crusade's scavenger hunt may seem ethically innocuous, particularly when compared to more flagrant missionary and proselytizing tactics. But while I think this scavenger hunt is not without morally problematic features, as are the more flagrant cases, I think we will encounter some quite challenging problems as we try to say why this is so and begin to examine the more general ethical issues raised by religious conversion activities.

### *Moral Problems in Convert Seeking*

The effort to convert people is like commercial selling in many ways. It is unlike it in one central respect: commercial selling is conducted by the seller for his or her own benefit or for that of the firm, while religious "selling" is supposed to be conducted by the missionary with the benefit of the "buyer" in mind. In spite of this disanalogy—and in part because of it—inspection of the scavenger hunt strategy used by the Campus Crusade for Christ with the apparatus of ordinary and applied professional ethics—and especially of business ethics—readily reveals morally problematic features.

The scavenger hunt is an opening-gambit strategy. Its purpose is to enable the missionary to establish contact with the target of the conversion effort in a way that would rarely be possible if the purposes of the contact were to be announced in advance. Door-to-door missionizing is a common feature of contemporary religious activity, but missionaries who announce themselves as missionaries often find doors closed in their faces and the proportion of successful contacts is very low. Door-to-door convert seeking is hard, inefficient work, perhaps even harder and less efficient than door-to-door sales of vacuum cleaners, encyclopedias, or other consumer goods. The problem, as door-to-door salespeople all know, is to get a foot in the door.

The Campus Crusade's scavenger hunt gambit employs a strategy of "indirection" or deception for overcoming this primary obstacle. Target persons are not told the real purpose of the call; instead, their attention is gained, and their interest held, by announcing a different objective. This is a form of the "bait-and-switch" technique common among merchandizers: the potential customer's initial interest is aroused by promoting a bargain and then rechanneled to another, usually more expensive item. In the scavenger hunt strategy in religious missionizing, the "customer's" interest is aroused not by a bargain item for purchase but by a particular project, yet the same effort is made to rechannel interest from the circumstance in which it was originally elicited to one serving the interests of the "seller." These scavenger hunters do not really want paper clips or bits of thread; they want souls. That the ultimate objective of the "sale" in religious conversion is supposed to be the benefit of the convert does not obscure the use of a familiar and manipulative commercial strategy.

The scavenger hunt is a device remarkably well suited as an opening gambit in convert seeking. It draws on a traditional game form, one that works by enlisting the voluntary cooperation of those from whom ojects are solicited. In finding and contributing objects to the players, the persons approached participate in the project of the game. Participation is possible in part because the conventions of scavenger hunts are widely understood in the culture: that the items requested will have little or no monetary value, that they will be of trivial personal significance to the donor, and that they will not seriously violate the donor's privacy. Furthermore, it is a game that requires no equipment, no special location (such as a playing field), and no other special arrangements. As a result, it is one of the (few) traditional American participatory games that resists commercialization. Furthermore, and most importantly, it is a game that is structured around contacts between the players and strangers, but in which the strangers are more than onlookers; they are brought into temporary, but genuine, personal contact with the players. This occurs as the strangers locate the objects sought and turn them over to the players. Thus, the strangers become contributors to the players' success. In a limited way, they are participants in the game.

It is here, I think, that the morally problematic features of using a strategy like the scavenger hunt for seeking converts are most prominent; there are clear ways in which this indirect approach appears to violate moral norms. The strategy is deceptive; specifically, it involves a type of deception that is associated with distortion or appropriation of an ordinary human relationship to serve one party's purposes. The little "cooperative, contributory delight" experienced by the person who gives the paper clip, length of blue thread, or whatever object is requested and the associated positive feeling toward the players that giving is likely to engender are exploited in the attempt to convert; they are used to elicit the stranger's interest in the players' project.

Within the conventions of the scavenger hunt game, however, this relationship and the positive disposition it engenders are not pursued. The donor does not usually know whether the side he or she has contributed to has won, and there is no mechanism within the game for informing the donors or returning the objects contributed. The transitory relationship usually ends with the donation, even though it has involved a genuine interaction between donor and players. In the conversion-oriented scavenger hunt for souls, however, the relationship is exploited as an opening to introduce the missionary message, and the game is intended to be the beginning, not the end, of a continuing relationship. This continuing relationship will then be redirected from a relationship with the players to a relationship with the players' church.

Furthermore, although the objects requested under the convention of the game are to be trivial, without monetary, personal, or other value, they can be informative. While all of the objects that the Campus Crusade scavenger hunters requested satisfied the convention of triviality, only the paper clip and the length of thread were genuinely insignificant; the turkey wishbone, the cigarette butt, and the European road map served distinct ulterior purposes. They were not simply trivial, hard-to-find objects. The turkey wishbone provided an occasion for the players to ask what wish I was planning to make with it; they interpreted the cigarette butt as evidence that I had undesirable, sinful habits; and they viewed the European road map as both evidence of cosmopolitan experience and a desire for something beyond one's present life. Thus, these objects were not requested innocently, but to elicit information essential in pursuing the opening gambit. The information would provide a way of directing the emerging brief relationship to personal terms. Once more personal contact was established, the real missionary effort could begin.

The Campus Crusade's scavenger hunt may seem an innocuous strategy: after all, when you discover its real purpose, it is easy enough to send the "players" away. But its character is not innocent, and—like many of the practices examined in earlier chapters—this strategy has multiple morally problematic features. Its bait-and-switch opening gambit is deceptive; its use of requests for items that have informative value is invasive of privacy; and it exploits an ordinary human relationship to serve ulterior purposes. To be sure, it does these things in quite a mild way. Nevertheless, the tactic provides an illuminating introduction to other, more aggressive proselytizing practices, for these morally problematic features will recur in many more pronounced forms in other religious conversion contexts.

Consider, for instance, the efforts of Henry Clay Trumbull, a man known around the turn of the century for his perseverance in "soul-winning." At one point, Trumbull converted a young man "of pronounced agnosticism" to Christianity; he did so in the following way:

> A young man of pronounced agnosticism but of scholarly scientific interests one time came into Dr. Trumbull's horizon. There was no common ground at all, in spiritual matters, to begin with. The older man, however, learned—by making it his business to learn—that the younger student was deeply interested in a certain line of scientific study. Promptly he set out to know something of that subject himself. He spent some weeks in reading it up. He gathered books on it, every one he could lay his hands on, and put them by. Then one day he mentioned to the young student that he had several books in that field at his office, and he invited him to avail himself of them whenever he cared to look them over. The subject became a theme of mutual interest, and the younger man eagerly seized opportunities of discussing it with one who knew so much more about it than most persons he met. From that common ground, reached only by the costly sacrifice of time and study by the soul-winner, it was not difficult to lead on to spiritual matters; and the day came when the once-agnostic thanked God and his confessed Saviour that one man had been willing to be "all things" to him.[1]

Like the Campus Crusade scavenger hunters, Dr. Trumbull began with a bait-and-switch strategy of indirection. He led the prospective convert to the discussion of religious matters by whetting his interest in another topic, a particular line of scientific study. Trumbull deceived the prospective convert by intentionally leading him to think that Trumbull was genuinely interested in the scientific matter, when in fact the scientific matter was of extrinsic interest only to him, as a means to facilitate his goal of converting the young man. What Trumbull did, much like the Campus Crusade scavenger hunters, was to first elicit the target person's interest in a particular area, and use it to engender a positive disposition toward himself, and then gradually rechannel the interest to an area suited to his actual purpose. Both Trumbull and the

Campus Crusade approached prospective converts in much the same way: by initiating what appeared to be an ordinary human relationship, one between two persons engaged in the exploration of a matter of common interest, but which was to be exploited to serve their purposes in convert seeking.

Examples of similar strategies are to be found in a wide range of religious groups. Members of the Unification Church, or "Moonies," have used a technique that involves vague, nonspecific invitations at the time of initial contact ("Are you lonely, would you like to come and spend an evening with some young people just like you?"[2] or "Are you interested in a meaningful way of life?"[3]) to interest prospective converts in further contact with the organization, though neither the identity of the organization nor the purpose of the invitation is mentioned at the initial contact and only later is it gradually revealed.[4] The Moonies have also used door-to-door "surveys" of attitudes toward world problems,[5] as has the Campus Crusade for Christ, initiating contacts with prospective recruits. Scientology, announcing itself as offering help to people with psychological problems, interests prospects by administering a simple personality inventory. This is sometimes circulated as an insert in newspapers; sometimes an apparatus called an "E meter" is used on people approached on the street. In either case, persons whose interest is solicited in this way are then told that the results of the tests show a need for improvement— which improvement can be achieved by undergoing Scientology's courses.

Sometimes whole groups, rather than single individuals, are the mass targets of this bait-and-switch strategy. In one of the cruder examples, evangelist Jerry Johnston persuaded school officials in Clearwater, Florida, to let him address middle and high school assemblies on the topics of drug and alcohol abuse and teen suicide, but used the occasion primarily to invite his audience to a free "all-you-can-eat pizza blast" at the stadium. What he did not tell the students, of whom nearly four thousand showed up, was that they would have to listen to a two-hour revival service before they could get to the pizza.[6]

Similarly, "lovebombing" or "befriending"—a tactic practiced under a variety of names by a variety of groups—consists in showering a prospective convert with incessant personal friendliness and affection but then channeling his or her response into interest in the group. A former member of the Boston Church of Christ, a group that, under evangelist Kip McKean, has been pursuing an aggressive "campus outreach program" to convert students at Harvard, MIT, Boston University, and other area colleges, claims that McKean's followers "would go onto a campus and latch onto freshmen who were away from home for the first time and had no friends. They'd make the students think that they were their best friends, give them about six weeks to learn what the church members believed the Bible had to say, and if they hadn't accepted the lessons by then, the recruiters would drop them and go on to the next convert."[7] Like Henry Clay Trumbull in pursuit of the scientific young man, the recruiters from the Boston Church of Christ focused on the uses that can be made of friendship, or at least what appears to the target individual to be friendship. Of course, friendship is a human relationship that is of substantially greater significance than the transitory, participatory interest that develops between scavenger hunters and the donors they approach, but all of these cases of convert-seeking strategy—from the Campus Crusade to the Boston Church of Christ—have in common the exploitation of human relationships for ulterior religious purposes.

Perhaps the most flagrant example of the strategy is the development among the Children of God of a practice called "flirty fishing." Introduced around the end of 1973 by the group's leader, David Berg, known as Moses David or "Mo," the practice began with Mo sending his second wife or mistress, Maria, out onto the dance floor in a London dancing school as "bait." At Mo's urging, Maria struck up a relationship, which quickly became sexual, with an Englishman named Arthur. Once Arthur was firmly "hooked" he was passed on to one of Mo's other wives. Maria was then commissioned to catch another "fish." According to Mo's later disaffected daughter, this became a regular practice, with Maria regularly seducing men and Mo and his team getting nightly reports, which they recorded, transcribed, and edited for eventual publication.[8]

Flirty fishing had its roots in Moses David's reading of the Old Testament, which he took to permit nonmonogamous sexual relationships.[9] He viewed monogamous marriage as a potential obstacle to total commitment to God and held that sexual activity should be assessed on the basis of whether it contributes to or hinders God's work. But he also had intensely evangelical intentions for the group, made urgent by his belief that the anti-Christ would soon appear and attempt to destroy his following, and thus developed what he called his "exciting but dangerous new ministry of flirty fishing" (called "FF'ing" for short) to promote rapid, effective proselytizing. Mo and a group of female followers, married and unmarried, would visit bars and discotheques, striking up relationships, proceeding beyond friendship and companionship to sexual relations "where meeting the person's sexual needs was seen as the only effective means of presenting God's message."[10] The group eventually moved from conventional England to Tenerife so that its members could practice FF'ing more freely. As one observer remarked, FF'ing "was developed and refined practically into an artform."[11] Mo was questioned and a group of FF'ers were arrested for prostitution; Mo left the island (leaving the women behind to stand trial), but flirty fishing prospered elsewhere. Mo's annual statistical newsletter for 1979 reported that "Our dear FF'ers are still going strong, God bless'm, having now witnessed to over a quarter-of-a-million souls, loved over 25,000 of them and won nearly 19,000 to the Lord, along with about 35,000 new friends."[12]

This is a considerably more elaborate enterprise than the Campus Crusade for Christ's simple scavenger hunt, but its strategy is in essence the same. They differ only in the degree of aggressiveness with which the strategy is pursued, the period of time over which the deception is maintained, and the nature and significance of the human relationship that is exploited.

## The Scale of Aggressiveness

These examples of convert seeking have not only been described but arranged along a loose continuum of practices involving the exploitation of ordinary human relationships. This forms a scale that reflects the degree to which these practices violate a specific moral norm. On this scale, the Campus Crusade scavenger hunt falls at the lower, minimal end, since the way it exploits human relationships, while real, is minor; Trumbull's pursuit of the scientific young man is a little farther along the scale; love-bombing tactics are still further along; and the Children of God's flirty fishing scheme serves as the most pronounced example, at the opposite end of the continuum. Conversion practices that involve the exploitation of ordinary relationships constitute one kind or type of convert seeking, defined in terms of the moral norm they most centrally violate, and this type includes specific practices that range from mild to extremely strong, highly aggressive varieties. When we want to say what is wrong with a particular variety of convert seeking, appealing to the canons of ordinary morality, it is to central features such as exploitation that we will point.

Of course, not all convert seeking involves the exploitation found in bogus scavenger hunts, Trumbull's deviousness, or flirty fishing. Turn-of-the century "buttonholing for Jesus," for example, does not; it is a straightforward, confrontational practice that does not involve deception or exploitation. Strategies of accosting, like buttonholing, haranguing, and some forms of reductive theological debate, are morally problematic in other ways—for instance, they invade privacy and characteristically involve a deliberate attempt to disrupt a person's previously held framework of belief. Nevertheless, they are distinct in strategy from methods that operate primarily by exploiting human relationships.

Still another type of conversion strategy involves indirect manipulation through a second party. Weaker forms of this technique involve the classic foreign-mission strategy of converting the tribal leader in order to convert the tribe, while more aggressive versions of the same tactic can be seen in the use of children as leverage in the conversion of adults. Writing in 1905, Phidellia P. Carroll congratulates herself on her successes with this technique: "The writer has again and again led children to Christ one by one in the homes of their parents . . . With these strong incentives brought to bear on non-Christian parents, many of them may be brought to a realization of their need of salvation, and induced to surrender to Christ, who could not be thus influenced were their children not in the fold."[13] Similarly, during the early

1960s, Mormon missionaries in England organized "baseball clubs" for school-age boys.[14] The boys were permitted to play baseball in these clubs only if they would allow themselves to be baptized; once baptized, they were expected to persuade their parents to be baptized into the church too. (This practice has since been discontinued by the church.) The form of manipulation at work in these cases involves placing indirect pressure on the target party by converting someone else in a position to influence the prospective convert's circumstances and thereby changing the target party's conditions of choice. For instance, when a tribal leader converts, members of the tribe may wish to emulate their leader, but they will also find the social circumstances of unconverted members of the tribe suddenly changed. Of course, they too may really be persuaded by the new beliefs the leader has embraced. But it may also be that they can no longer prosper or even survive in a community where they continue to adhere to a belief system that the leader has rejected; thus, they also must convert to maintain their place within the community—even though they would not voluntarily have converted to the new belief system. Similarly, parents whose child is converted face a changed circumstance not of their own making: they must now weigh their disinclination to believe the new religious claims against the costs to family harmony where child and parents are separated along religious lines. They may try to "deconvert" the child, of course, but if they are not successful, they will find themselves forced to choose between their own conversion and continuing family friction. Whichever way they move, the situation is hardly conducive to voluntary, unfettered choice.

These examples, too, form a spectrum of cases distributed along a continuum identified by a characteristic morally problematic feature—the cases' central "wrong-making trait." In these examples, what makes them wrong, prima facie, is that they all involve circumstantial manipulation accomplished through an intermediate party.

A given conversion practice may have more than one morally problematic feature. For instance, the Mormon baseball clubs involved not only circumstantial manipulation but also deception: apparently, the boys thought—and were allowed to think—that baptism was a sort of initiation ceremony required for playing baseball. The practice also involved what might be called undue inducement or bribery; baptism was promoted as a prerequisite for being allowed to play the exotic American game of baseball. As in the case of bogus scavenger hunts, these multiple morally problematic features occur in comparatively mild form, but they can all be discovered in much more pronounced versions in overtly proselytizing practices.

Still other conversion-oriented practices, often associated with recent or current groups such as the Oakland Family Moonies, the Alamo Foundation, the Hare Krishna, and others—are said to involve physical intervention, including isolation, sequestering, deprivation of food and sleep, disruption of contact with family and other outsiders, continuous surveillance, and so on. Still stronger versions of physical intervention may involve physical threats of punishment, torture, or death, like some of the Spanish conquistadores' tactics in converting Indians in the Americas. As with other types of proselytizing practices, these too can be described along a continuum that identifies their central morally problematic feature—physical coercion—ranging from comparatively mild cases to very aggressive ones.

In general, then, those forms of convert seeking that centrally involve the exploitation of ordinary human relationships form only one type of conversion activity. A full-scale survey of conversion practices across the range of religious groups would permit the grouping of practices under a remarkable variety of types, identified according to central morally problematic features or wrong-making traits— deceptiveness, invasiveness, manipulation, bribery, exploitation, and physical coercion being but a few. Within each type, some practices exhibit the moral violation that defines them more mildly, some in a pronounced way. These types are not meant to constitute a rigorous typology but rather provide a loose framework illuminating the problematic features of those practices that are subject to ethical scrutiny here. The terminology popularly used for various conversion practices tends (though not fully reliably) to reflect these scales and the pre-critical assumptions built into them about the ethical features of the practices. Terms without negative ethical connotations—for example, "evangelism," "outreach," and "missionary work"—are reserved for practices at the milder ends of the scales; "missionizing," a term that retains the flavor of active nineteenth-century conversion programs, falls somewhere in the middle; and "proselytism," a term with highly negative connotations, is applied to practices at the stronger, more aggressive ends of each of the scales.

An exhaustive analysis of conversion practices would of course be enormously complex. To be fully descriptive, each scale would have to permit the ranking of discrete components of various convert-seeking styles in order to accommodate practices that are, for instance, less deceptive but more intrusive or vice versa. No one group would be likely to score highest in all categories, and some categories might exclude one another. Furthermore, such scales, fully developed, would have to take into account the relative sophistication or naïveté of the people or groups to which conversion strategies are directed. For instance, approaches involving manipulation and inducements, especially among the televangelists of the "electronic church," are less aggressive in character when used with people or in cultures already familiar with slick merchandizing techniques; on the other hand, even very mildly deceptive approaches can be aggressive when used on particularly vulnerable individuals, such as adolescents undergoing identity crises or recently bereaved adults.

However complex a specific scale might need to be to describe fully the varieties of actual practice, and however many different subscales might be required to account for the multiple forms of moral problems in different evangelizing, missionizing, and proselytizing practices, we can nevertheless speak of an overall, composite scale of aggressiveness in religious convert seeking, where "aggressiveness" designates the violation of moral norms. This scale ranks conversion practices generally in terms of the degree to which they exhibit their central morally problematic feature, whatever it may be. The scale runs from those practices in which the violation is minimal (at the weaker end) to those in which it is most pronounced. Thus, some practices can be said to be weakly aggressive and others strongly aggressive, regardless of the specific moral wrong-making feature involved.

## *Invitational Convert Seeking*

While it is possible to describe a scale or set of scales of aggressiveness in convert seeking, some forms of convert seeking are barely aggressive at all. Although conversion-oriented in character, they involve virtually no violations of ordinary moral norms or do so only in a very slight way.

This "new," nonaggressive variety of convert seeking began to be discussed within mainstream Protestant groups around 1912, largely in response to perceived excesses of the large-scale foreign missions of the nineteenth century, and was widely accepted within Protestant groups. A similar conception of missionizing without violation of moral norms was embraced by the Catholic Church at the Second Vatican Council. The foreign missions of the nineteenth century clearly would have ranked high on a scale of overall aggression, involving as they often did extraordinarily problematic techniques. For example, these missions often deliberately disrupted personal relationships, communities, and cultures. They solicited interest with inducements ranging from trinkets to employment and housing. They deliberately attempted to destroy the existing belief systems of individuals and displayed little regard for the protection of voluntary individual choice. Questioning the methods and the destructive effects of foreign missions on native cultures and communities, both mainstream Protestants and Catholics gradually moved to replace the old style of aggressive proselytism with nonaggressive, primarily invitational missionary outreach. The transition was by no means abrupt, and Catholicism, in particular, continued to assert its commitment to the conversion of unbelieving peoples. Nevertheless, there was a substantial change in strategy: missionaries might serve as models of Christian belief and practice, both Protestants and Catholics asserted, but ought not employ aggressive, morally problematic techniques to convert people to Christianity. As Vatican II decreed, "the Church strictly forbids forcing anyone to embrace the faith, or alluring or enticing people by unworthy techniques."[15] Theologians in both traditions stressed that these changes were not discontinuous but rather involved bringing forward a different strand of past tradition. Nevertheless, the gradual transformation in mainstream missionary styles during this century has been profound.

The new missionaries have increasingly curtailed interventionist efforts to change the beliefs of prospective converts and have instead begun to represent themselves as models or examples of faith. While the foreign missionary typically provides practical assistance to the community where he or she works—such as medical care or agricultural advice—this new missionary does not present himself or herself as a "saver of souls" but rather as a person for whom religious faith is a central commitment. Evangelism, in this newer model, consists in acting in a way that expresses one's own religious beliefs: living one's beliefs is in itself a way of announcing them to others. Although it can be wholly nonaggressive in the sense just identified, invitational evangelism is still a convert-seeking activity; it is done under the assumption that for a nonbelieving individual simply to see or interact with someone for whom faith is central may be sufficient to bring faith to that individual. This might be considered a "contagion" as well as an invitational model; it assumes that acting in a way that reveals or exhibits one's own faith will tend to spread it to others.

Much domestic convert seeking also reflects this newer, nonaggressive character. The missionary sets up a booth in a shopping center or goes door-to-door distributing leaflets; unlike the Campus Crusade for Christ in its simple scavenger hunt, however, he or she announces the purpose straightforwardly and moves politely away if not invited in. In line with the mainstream denominations' gradual move away from evangelism to social activist projects in the late 1960s and 1970s, many domestic missionaries avoid direct convert-seeking activity altogether, concentrating instead on social service involvement with youth groups, soup kitchens, sanctuary homes, and similar projects.

A particularly remarkable example of the new missionary is Sister Emmanuel, aged seventy-four when she was celebrated by *Time* several years ago, who had been living for ten years among the ten thousand garbage pickers of Cairo. Sister Emmanuel, a Roman Catholic nun, was conducting a school for the children of families living in the garbage dump, and while she preached about cleanliness in a world of rotting garbage and broken glass, she said she did not attempt to convert the Muslim children in her school to Christianity. "Today we don't talk about conversion any more," *Time* quoted her as saying. "We talk about being friends. My job is to prove that God is love, to bring courage to these people."[16] Insofar as she wishes to bring these people an understanding of God as love, and with this to bring them a new fundamental attitude toward life (an attitude that she calls "courage" but that is best understood as faith-based hope), her effort is clearly missionizing, but she is correct in thinking it is a long way from seeking to convert these people to a new set of theological doctrines.

Invitational convert seeking of this type is particularly attractive as an antidote to the personal and cultural damage aggressive practices can produce, especially where they reinforce colonialist, imperialist policies. Rather than targeting isolated individuals, the new missionaries direct their efforts toward groups. They work to avoid disruption of the family, even when one member converts without the others, and they work particularly hard to avoid wholesale destruction of indigenous cultures. Unlike earlier missionaries, who had both intended to and succeeded in disrupting local cultures enough to replace tribal values and practices with Christian ones, the new missionaries seek to accommodate Christianity as much as possible to existing practices, stripping Christian belief as completely as possible of Western cultural trappings and translating its essence into the local idiom. Under this newer model too, missionaries not only avoid making missionized peoples economically dependent upon them but they also avoid creating dependence upon a foreign religious hierarchy. Indeed, many missionizing groups now seek to train native clergy in order to develop self-sufficient indigenous churches.

Both for these reasons concerning the effects of missionizing on local communities and cultures and also for reasons having to do with the character of the missionary's interaction with the prospective convert, the newer model of convert seeking seems in harmony with both ordinary moral norms and with those specifically relevant in contemporary professional ethics. The new missionary style does not deceive individuals or groups. It does not exploit ordinary human relationships for the ulterior purpose of conversion, nor does it engage in circumstantial manipulation or other coercive strategies. It does not offer unfair inducements or bribes. Insofar as it addresses the individual at all, rather than the community more generally, it emphasizes respect for the integrity of the individual, including respect for cultural affiliations, familial and social relationships, and even prior religious beliefs. It attempts to introduce a new dimension into the group's and hence its members' lives by introducing them to faith without disrupting or destroying their personal or social equilibrium. It respects the values and rights of other persons within an individual's familial or cultural spheres as well, by not forcibly removing the individual from them. Most importantly, it places much greater emphasis on the autonomy of the individual and on the individual's capacity and right to determine his or her fundamental values, including religious values. On all these grounds, the new, invitational model of missionary outreach clearly seems to represent a moral advance over the practices of aggressive conversion tactics.

The new model of missionary practice is often coupled with a new theoretical model of how conversion occurs. In the traditional conversion model, the candidate for conversion was seen as passive, subject to external or internal forces that would effectuate changes in his or her beliefs. Under the earlier deterministic model, conversion was understood as the outcome of a causal process initiated by the proselytizing agent. According to the newer paradigm,[17] in contrast, the subject is active: a meaning-seeking individual who exercises volition in deciding to convert. At the time of the encounter with the missionary, this individual is already seeking to alter or develop his or her personhood; he or she simply responds to a religious suggestion or invitation to do so in a specific way. James Richardson, describing this paradigm for conversion to the new religions, talks not about how people are converted, but about "how people go about converting themselves."[18]

Under the newer paradigm, of course, a great deal more of the responsibility in conversion matters is assigned to the subject: he or she is no longer the passive target of forces that are causally sufficient to bring about conversion but is an active participant in the process. In this sense, he or she also seems to be a voluntary, willing participant in the process: at least, the person is antecedently predisposed to undergo an experience that would convey meaning and develop personhood, even if he or she may not antecedently intend that it take the form of religious conversion. Consequently, under this paradigm, the missionary does not *cause* the subject's conversion, except in an accessory, occasional way; the missionary simply provides the stimulus, to which the person, already ripe for conversion, responds. Under the new paradigm, unlike the old, conversion strategies can no longer be understood as *making* believe, and "convert" is no longer understood to be a transitive verb.

This does not, however, remove the missionary's methods and objectives from potential ethical critique. If the paradigm is correct, it merely suggests that one may have to look more perceptively for the missionary's contribution to the conversion process. To say that an individual was already "seeking meaning" does not diminish the missionary's responsibility in channeling the individual's search in one direction or another, nor does it excuse the missionary for using "unworthy techniques" to take advantage of whatever suggestibility or vulnerability the individual displays. The issue of moral constraints on convert seeking and interference in religious belief remains before us, whichever paradigm we employ.

The new variety of convert seeking in the Catholic and Protestant mainstream represents a rejection of problematic techniques and a move away from aggressive proselytism in principle. It is a move toward the use of invitational missionary work only. Inasmuch as it rejects strategies that involve violation of ordinary moral norms, the move appears to represent a moral advance. The distinction between aggressive and invitational conversion activities, reflected in the overall scale of aggressiveness just described, suggests that the changes in missionary strategy among mainstream Christian groups from the nineteenth to the twentieth century represent moral progress, and that the recent appearance of much more aggressive tactics among the cults and new religions is a moral setback.

The scale of aggressiveness allows us to rank groups directly (although the ranking may be complex) according to the degree to which they violate or respect moral norms. Both historical groups like the

Spanish conquistadores and contemporary ones like the Oakland Family Moonies rank very high on this scale, even though their methods and effects differ in many important ways. At the opposite extreme, those groups whose practices put them in the lowest ranges of the scale are, typically, the mainline Protestant groups within the National Council of Churches, groups whose missionary efforts have consisted, at least until recently, almost entirely in service to the disadvantaged and who make virtually no effort to alter belief. Some post–Vatican II Catholics rank a little farther up the scale: many Catholic missionary groups still actively seek conversion, but do so in a comparatively nonaggressive way. The Mormons, whose extensive missionary program involves sophisticated persuasive techniques, might score in the midrange: although their door-to-door canvassing is both uninvited and confrontational, and inducements for membership—including access to social services provided by the church—often manipulative, this group clearly rejects outright coercion. The numerous contemporary evangelicals in foreign missions, many associated with the relief agency World Vision, rank in midrange for slightly different reasons: while they often resemble the new mainstream Protestant missionaries in providing such things as medical and agricultural assistance, they may be more duplicitous in their reasons for providing assistance and less ready to acknowledge that their real purpose is to win the confidence of the people and thus gain an opportunity to make converts. The electronic church in its various forms might also rank somewhere in midrange; while evangelizing efforts that operate largely through radio and television (often supplemented by direct-mail campaigns) have little opportunity to be directly coercive, they can be highly manipulative in offering inducements. Finally, some groups are not even on the scale: off the scale at the low end are those groups that generally eschew convert seeking—for instance, Unitarian Universalists, Quakers, and, except for the so-called return movements, most groups within Judaism. But in spite of the apparent conspicuousness of moral violations among the more aggressive proselytizing practices and the evident innocuousness of the invitational, nonproselytizing ones, judgments like these, ranking groups and their convert-seeking practices from least to most aggressive, raise a new and difficult issue.

The problem is this. On what basis can it be said that rankings on this scale reflect moral *wrongness?* The scale has been constructed to reflect what are prima facie morally wrong features—deception, manipulation, coercion, and so on; it would seem that the scale could be interpreted as an index of moral reprehensibility as well as of aggressiveness. If so, the high scorers—for instance, the Spanish conquistadores, the Oakland Family, and the flirty fishers—like other practitioners of highly aggressive proselytism, could be said to employ highly unethical practices, whereas the low scorers—those, generally, who respect individual autonomy and rights, who do not disrupt societies or familiar relationships, and who do not force change on a person but simply invite it, like the nun in the Cairo garbage dump—would be those who receive the highest ethical marks. We have been speaking in this precritical way as if the scale of aggressiveness also served as a scale of ethical repugnance, and that, therefore, the more aggressive a practice, the more morally problematic. To assess convert-seeking activities in this way is to evaluate religious practice directly with the categories of ordinary morality—that is, to employ one prong of the pincer apparatus developed here. But we do not yet have any warrant for using this apparatus in this direct way. We cannot simply suppose that ordinary morality, any more than professional ethics, can be applied directly to religious practices. Instead, this matter returns us to the methodological issues with which we have been constantly confronted. Although ordinary morality suggests that the aggressiveness scale is a scale of ethical reprehensibility, it may show something quite different indeed.

## Methodological Issues

It may seem that the issue of aggressive convert seeking will only invite doctrinal dispute. Rather than accept the ethical disapproval such a scale invites, the highly aggressive groups will point to scriptural passages to provide support *for* such practices, insisting that the scale of aggressiveness cannot be interpreted as a scale of moral reprehensibility. For instance, at Matthew 10:35–37 Jesus says: "For I have come to set a man against his father, and a daughter against her mother, and a daughter-in-law against her mother-in-law; and one's foes will be members of one's own household. Whoever loves father or mother more than me is not worthy of me." Some groups will cite this as evidence that not only are intrusive, aggressive conversion tactics not to be disapproved—including the disruption of domestic relationships and enforced isolation of a prospective convert from family members—but that they are religiously commanded. On the other hand, the nonaggressive, invitational groups will point to the clear respect the scriptures are said to show for cultural and familial values, arguing that Matthew 10:35–37 does not mean that the missionary should disrupt social and family relationships, but only that the believer must be prepared to value God above all. Clearly, to try to resolve the *moral* issues in convert seeking on scriptural grounds would invite a protracted, dogmatic battle, a battle that has in part already been actively waged within various theological traditions.

As in the earlier discussions of confidentiality and risk taking, however, our typology of doctrinal claims will allow us to avoid doctrinal dispute. Ethical critique of a group's practices need not begin with an attack on its most basic doctrinal tenets; the group's 0-level doctrines can remain unchallenged, with neither a positive nor a negative truthvalue assigned to them or to the background metaphysical claims on which they rest, and attention is directed instead to the upper-level practices and claims that develop as these imperatives are put into practice.

For most Christian groups that engage in convert seeking, it is Matthew 28:19 ("Go therefore and make disciples of all nations") that functions as the fundamental, 0-level imperative commanding these practices. But, as discussed earlier, a fundamental, 0-level imperative does not typically dictate *how* it is to be put into practice, nor what moral constraints govern its exercise. As a staunch supporter of foreign missions insisted in 1889, "There is no one method of evangelization enjoined on us in the New Testament."[19] To say that the scriptural texts enjoin no one method is not to say, however, that the methods employed cannot be evaluated; we can examine the strategies of conversion without criticizing (or approving) the underlying project. We can ask which styles of convert seeking are ethically preferable to others, independently of whether convert seeking is morally defensible in the first place, and do so in a way that avoids appeal to basic-level doctrine. This will allow us to make moral differentiations between the conquistadores' threats of death, the Children of God's prostitution, the Campus Crusade's scavenger hunt, and the seemingly saintly example of the nun in the Egyptian garbage dump, even though they are all practices that develop in response to the fundamental imperative in Matthew 28.

But there is a further limitation. In the discussion of decision making under risk in chapter 2 we identified restrictions in the range of religious practices subject to normative critique: only those practices can be critiqued in which the religious practitioner is obligated to satisfy the fiduciary principle—to act in a way that is worthy of the client's trust and does not undermine those interests with respect to which the client consults him or her. However, appeal to the fiduciary principle takes the relationship between professional and client as a background model, and it may seem that the interaction between the religious missionary and the prospective convert does not fit this model. In many ways, the relationship between missionary and prospective convert more closely resembles the relationship between commercial seller and buyer. Nevertheless, some features of the professional-client relationship do have analogues—though weak ones—in the missionary-convert relationship, and these can be used to consider whether the principle that a religious practitioner ought not undermine a client's interests can be generalized to a much wider range of cases—including the present one of convert seeking.

In the central, core cases of convert seeking, the nature of the missionary-convert relationship shares important characteristics with secular professional-client relationship. For instance, the missionary responds to and helps to identify a deficiency in the prospective convert (often diagnosed as emptiness, loneliness, or despair, which in the missionary's view results from a lack of faith); this process is much like the physician's diagnosing a patient's illness, as well as antecedently determining what is to count as illness, or the attorney's identifying a client's degree of legal jeopardy. The missionary brings to bear a specialized body of knowledge (the truth or falsity of which we are not permitted to challenge under our methodology)—namely scripture and religious history—to address the prospective convert's problem, much as physicians and attorneys employ specialized knowledge to address their patients' or clients' problems. The missionary attempts to alter the prospective convert's attitudes and recommends that these changes in attitude be coupled with action—namely joining the church—much as a physician prescribes drugs or surgery and an attorney advises a client what to say on the witness stand. Furthermore, the missionary's institution—the church—accepts any offerings that may be made by a convert in gratitude for the services the missionary has rendered in bringing him or her new faith, not entirely unlike the physician or the attorney receiving fees for services performed, and the missionary's institution can also expect additional contributions from the new member in the future. There are many disanalogies between the secular professional and the missionary in the field. But if some components of these parallels between the missionary and the secular professional are persuasive, given the results in chapter 2, the missionary will also be subject to fiduciary obligations, just as other religious and secular professionals are. Thus, the missionary ought not undermine a prospective convert's interests, nor violate moral rules such as honesty, respect for autonomy, and confidentiality in his or her treatment of the person. On these grounds too, it seems, aggressive convert-seeking strategies—those that involve deception, coercion, unfair inducement, and so on—are proper candidates for normative assessment and must be assessed as morally wrong.

This conclusion introduces the problem of paternalism, the central ethical issue in religious convert seeking, since application of the fiduciary principle presupposes a claim that the paternalist rejects. The claim is that the conception of the client's interests, key to the application of the fiduciary principle, can be identified straightforwardly according to why the client approaches the professional. The paternalist sees it differently, believing that the client is mistaken about what his or her interests really are and that it is the professional's job to serve the *true* interests of the client.

## The Paternalist Argument for Aggressive Conversion Activities

Even if, as seems to be the case, the deceptive, manipulative, coercive methods of aggressive convert seeking are prima facie morally wrong (either weakly or strongly), we must also consider whether they can be justified on paternalist grounds. If we begin with the working assumption that convert seeking, on even a weak analogy to other professional services, should benefit the person to whom the possibility of conversion is offered, the principle of paternalism may license aggressive practices after all.

Under the classic view of human liberty and moral rights developed in the liberal tradition of the eighteenth century, an individual's liberty and other rights may be violated only under the harm principle, that is, only to prevent the individual from causing harm to others. According to the principle of paternalism, however, which challenges the liberal view, an individual's liberty and other rights may also be violated for that person's own sake. Paternalism may involve protecting someone from causing harm to himself or herself; it may involve keeping the person from failing to prevent a harm that would otherwise happen to himself or herself; or, more controversially, it may involve making the person act to benefit himself or herself or act not to prevent a benefit to himself or herself that would otherwise occur. The severity of the violation of liberty or breaking of other moral rules is justified in proportion to the level of interference required to protect the individual's interests and to the degree of harm done to the individual by the interference. Interference that is more coercive than necessary is not justified. Interference is not justified at all if noninterfering methods of protecting the individual's interests exist. If there are no alternatives, however, there is no theoretical limit (other than death, if it is assumed that death thwarts all the individual's interests) to the extent of intervention justified, providing only that the costs to the individual of the interference do not outweigh the benefits of satisfaction of the interests protected. If, then, on this paternalist challenge to the traditional liberal view, converts are sought *for the convert's own sake,* even the aggressive methods of proselytism required to achieve conversion may be excused. Under the paternalist view, even conversion tactics that involve moral wrongs, such as deception, manipulation, and coercion, are morally justified.

Three types of convert seeking fall outside our focus here. These involve convert seeking that is not paternalistic or not centrally so—that is, it is not done primarily for the sake of the individual whose faith is at stake. First, some proselytism and missionizing is done primarily for the benefit of the missionary, to achieve whatever benefits accrue to him or her from converting others. Sometimes this is simply egocentric notching one's gun of the sort in which the missionary works primarily to increase the tally of converts to his or her credit. Some religious groups also institutionally encourage convert seeking either by imposing penalties for failing to meet quotas, or by stressing direct benefits to the person who makes converts, or both. In the Unification Church, for instance, members are normally eligible to participate in the mass marriages celebrated by Reverend Moon only after they have gained three "spiritual children," that is, only after they have recruited three new members into the group. In this group, making converts is a prerequisite (though now often waived) for being permitted to engage in sexual and reproductive relationships.

Second, some convert seeking also aims primarily to enrich or enlarge the religious institution that promotes it. In many groups it is assumed that increasing the strength of the church is an end in itself, and there has been considerable theological dispute on this issue. Objecting to such a view, for instance, one writer asserts that it is "misleading to say that the Church has a mission, as if the existence of the Church comes first. In truth it is because of the mission that there is a Church; the Church is the servant and expression of this mission . . . it is quite misleading to say that the purpose of the mission is the expansion of the Church."[20] But another writer insists that "strengthening a congregation" is a "valid end," and points out that evangelism is sometimes practiced to serve the "institutional needs of adding to the membership and budget of our churches."[21] Particularly among the foreign missions, as still another writer recalls, conversion programs were treated as a matter of numbers: "Conversion was a numerical affair and numbers were an important index of evangelizing a nation. Success was reported by counting visible things such as numbers of baptisms, numbers of confessions, numbers of communions."[22] It is a quick leap from counting numbers of converts to counting the increased size of a church. Where bottom-line objectives in augmenting a church motivate convert seeking, it can hardly be said to be paternalistic in character, though it is often excused on this ground.

Third, some convert seeking seems to be conducted as a form of social control, strongly associated with other colonialist, imperialist strategies, to subdue or pacify a political, cultural, or geographical region. The gun-notching, church-aggrandizing, and social-control forms of convert seeking may be uncommon; certainly they all raise substantial moral problems of their own. But it is comparatively purely paternalistic conversion efforts that raise the most difficult moral issues, and which will be the focus of discussion here.

The argument defending aggressive proselytism on paternalistic grounds would seem to be defeated by the basic tenets of the liberal view that the doctrine of paternalism challenges and from which political doctrines of freedom of religion have derived. Under the liberal view, each person is entitled to his or her own religious beliefs, both to hold them and to act on them, provided only that acting on them does not cause harm to others. There is to be no interference by government or by any other agency or individual with the freedom of religious belief. This tenet protects a central area of autonomy and a fundamental constitutional right. Other interests, which might be served by invading a person's liberty of religious belief cannot override it. In this view, then, invitational missionary work might be permitted, but aggressive, invasive, coercive proselytism designed to change beliefs could not under any circumstances be condoned.

## The Benefits of Conversion

This objection, which points to fundamental principles of freedom of religion as an argument against aggressive convert seeking, fails to take into account the benefits that missionary work, it is claimed, may provide for the person who converts—or the harms it may prevent.

Some of the benefits that acceptance of a new faith may offer are identified in terms of external social and material goods: membership in a particular group, sometimes living space and employment, or occasionally other inducements such as food, clothing, or other assistance. However, the personal benefits of religious faith may be considerably more profound. By providing an environment in which the individual is the focus of caring concern and by bringing him or her to accept a new faith, missionary work may alter the nature of the individual's existence in substantial ways. It may relieve fear and dispel a sense of loneliness or isolation. It may provide a sense of purpose in life. It may bring a sense of community and membership in a group, a feeling of being connected, wanted, and of fellow feeling with others; it may make the individual understand in a new way what it is to be a human being.

The claims and testimonials made by converts clearly suggest that there is something more than trivial, external advantage at stake. Converts speak of "opening doors," "becoming myself," "adding new depth to my life," "wholly transcending my former existence." Sometimes the scope of these benefits may be very broad, affecting all areas of a person's life. In foreign missionizing, for instance, the transformation of belief systems can be profound. Conversion away from an animistic belief system based on fear and an unpredictable, implacable threat to a Christian belief system, emphasizing acceptance and inclusion in a benevolent divine plan, may make an enormous difference in the character of the lives of those converted, since the new belief system provides a sense of security and purpose the old one did not.[23] Writing in the 1880s, Miss Gordon Cumming emphasized similarly profound changes in the character of everyday life in describing the transformation of Fiji:

> I often wish that some of the cavillers who are forever sneering at the Christian missions could see something of their results in these islands. But first they would have to recall the Fiji of ten years ago, when every man's hand was against his neighbor, and the land had no rest from barbarous inter-tribal wars, in which the foe, without respect of age or sex, were looked upon only in the

light of so much beef, the prisoners deliberately fattened for the slaughter, dead bodies dug up that had been buried ten or twelve days, and could only be cooked in the form of puddings, limbs cut off from living men and women and cooked and eaten in presence of the victim. . . .

. . . Just think of all this, and of the change that has been wrought. . . Now you may pass from isle to isle, certain everywhere to find the same cordial reception by kindly men and women. Every village on the eighty inhabited isles has built for itself a tidy little church and a good house for its teacher or native minister . . . and the first sound that greets your ear at dawn, and the last at night, is that of hymn-singing and most fervent worship rising from each dwelling at the hour of family worship.[24]

Miss Cumming's claims are no doubt extravagant, and much religious conversion involves changes less dramatic than renouncing cannibalism and reforming a world of unremitting cruelty. Nevertheless, profound, enduring benefits are claimed by converts even in a comparatively civilized society, as they find their outlook and expectations radically altered. Converts to a wide variety of religious groups say, "this has transformed my life."

Gaining religious faith may also prevent conditions that constitute life's more profound harms—the sense of purposelessness, meaninglessness, and sinfulness often described in religious literature as despair. In the religious context, despair does not merely mean a temporary psychological depression, but a much more consuming, self-destroying, wholly negative and painful condition of life. By converting a person, the missionary acts in that person's most basic interests, helping him or her avoid these harms.

It may be objected that this is hardly an adequate argument for aggressive religious proselytism, especially if it involves serious moral wrong. There are two principal components to this objection. First, though in some cases religious conversion may provide advantages, these advantages could also be attained through psychotherapy or other forms of mental and emotional care, changes in social or political conditions, and so on. Peoples with animistic belief systems do not need religion—the argument goes—they need exposure to science. The lonely need friends; the insecure need reinforcement that improves self-confidence; and those with deep-seated fears need psychotherapy, not preaching about love. Second, to assess the benefits and advantages of religious faith in this way is to dictate values to the individual; this is, itself, an indefensible move. It may be true that many people do value community, purposefulness, freedom from fear, and so on, but this scheme of values ought not be *forced* upon anyone. In general, paternalistic intervention that restricts a person's liberty or violates other moral rules in a way that makes him or her act to enhance specific values is warranted only if that person's thinking is impaired or if, for some other reason, his rationality is compromised and he is unable to pursue those values that are his own.

This so-called soft or weak paternalist view, which countenances intervention in a person's liberty for his or her own sake only when the person is rationally impaired and cannot act on his or her values (the view accepted under the traditional liberal stance), does not permit aggressive proselytism using deceit, manipulation, coercion, or other liberty-infringing measures to change someone's religious beliefs. In holding certain beliefs already, the individual is exercising precisely those values that are already his or her own. "Invitational" convert seeking that consists in passive evangelism would be permitted since it enlarges the range of information about religious views and institutions a person has in developing religious beliefs and values but does not alter the way that person chooses. Aggressive proselytism, on the other hand, is wholly unwarranted in the soft paternalist view, and the moral excesses of aggressive proselytism cannot be excused. Thus, the rough scale of aggressiveness constructed earlier seems to serve after all as a scale of ethical reprehensibility: the more aggressive proselytism is, the more clearly it is morally wrong; the more purely invitational, the more plausible a candidate it becomes for moral approval.

## *Afterlife Claims: Salvation and Damnation*

The paternalist must object, however, that the issue here is *religious* paternalism, and we have not yet taken account of the most central religious claims. Under the traditional set of basic Christian and quasi-Christian theological assumptions (of which we will assert neither truth nor falsity), more is at stake for the prospective convert than feelings of membership, emotional comfort, and purposefulness. Traditional Christian belief holds that what is most centrally at stake are afterlife outcomes—salvation or damnation of the individual's soul. Thus, the issues in paternalistic convert seeking are much more serious. For the missionary, what is at stake for himself or herself in converting a person may be a feeling of accomplishment, praise for the effort, and perhaps other transitory rewards; but what is at stake for the person converted or not converted is whether his or her soul is saved and thus, whether he or she will go to heaven or to hell. What the missionary does for the convert is no small thing. Salvation is not a trivial benefit, in this traditional belief system, and damnation no trifling risk. On the contrary, as a conceptual truth among religious claims, salvation is the best thing that could happen to a person, damnation the worst: one is maximally good both in character and duration; the other maximally bad. Conversion thus involves the double substitution of values discussed in chapter 2: afterlife outcomes, if a person comes to believe them to occur, will now carry the greatest weight in the individual's economy of values. No other interests or values, no matter how deeply held, can possibly outweigh these, and no sane, rational person could conceivably choose damnation over salvation—under the assumption that one or the other will actually occur—except in a demonstrably mistaken short-term tradeoff.

However, this changes the missionary's position radically. Although the soft paternalist position widely accepted in liberal political theory and in the secular professions would license interference in an individual's liberty when the individual's choice-making capacities are impaired but would not allow interference to protect him or her from what the paternalizer takes to be great harm, even though it is in accord with the individual's values, soft paternalism simply is not a tenable position in this special religious case. Under the traditional bipolar religious schema, the stakes are too high, and the value rankings a person holds cannot possibly be other than to prefer eternal bliss to eternal torment. Someone might jokingly maintain that the company in hell will be more interesting, or that eternal life in heaven would be tediously pure, but anyone who understands the grammar of these terms as denoting maximally good and maximally bad states and also understands that they are of infinite duration cannot possibly prefer hell to heaven. A hell in which the company is enjoyable is not a real hell, nor is a boring heaven heaven. The soft paternalist's insistence on the ultimate subjectivity of values is completely implausible here. No amount of liberty to act on one's own values or to determine the course of one's life can outweigh the disbenefit of hell—infinitely continuing maximal bad for oneself. Thus, paternalist intervention in religious situations, under the traditional schema, must always be hard paternalism, acting not simply to counter rational impairment but to prevent the greatest of all possible harms. No intervention of any sort, regardless of how deceptive, invasive, coercive, or otherwise seriously morally flawed, would be out of bounds if it were required to save someone's soul.

One way to defeat this startling argument might be to assert that traditional religious claims about heaven and hell are false. But under the general assumption required for the examination of ethical issues in religious practice, we cannot assume such beliefs—either the 0-level imperatives or the background metaphysical claims on which they are based—to be either true or false; no valuation of such claims can be either assigned or presupposed. Unless we can assert that these claims are false, however, the argument reaches a seemingly outlandish conclusion: aggressive proselytism is not only *not* morally wrong, despite the extreme violations of moral norms it often involves, but justified— perhaps even obligatory—in any case where it could mean the difference between a person's going to heaven or to hell. Thus, the aggressiveness scale constructed above becomes an index of moral *rightness,* not wrongness, after all, and the paradox the issue of paternalism introduces is that those conversion tactics that, under ordinary ethical norms and nontheist assumptions, look most reprehensible turn out to be, when the traditional theological assumptions are introduced, those that are morally best. Analysis with our pincer apparatus of ordinary and professional ethics seems to be not only useless, since it gives us the contrary result, but misleading in the most profoundly disastrous way. The practices of the Spanish conquistadores in converting a populace at gunpoint must be commended, if these measures were required to be effective in producing conversion, and the only moral risk was that they might have backfired by producing death before they produced belief. Similarly, the Unification Church ought not repudiate the earlier practices of the Oakland Family, as it now does, but should view this as the most ethically commendable of its divisions. If the Children of God find flirty fishing the most effective way of bringing converts into the fold—and as we saw, they claim to have converted nineteen thousand of the twenty-five thousand with whom they had had sex— this bit of duplicitous prostitution is to be strongly commended, no matter how sordid it may seem.

Furthermore, this conclusion leads us to see that mere invitational outreach is completely inadequate, since it makes no attempt to alter the values and beliefs of people who are not predisposed to have them altered in any case. Groups that have tamed their missionizing practices, including the Protestant members of the National Council of Churches and post–Vatican II Catholicism, should on these very grounds be morally condemned. What looked like historical advance—from the conquistadores and the ruthless foreign missions to a nun talking only of love, not conversion, in the Cairo garbage dump—now seems to reflect moral defeat.

## Generalizing Pascal's Wager

The methodology developed here for examining ethical issues in organized religion, which precludes assigning a truthvalue to the background metaphysical assumptions common to religious belief, requires us to refrain from supposing what is or is not the case. Of course, the missionary does not see it this way. The missionary, we may assume, believes that it *is* true that God exists, that there is a heaven, that unbelievers go to hell, and other teachings of his or her religious group. It is therefore tempting to suggest that if the missionary sincerely believes that these teachings are true, then as a matter of *moral* obligation he or she must act in accord with them since to do otherwise would be to act contrary to what he or she believes is true. This argument, it seems, would provide moral justification for the missionary's attempts to persuade others of the truth of these beliefs. Against this, it can be argued that the conscientious missionary must also recognize that however sincere his or her beliefs, they involve subjective certainty only; the missionary cannot have objective proof of nonempirical realities. This is, after all, what it is to have *faith*. On this counterargument, the missionary has no justification for imposing his or her beliefs on others or for violating moral rules with respect to others in attempting to get them to believe, as distinguished from simply announcing what he or she does believe and inviting others to do so, too. Without objective certainty of the truth of the religious claims, this counterargument holds, the missionary is not justified in any aggressively proselytizing activities, though purely invitational evangelism would be acceptable. But neither the initial argument nor the counterargument will work; both give way to a much stronger argument independent of claims about whether the missionary can be certain of the truth of what he or she believes. Examining this argument reveals that the case for aggressive morality-violating proselytism is much stronger than we have supposed.

As Pascal pointed out in his famed discussion of the wager of belief, certainty is by no means required to make it prudent to adopt a faith, and even a comparatively small chance that the doctrines are true may still make it reasonable to adopt that belief—or, since this may not be possible directly, to do things that will foster that belief. In Dan Wikler's paraphrase, the wager is this:

> Agnostics should adopt the habits that would foster their own belief in God. If they do and God exists, they will receive the infinite rewards of paradise; if they do and God does not exist, they were only wasting the efforts of conversion and prayer. If they do not try to believe in God, and religion is true, they suffer the infinitely bad fate of hell; whereas if God does not exist they have merely saved some inconvenience. Conversion is the rational choice even if agnostics estimate the chances of God's existing as very remote, since even a very small probability yields a large index when multiplied against an infinite quantity.[25]

Pascal's wager is familiar as an exercise in rational prudence.[26] But Pascal poses it in a self-respecting version only; he is concerned just with the risks and benefits *to himself* from belief and unbelief. What he does not consider is a generalized version of this argument to other-respecting cases. Yet if there are reasons for fostering one's own belief, similar considerations will also apply to fostering belief in others— that is, doing whatever one can to bring them to believe—since the same risks and benefits presumably attend other people's believing or not believing as one's own. If you do not believe and there is a God, you go to hell; if others do not believe and there is a God, they go to hell too, and the risks of this horrendous outcome outweigh whatever small costs there are to belief. But when the wager is generalized in this way and it is supposed, as the missionary does, that efforts by one person can affect another person's beliefs, the issue takes on a new dimension. In Pascal's self-referential case, the matter is one of rational prudence: I protect my interests best by getting myself to believe. But, where it is possible for me to do so, getting others to believe is not merely a matter of rational prudence; it is a circumstance with distinctively *moral* features. To get someone to believe is to confer an enormous benefit on that person, as great a benefit as I confer on myself in succeeding in believing; to let that person persist in unbelief when I could get him or her to believe is to consign that person to a cataclysmic harm. Aggressive convert seeking, thus, is to be recommended on moral grounds.

But the argument is still stronger. Given the infinite magnitude of the possible rewards and the catastrophic nature of the potential penalties, bringing others to believe cannot be merely morally optional, but is clearly obligatory. After all, securing salvation for somebody is not like securing a pair of theater tickets for him or her. Nor is preventing another's damnation like preventing the person from being run over by a bus: being killed is a great harm, but—under the traditional assumptions—being damned is (literally) infinitely worse. It may be seriously imprudent to fail to take precautions against damnation in one's own case, but it is profoundly, maximally *immoral* to remain unconcerned about what happens to others, if one is in a position to influence this outcome.

Hence, just as in this context of traditional religious assumptions soft paternalism is not a tenable stance, so the distinction between optional, supererogatory, and morally obligatory action fades as well. It is not simply that bringing someone to believe would be a good thing to do, though not morally required; it is, from a moral point of view, completely untenable to suggest that where an agent could make the difference in whether another person is saved or damned, that doing so is supererogatory—a nice thing to do, but not required. It is also untenable to suggest that if this imposes inconveniences or costs on the agent, he or she is under no obligation, since whatever the magnitude of the cost to the agent, it is trifling in comparison to the magnitude of the eternal outcome for the person involved. What is at stake for that person, in the traditional view, is an *infinity* of bliss—"an infinity of infinitely happy life," as Pascal puts it,[27] or an infinity of infinitely severe torment, and it is morally heinous to suggest that making this difference could be merely optional for an agent— something the agent can do if he or she feels like it, but something he or she cannot be morally criticized for choosing not to do.

Furthermore, on this view, the missionary—or any believer, for that matter—has a moral obligation to attempt to convert as many people as possible, whenever failing to do so would risk their being consigned to hell. Similarly, the missionary ought to intervene in any act that might seem to jeopardize someone's salvation—even if the person seems to be doing it in accord with his or her own values, of his or her own free will. Where the stakes are this high, omissions are as significant as commissions, and the missionary who fails to prevent such cataclysmic harms is morally at fault.

But this too seems to presuppose that it is certain that the agent's intervention guarantees these outcomes. Of that, of course, there is no objective proof. The missionary does not question the truth of the religious faith he or she is promoting, but in assessing the missionary's practices from an ethical point of view, the fact that the beliefs could be false must be considered. Yet this does not seem to undermine the argument in favor of aggressive conversion practices since, in structure, the missionary's deliberations parallel exactly those a Pascal would make on his or her own behalf, except that he or she must take into account whatever additional costs to the prospective convert there are from being coerced. Even if these are considerably more substantial than the trivial inconveniences Pascal took into account, they will still weigh virtually nothing against the magnitude of infinite benefits or harm.

Thus, the problem in conversion practices under consideration here yields a generalized version of Pascal's wager, in which the agent is fostering belief not just for himself or herself but for others as well. It is a version that is a good deal more disturbing. Pascal's own self-affecting wager involves no invasion of liberty, since it involves only Pascal's deciding for himself whether to foster his own belief and assuming for himself the small costs of doing so. But the proselytism case at issue here involves deciding for others whether their beliefs shall be promoted and acting to bring about such belief by converting them— if necessary, by means that are forcible, duplicitous, or in other ways apparently unethical. Of course, the disbenefit is much larger if the belief is false; it includes not only the inconvenience of religious practice for naught, but also the costs of having been coerced. But if the stakes could be *maximally* high, as the traditional claim goes, then even the additional disbenefit does not tip the balance the other way.

This conclusion may seem utterly bizarre, repugnant both in the secular climate of ordinary and professional ethics and in the religious atmosphere of tolerance and respect for individual choice now characteristic of most contemporary mainstream churches. This conclusion is, nevertheless, extraordinarily hard to avoid if our methodological requirement is preserved that fundamental religious doctrines and underlying metaphysical claims not be assumed to be either true or false. In what follows, I'd like to look at several attempts to defeat this conclusion—none of which succeeds. This will force us to take a new look at the nature of the problem itself.

## Defeating the Case for Aggressive Proselytism

In the face of the apparently outlandish conclusion to which the paternalist argument has led, it is tempting to reject the underlying bipolar schema of salvation and damnation altogether, since it is, after all, the schema that produces the bizarre results. As pointed out in the discussion in chapter 2 of high-risk decision making, rejecting this schema is just what the more liberal elements within many mainstream groups have done, and it is also what the new, invitational-model missionaries are doing. "Today we don't talk about conversion any more," *Time* had quoted Sister Emmanuel, the Catholic nun in the Cairo garbage dump, as saying. "We talk about being friends." Father Walbert Buhlmann, the Rome-based mission secretary of the Order of Friars Minor Capuchin, says still more directly: "In the past, we had the so-called motive of saving souls. We were convinced that if not baptized, people in the masses would go to hell. Now, thanks be to God, we believe that all people and all religions are already living in the grace and love of God and will be saved by God's mercy."[28]

But of course this assertion simply rejects the traditional view; it does not solve the moral problem that the traditional view generates. Thus, it does not satisfy the antecedent condition stipulated here that basic religious claims not be assumed to be either true or false; it supposes that they are false. Incidentally, not only would this posture leave little for the aggressive proselytizer to do, since no one would be in need of his or her services, but it would also undermine whatever preferential justification might be produced for even the mildest invitational outreach.

A related objection attempts to challenge the theological claim that conversion brings salvation, while failure to believe risks damnation. This objection denies that conversion or nonconversion has any role in determining afterlife status and so would completely undermine any justification for conversion activities. Different religious groups understand this issue in different ways. Some, like Catholicism, stress the role of divine grace in salvation, so that belief alone is not a guarantee of salvation, nor is nonbelief a certain ticket to hell. Many fundamentalist and evangelical groups take the relation to be much more direct. In any case, unless it is held that conversion plays *no* role in afterlife outcomes, the problem that paternalism poses remains.

It might be insisted that the case for aggressive convert seeking cannot succeed because religious belief must be *voluntary* if it is to play a role in afterlife salvation; it must be the product of free choice. However, under traditional assumptions, it is the condition of believing, or the act of belief, that is central, not the causal route by which a person comes to be a believer. Adults brought up with specific beliefs inculcated since childhood are not thereby said to believe involuntarily, provided only that they willingly confirm their beliefs in various assertions, actions, and participation in rites in adulthood. Thus, the aggressive proselytizer might coerce, cajole, manipulate, trick, or bribe someone into adopting certain beliefs, but under traditional assumptions, once the belief has been embraced and is thereafter continued in a voluntary way, it is the belief, not the manner of acquisition, that is central. Belief need not be acquired in ways that preserve autonomy to play the central role in salvation that the tradition assigns it.

Of course, the means by which belief is promoted may affect the degree to which it is absorbed. It is possible that aggressive proselytism is not more effective, as we have been assuming, in producing conversion than a soft-sell, invitational approach to prospective converts. But this is merely an empirical question, not an adequate answer to the ethical issue raised here. Invitational conversion strategies may actually be more effective, either on the home front or in foreign missions, than the aggressive variety, coupled as the aggressive variety so often is with domineering, imperialist, often racist Western cultural attitudes that alienate prospective converts. Discreet invitational witnessing is, of course, also more effective in a political region where overt proselytism is outlawed. Invitational conversion activities may also appeal more effectively to certain temperaments or to people made wary by hard-sell techniques in commercial advertising. It may even be that the current trend away from aggressive proselytism and toward invitational missionary work in the mainstream churches has resulted more from a perception that invitational conversion activities are of greater effectiveness in the contemporary world than from a repudiation of aggressive proselytism's apparently unethical methods. Nevertheless, aggressive proselytism can be extremely effective: virtually all of Central and South America, for instance, was originally converted in this way, and the most rapid growth in contemporary religious groups is among conservative, evangelical, and pentecostal groups, which typically use moderately to vigorously aggressive techniques. But if there remains any situation in which aggressive convert seeking is equally or more effective than a mild-mannered version, then the moral problem that paternalism raises recurs.

Nor will it do to suggest that proselytizing methods that involve deception, the exploitation of relationships, coercion, other wrong-making features, or specific morally unacceptable practices like bribery or prostitution, are intrinsically immoral, "un-Christian," or inherently wrong. They may indeed not only violate traditional secular moral codes but run counter to traditional Christian codes as well. But unless they are an *absolute* bar to salvation, for which repentance is not possible and forgiveness not forthcoming, the problem remains. This is so whether the apparent immorality of the practices is taken to stain the proselytizer or the proselytizee, or both. They may be wrong, but that wrongness—it can in every case be argued—is excused or overridden by the incalculable good accomplished in the achievement of salvation.

If the paternalist argument for aggressive proselytism cannot be defeated, it may seem to invite mutual aggressive proselytism that could be called "poaching," where the missionaries of one group try to convert the members of another, the missionaries of the second group attempt to convert the members of the first, and so on for all the various religious groups. This would result in a kind of generalized religious piracy, a universal rapaciousness, intolerance, subversion, undercutting and reundercutting of belief, or, in general, complete religious anarchy and chaos. The "Jews for Jesus" movement, specifically intended to convert people whose background is in one faith to another, might be just one among many groups dedicated to the deconversion of people from one group and reconversion to their own. No individual would find himself or herself safe from the well-meaning but earnest aggressions of another, nor could he or she expect any stability in religious life. To be sure, the person might resist the efforts of missionaries who pursued him or her, but where genuinely aggressive proselytism is practiced, the costs of resistance could be fairly high. Nor is this an idle prediction; the history of the world displays numerous examples of the chaotic and painful results of condoning aggressive conversion programs.

We might thus argue from the social benefits of mutual religious tolerance and respect for one another's religious views that only invitational missionary work be countenanced. An individual may be provided with the opportunity to change his or her beliefs, in this view, but should in no way be coerced, manipulated, or have his or her privacy invaded. People must be free to choose their religious affiliations without interference, or to have none at all; their autonomous choices must be respected in religion as well as elsewhere. This, of course, is the picture of religious liberty we have come to expect as the legacy of traditional liberalism, evident in much of contemporary Catholicism and mainline Protestantism. It is precisely the background principle of autonomy familiar in both ordinary normative ethics and in the specialized considerations of professional ethics, to which this study has made repeated appeal.

But this is hardly a satisfactory solution to the problem. It gives primacy to "this-world" considerations over afterlife ones, something which, under the traditional assumptions of the argument pursued here, it is irrational to do with respect to oneself and immoral to do with respect to others. It is a short-term tradeoff, badly chosen against an infinite loss or gain. Furthermore, on a view analogous to that form of utilitarianism that averages hedonic gains across all persons affected, this argument might be used to hold that even if only comparatively few people were to gain salvation as a result of aggressive proselytizing measures, the magnitude of the benefit to them would still outweigh the disbenefits of social discord since the benefit to those few is an infinitely great one. In any case, even without this utilitarian argument, it is evident that an argument from social benefits against mutually aggressive proselytism cannot succeed, even though it is undeniable that the latter world would be dreadful, and that a world of peaceful religious tolerance would be much more pleasant to inhabit.

There is, however, a final set of arguments that may resolve some of the ethical issues posed by a paternalist view of aggressive proselytism. The issue poses a generalized version of Pascal's wager. But Pascal's wager considers tradeoffs between just two beliefs, the traditional theist position that God exists and the atheist view that God does not exist. In the real world, there are many different religious groups, each promoting different religious beliefs, appealing to differing conceptions of religious entities, providing different reasons for believing religious claims, and making different assertions about the afterlife outcomes of belief and unbelief. They also typically claim to be uniquely true and incompatible with each other. Now we may ask whether the sheer multiplicity of claims changes the nature of Pascal's wager. After all, neither the proselytizer nor the proselytizee has any objective way of knowing whether the new faith the convert is about to accept, the old one the convert is about to reject, or some other faith is the true one, or none at all. Although this may seem to lower the likelihood that the faith the proselytizer promotes is true, it does not. There is no way to determine an objective probability that a particular faith is true. The fact that there are, as noted earlier, some 218 different churches and several thousand additional sects and cults in the United States does not alter in any way the probability that, for example, Catholicism or Presbyterianism or the serpent-handling Holiness churches or the flirty-fishing Children of God is the uniquely right group. Not all religious groups claim to be uniquely true nor do all (particularly the Eastern-influenced cults) promise a personal afterlife. But the problem is not altered by the precise number of groups, since the likelihood that any one of them is true is not affected by the number of contenders for this status.

Nevertheless, the sheer multiplicity of religious claims may provide a way to undercut the bizarre conclusion to which the problem of paternalism leads. In those cases that involve converting an individual from one faith to another, since there can be no guarantee that the new faith is more likely to be true than the old one, the proselytizer must take into account the possibility that he or she is converting the proselytizee *away* from eternal bliss, toward eternal hell. Provided only that the proselytizee's commitment to the old faith was not merely nominal but involved genuine belief, the paternalistic proselytizer has no basis for claiming to bring the proselytizee a benefit rather than harm, or for claiming that if this is wrong, the costs will be trivial compared to benefits that might have been gained. Thus, although Pascal's wager does apply to converting others as well as to choosing one's own beliefs and when applied to others introduces moral as well as prudential claims, it does not work in the same way when there are more than one possibly true faiths. It is not only a matter of the costs to an individual being much greater if he or she must foster belief in every deity for which the chance of existing is greater than zero, as Dan Wikler points out,[29] but of not having an objective, non-faith-based way of knowing whether a person's converting from one faith to another will advance self-interests or harm them. Yet if the proselytizer cannot know this (though he or she is unlikely to recognize it), then he or she can have no moral obligation to attempt to convert others.

Although this would seem to be an adequate reply to the bizarre conclusion that aggressive convert seeking, involving clearly immoral methods, is morally preferable to invitational outreach, it could be only a partial success. For while this objection tells against attempts to convert those who already sincerely believe in one faith, it does not tell against attempts to convert atheists or those whose religious affiliation is nominal. Hence, aggressive proselytism will still be morally obligatory in some cases, particularly among those who seem least interested in and most resistant to religion. Such a position would, then, legitimize aggressive proselytism toward nominal believers and nonbelievers—proselytism from all sides, on a continuing, sustained, relentless basis, protecting only those whose religious commitments are already firm.

However, expanding this defense may change the outcome. In mentioning the multiplicity of religious beliefs, this argument has counted only those usually put forward by recognized religious groups. There are other possible religious beliefs—religious in the sense that they presuppose the background religious metaphysics left unchallenged here, though certainly not beliefs advanced by familiar religious groups. For instance, as critics since Diderot have pointed out, we cannot be certain that, even if there is a God, it is one who favors Christians,[30] or for that matter who favors the members of any religious group. One might hold the *religious* belief that there is a God and that there is such a thing as salvation, but that God grants salvation only to those tough-minded persons who do not rely on faith, who pursue courageously atheistic visions of the world, who do not base their conceptions of moral obligation on expectations of divine reward or punishment, who do not join religious groups, and so on. Still without supposing that the background metaphysical assumptions are false, then, one might hold that the usual proselytizer's claim that belief leads to salvation, unbelief to hell, is backwards.

This argument technically undercuts the conclusion that troubles us here, for it undermines the assumption that engendering some belief in preference to none would be more, rather than less, likely to promote salvation. The paternalist argues on expanded Pascalian grounds that if there is any chance that conversion will promote salvation, it is both morally justified and morally obligatory. This new argument points out that since there is no way to assign probabilities to the truth of either the conventional view that belief promotes salvation or the unconventional view that it is nonbelievers who will be rewarded—that is, to whether belief and salvation are positively or negatively associated—the conclusion that aggressive, belief-promoting proselytism is morally justified and obligatory does not follow. On the contrary, one could just as well argue—still without challenging background metaphysical claims—that it is both morally justified and obligatory to attempt to deconvert current believers in order to increase their chances of salvation.

Thus the issue ends in a draw. It is a draw that will hardly persuade believers, who appeal to the ubiquitous nature of the conviction that belief is positively rather than negatively associated with salvation as evidence for its correctness. Nor will it persuade nonbelievers, who find the background metaphysical assumptions implausible to begin with. But perhaps there is something in the nature of the problem that defies resolution and results in this draw, even though the problem was originally posed in a way that reflects traditional religious assumptions and even though a carefully reserved posture as to the truth or falsity of these claims has been maintained.

## The Nature of the Problem

The result reached, an unsatisfactory draw persuasive to neither believers nor nonbelievers, invites reinspection of the problem itself. This is a *moral* problem, a problem about which convert-seeking activities (if any) are morally permissible or obligatory and which are not. What is crucial to observe is how traditional afterlife claims that generate the problem function in the argument.

Two factors are central: first, traditional afterlife claims are claims for which there is no doctrine-independent, non-faith-based, objective evidence for their truth, either that there are such states or that belief and conversion are relevant in attaining them. Second, they are also *self-interest-gratifying* claims: they promise an outcome the person strongly seeks and, hence, has reason to want the claims to be true. Yet, although these claims are both unprovable and self-interest-gratifying, all other moral considerations seem to be trumped by them. This is because they are "off-scale"; they introduce into the argument bipolar outcome predictions with such extreme positive and negative values that they override all other considerations. This phenomenon in the risk-taking choices of Jehovah's Witnesses was considered in chapter 2; here, we see how off-scale values trump other considerations not only in the context of an individual's prudential choices, but in any independent assessment of the practices of religious groups altogether. Although we did not find a basis for *moral* objection to an individual Jehovah's Witness's choice to refuse blood transfusions—even though such a choice is based on unprovable, self-interest-gratifying, off-scale beliefs about afterlife outcomes—the picture changes when we look at the way religious groups employ such beliefs to license treatment of persons that would otherwise involve seriously unethical practices. What is problematic is the relation between the incentive to believe in these claims and their status as excuses for what would otherwise be moral offenses against the believer. Unlike ordinary paternalist excuses, there is no independent way to determine whether the paternalist's perception of the paternalizee's interests has any basis in actuality and so there is no way to rule out sheer self-interested solicitation of the paternalizee by the alleged paternalizer. The missionary puts forward a claim that the target person will want to believe, but also uses this very claim as an excuse for his or her treatment of that person. Similarly, the aggressive religious group that promotes its missionaries' proselytizing strategies uses the same claim to justify these practices. These claims are then held to supersede all other moral considerations, even though they are both self-interest-gratifying and unprovable.

Not only with respect to convert seeking but in many other areas of religious practice, it is in the last analysis an ethical issue whether such claims should be allowed to function in this way. This is not to say that it is an ethical issue whether such claims are true or false, but rather that, given that their truth or falsity cannot be established, it is by default no longer an epistemological question but an ethical question what role these claims should be granted. It is true that these claims are faith-based. But they are also self-interest-gratifying, both in the belief of the individual who comes to accept them as a result of conversion and in the faith of the religious group that promotes the conversion, and hence carry with them a strong inducement to believe them to be true. Yet if primacy is given to these claims, then the way is open for them to function as a kind of religious blackmail, serving both to excuse the proselytizer's behavior and to shield religious authorities and the religious institutions that encourage what the aggressive pros-elytizer does from any moral scrutiny. On the other hand, under the terms of discussion here, it cannot be assumed that these claims are false.

After all, the moral principles that are allegedly overridden would otherwise be binding. This is because the convert-seeking practices in question are upper-order practices, not 0-level ones, and so open to moral critique. Furthermore, they are clearly addressed to the self-interests of the target person, at least in the pure form of convert seeking treated here and thus fall under the fiduciary principle articu-lated in chapter 2. The target person is approached with an appeal to his or her self-interests: this is what first makes conversion strategies possible, since after all the person has no antecedent, independent reason to believe the missionary's claim. Thus convert-seeking prac-tices in general remain candidates for moral critique in the light of the two methodological principles developed so far, and despite the high stakes and off-scale claims, can be examined with the principles of ordinary and professional ethics.

Doing so yields a third methodological principle for assessing the moral issues in institutional religion: *unprovable, off-scale, self-interest-gratifying theological claims are to be considered suspect when their central function is to excuse violations of moral norms*—that is, when they are employed to defeat moral principles that would otherwise be binding on the practices of organized religion and its representatives. In the ethical critique of organized religion, attention must be given to the *function* of particular claims, even when their content cannot by hypothesis be challenged, and this attention must be particularly alert when the primary apparent function of these claims is to defeat moral norms.

As a methodological instrument, however, the principle is inconclusive: it does not decide the issue in any particular case, nor yield a clear conclusion about the status of unprovable, off-scale, self-interest-gratifying theological claims. It merely asserts that the ways these theological claims are used are suspect. It cannot distinguish legitimate uses from illegitimate uses of these claims, beyond warning that they are particularly suspicious in certain circumstances, and hence less so in others. To say that such claims are suspect in a given context is not to prove them guilty; to say they are not under suspicion in another context is not to establish their innocence. In the end, however, we cannot show that religious claims are themselves unethical or are used unethically in excusing violations of morality without deciding for or against the truth of the background metaphysical claims and 0-level imperatives that generate the problem.

Nevertheless, when we observe such claims as they are actually used, especially third-order excuses offered for the moral problems generated by various practices, we note the varying light in which use or nonuse of such claims casts these practices. Consider, for instance, the sets of practices concerning confidentiality in confession examined in chapter 1. Catholicism's practice of absolute confidentiality poses endemic moral dilemmas concerning whether the priest ought or ought not prevent serious harm that the confessant intends when he could prevent it, if doing so would reveal information learned in the confessional. The excuse this tradition offers for its policy that the priest ought not intervene to prevent the harm is that the priest does not actually "know" what the confessant intends in any usual sense, but only "as God." This is an excuse that, while unprovable, does not employ self-interest-gratifying claims and does not make the person to whom the excuse is offered want to believe it. If this is contrasted to

Mormonism's excuse, offered in the Bishop's Handbook, for violations of confidentiality involved in taking a person's confession to a
disciplinary council or church court, it is evident that the Mormon
excuse is not only unprovable, but also appeals to self-interest: the
person to whom the excuse is offered—namely, the person whose
confession is not kept confidential—is told that "the first purpose of
Church discipline is to save the soul of the transgressor."[31] Submitting
to the violation of confidentiality that a court trial involves, this assertion implies, will increase one's prospects in the afterlife. But because
this excuse for harm imposed on an individual is unprovable, off-scale,
and self-interest-gratifying, it is ethically suspect. "Without formal
Church discipline," continues the Bishop's Handbook, "some transgressors may never experience the change of behavior and the change
of heart necessary to qualify them for redemption."[32] Of course, in
contrast, the Bishop's Handbook also acknowledges two additional
purposes for the practice of church discipline: "to protect the innocent," that is, other church members, and "to safeguard the purity,
integrity, and good name of the Church."[33] These additional purposes
do not promise the gratification of self-interests to the persons to
whom they are offered (at least not directly) and do not trade on
unprovable, off-scale afterlife claims. On the contrary, they provide a
comparatively straightforward account of the church's own interests in
maintaining its system of courts. Here, then, the apparent moral
abuses involved in one practice are defended by strikingly different
excuses, one profoundly ethically suspect, the other two much less so.
Unprovable, off-scale, self-interest-gratifying excuses also played a role
in the Collinsville Church of Christ's treatment of Marian Guinn. A
major point in the elders' defense of their actions was to show that they
had acted "out of love" and concern for Guinn's soul, a point that
Guinn herself acknowledged. Here, the elders' excuse involved indirect
appeal to off-scale outcome claims; the direct appeal was simply to
obedience to the biblical command, but as participants in this tradition
would believe, obedience to biblical command is a precondition for
salvation.

That an excuse includes an incentive for acceptance by the person to
whom it is owed does not, of course, establish that it is an inadequate

excuse. If we look at the various practices involved in religious convert seeking from the most weakly aggressive to the strongest, however, we see a curious feature. The excuse offered for virtually all of the various moral problems generated by differing convert-seeking practices is the same: it will help the target person to gain salvation. This excuse is utterly ubiquitous in conversion contexts, though it is phrased in vastly different theological ways. Yet other excuses for the moral violations involved in convert seeking could have been employed instead. For instance, it could be claimed that these moral violations are necessary to gratify the missionary, or that they are essential in aggrandizing the church, or that they permit the subjugation of lands and peoples—but these are hardly excuses that would be accepted by the targets of the practice, the persons to whom excuses are due. Yet if other explanations for the moral violations would not be accepted, there is surely something suspect about an explanation that comes with a built-in inducement to be believed—especially when it is the only acceptable explanation offered. Thus, it is not a casual observation that excuses for moral violations in convert seeking virtually always appeal to unprovable, off-scale, self-interest-gratifying claims about the afterlife benefits these practices provide; rather, it is an observation that invites more careful moral scrutiny of explanations religious groups offer for their practices in approaching potential converts.

It is this that arouses our suspicion of convert seeking as a whole and makes the problem of paternalism particularly acute. Given the methodological requirement of refraining from assuming truthvalues for the metaphysical assumptions on which conversion activities rest or for the fundamental imperative that commands them, we cannot decide whether the theological bases of these excuses are adequate or not. However, the *use* of such claims *as excuses* is itself a developed practice and, hence, invites ethical critique. It is in this sense that these claims are suspect. We cannot at any deeper level prove that they are fraudulent, but it is also clear that there is no adequate moral justification for the practice that has developed of using them in this way.

# CHAPTER 4

# Moral Problems in the Mainline Denominations

This study has undertaken to examine three moral issues in organized religion, issues that our pincer strategy of beginning with the view from professional ethics and ordinary morality has revealed: the issue of confidentiality, especially as it arises in connection with the practice of confession; the issue of informed consent in high-risk religious practices; and the issue of paternalism, raised in the context of convert seeking. We have looked at the practices of a wide variety of groups, including the Roman Catholic Church, Christian Science, the Jehovah's Witnesses, the Mormon church, the Churches of Christ, the Faith Assembly, the serpent-handling Holiness churches, the Moonies, the Children of God, and others. However, except for the Catholic church, all of these groups fall outside of what is traditionally regarded as mainstream religion. Of course, there is considerable bias in the way religious groups are viewed, in whether they are labeled mainstream or fringe, and in how the distinction between mainstream and fringe is drawn, but that does not diminish the issue here. The practices of mainline Protestantism, for instance, in such groups as the Episcopalians, United Methodists, Presbyterians, American Baptists, and Congregationalists, have not yet attracted our attention, even though we are examining ethical issues in the whole range of Judeo-Christian religion. There is a reason for this; to see what it is, we can begin with a particular but representative case from a clearly mainstream group.

## One Hand in the Plate . . .

One Sunday morning several years ago, a member of the Presbyterian church whom I will call Stephen Sanders was caught stealing from the worship-service offering. As the collection plate was being passed to him along the pew, Sanders pretended to deposit a donation, but instead retrieved a number of bills, concealed them under his hand, and withdrew them from the plate. A parishioner seated next to him in the pew noticed this and reported the matter to the minister.

The minister informed this person that in order to bring charges, it would be necessary, according to the *Book of Order,* which governs the Presbyterian Church (U.S.A.),[1] to make a written accusation. The person who observed Sanders supplied this. At the same time, the minister also recollected that about six months earlier, another member of the church had mentioned seeing Sanders in a back room of the church with a young child in what the person had perceived as a "questionable position." Putting these two reports together, the minister appointed three elders of the church to talk with Sanders. Sanders denied any wrongdoing with the child, and although he admitted taking money from the collection plate, insisted that he had put it back. The elders asked Sanders whether he had been receiving any psychological counseling; when he said he had, the elders told Sanders that they would "work with the counselor" and that he should refrain from attending church until they, in consultation with the counselor, "thought it was okay." Several months later, the elders invited Sanders to return, though they required that he remain in a restricted area of the church (excluding the back rooms), until they "felt good about his aims." At this writing, Sanders remains a member of the church, all restrictions have been lifted, and there have no further complaints.

This is a true story, involving the normal practices of an ordinary Presbyterian church. It is a less exciting story than others considered here from marginal and fringe groups, and certainly the practices involved seem much less problematic. Nevertheless, the earlier examination of ethical issues in religious groups outside the mainstream will have made us more sensitive to the issues this mild case raises. Several things about the practices used by the Presbyterian church in responding to Sanders' activities are now evident. First, the minister acted on reports about a member of the church by other members of the church, and although he required a written accusation in the matter of the alleged collection-plate theft, he also responded to an older, unconfirmed report about the member's behavior in the back room. If this reminds us of anything, it may be of the Collinsville Church of Christ's readiness to listen to rumors and reports by one member about another in the case of Marian Guinn. Thus, the Presbyterian practice raises some of the same issues about sources of information, about their reliability, and about the degree to which a religious institution should permit or encourage its members to monitor each other's behavior.

Second, the minister of the Presbyterian church appointed a group of three elders to talk with Sanders; this is much as when the Collinsville Church of Christ sent its three elders to confront Marian Guinn—though the Presbyterian elders did not accost Sanders in a laundromat or at night on the lawn of his home. In addition, the Presbyterian elders asked Sanders about his behavior and about other details of his private life, specifically including whether he was seeing a counselor; this recalls many other practices involving probing by religious officials into individuals' personal lives, ranging from Mormonism's annual "temple recommend" interview to the Campus Crusade's strategies for eliciting personal information by means of a scavenger hunt. These practices raise issues about the extent to which religious officials are morally justified in eliciting personal information that is not volunteered and whether the purpose of the attempt, the status of the individual as a member or nonmember of the church, or any other matters are relevant to these ethical issues.

Equally significant are the issues the practices of the Presbyterian church in the case of Stephen Sanders do *not* raise. That charges had been brought against him was immediately disclosed to Sanders, and there was no issue about a secret investigation. No promises of confidentiality were made to Sanders, nor was he interviewed in any situation (like a confessional booth) that might seem to have promised confidentiality. The church did not lie to Sanders about its motives in questioning and disciplining him, nor did it excuse its practices in this way. It did not coerce or trick him. Although it did ask Sanders to account for his behavior, it did not attempt to extract a confession by using unprovable, off-scale claims about the afterlife (even though Presbyterian faith includes such beliefs), and in particular it did not use claims about possible damnation as threats. Finally, it did not avoid the issue about preventable harm to other persons, and while it did not act quickly—the report about Sanders in the back room with the child had been received six months earlier—it did act to prevent further possible harm by prohibiting Sanders from attending church and later restricting him while there. It also acted to prevent further harm by informing Sanders that it would consult with his counselor about the charges, knowing that the counselor (unlike the religious official) would be bound by state law to report any evidence of child abuse.

In looking, then, at a routine case of mainstream church practice, we see that while ethical issues clearly do arise—the minister acknowledged that he and the elders were torn between responsibility to Sanders and to others, including children Sanders might molest and the parishioners as a group whose contributions he might steal—they are not like the stark issues raised in fringe groups. Nor do they involve the same glaring ethical abuse. If the case of Sanders and the Presbyterian church does at all represent the moral problems that arise in mainstream groups—and it is fair to assume that it does—then an explanation is needed of why there seems to be such a striking difference between it and problems at the fringe.

## *The Apparent Absence of Problematic Practices in Mainstream Denominations*

That fringe groups have played a prominent role in this inquiry while mainstream groups have been virtually absent, and that the moral issues observed in the mainstream seem much milder than those at the fringe, suggests that the practices of mainstream groups simply do not give rise to substantial moral problems. We have identified moral issues associated with religious practices using professional ethics and ordinary morality—employing the pincer strategy—and found numerous violations of moral norms in groups outside the mainstream: deception, coercion, aggressive persuasion, breaking promises, manipulating choices, and so on. In many cases, these ethical violations were conspicuous. None of these violations, however, seems to characterize the practices of the mainstream; on the contrary, the mainstream is often taken to be the very model of morality, free from precisely these abuses. It is often claimed that religion, as embodied in mainstream institutions, is the source and standard of morality by which other human practices and institutions are to be judged. The reason moral problems are not seen in the mainstream, it seems, is that there are none.

This does not mean that there are no real moral problems in the mainstream groups. Acutely painful dilemmas arise when, for instance, a church secretary embezzles, a minister misappropriates church funds or inflates membership rolls, or a pastor becomes sexually involved with a member of the congregation. These embarrassments occur in every denomination; the mainstream is no exception. There are currently several dozen pederasty cases pending against Catholic dioceses in the United States. These aberrations, however, are not of philosophical interest to us, except in how a denomination responds to them, because they all involve delinquent or deviant practitioners who do things that are not recognized as practices of the group. What is of interest are the ways in which the central, accepted, legitimate practices of a group, faithfully and conscientiously performed, nevertheless give rise to moral problems. Our concern is with systemic moral dilemmas, not adventitious ones, and in the ways that entrenched, established, ordinary practices generate ethical issues.

It seems, then, that major, systemic moral issues do not arise in the mainline groups, as they do in the intermediate, marginal, and fringe groups, because mainstream groups simply do not engage in the same problematic practices that groups outside the mainstream do. Indeed, the specific institutional practices that give rise to the three major moral issues under discussion here either do not exist in the mainstream groups or exist only in limited ways.

*Confession.* First, with certain exceptions, the mainstream groups, except Catholicism, do not practice confession and so are not torn by dilemmas over confidentiality. Confession is not a sacrament in the mainline Protestant groups; except for the corporate or general confession that is part of worship services in some of these churches, there is no ritual confession. The sacraments and ritual practices do not include required private, auricular confession in which the church member is expected to confess things to an official of the church that he or she finds embarrassing or shameful. Nor is there a formal setting, like a confessional booth, that promises anonymity and privacy. Of course, in recent years there has been renewed interest in individual confession among certain Protestant groups and some have discussed the possibility of either introducing or reintroducing it. The rite of individual confession is available on an optional basis for Episcopalians and Lutherans. Nevertheless, it would be incorrect to say that the practice is representative of the mainstream. The Greek Orthodox and Roman Catholic churches continue to practice confession, but even in Roman Catholicism, the use of confession has declined radically in recent years—despite Pope John Paul II's repeated reaffirmation of its importance, underscored in the 1984 papal document "Reconciliation and Penance." Except for Catholicism, then, the mainstream does not practice confession as an obligation of faith and certainly does not make it central among its practices.

Furthermore, mainstream churches do not routinely examine members about their personal lives. They do not make a probing personal interview prerequisite to entering the sanctuary, as in the Mormon church. Nor do they pursue or respond to rumor, as at the Collinsville Church of Christ, as a matter of standard practice for enforcing certain standards of moral behavior, in a way that involves having church officials confront and request—or extract—confessions from the person whom the rumor concerns. Mainstream groups are typically non-interventionist: while they do encourage members to lead morally responsible lives and provide help when requested, they do not pry.

Many mainstream groups, including the Catholic, Episcopal, United Methodist, Presbyterian (U.S.A.), United Church of Christ, and American Baptist churches,[2] have internal church court systems that may resemble the Mormon system examined in chapter 1; it might seem that these court systems would raise many of the same issues about confidentiality. However, there are substantial differences between the church courts in the Protestant mainstream and the Mormon disciplinary system. For instance, while the Episcopal church does have an ecclesiastical court system, it is used principally for trying bishops and rectors who have violated the requirements of their offices; neither the national nor Missouri diocesan standards appear to provide for trials of lay members.[3] The United Methodist Church guarantees its clerics and lay members "the right to an ecclesiastical trial,"[4] but differentiates between the offenses for which clerical and lay members may be tried. American Baptist churches also use disciplinary measures against members, although because local churches are basically independent, there is no authoritative declaration of how ecclesiastical trials are to be conducted,[5] and for some offenses the penalty is immediate excommunication without trial.[6]

Among the Protestant mainstream, it is the internal court system of the Presbyterian Church (U.S.A.) that is perhaps the best developed; it is here that the case of Stephen Sanders might have been referred if the actual, satisfactory outcome of the case could not be achieved. The Presbyterian system involves an elaborate, sophisticated structure for trying remedial and disciplinary cases of both clerical and lay members. It stipulates procedures for initiating cases, filing charges, assessing evidence, notifying the alleged offender, informing the accused "of the right to remain silent and to be represented by counsel,"[7] stating the charges, requiring witnesses to appear, and so on. This system is described in detail in the church's *Book of Order,* which is available to members of the church and to any nonmembers expressing interest in the church.

Lay members, like Stephen Sanders, are tried by the Session, the governing body of the local church, which consists of the pastor, associate pastors, and elders, while ministers are disciplined by the presbytery of the relevant geographical region. The preliminary procedures in a disciplinary case can be initiated by another member or by the person involved; the charge must be made in writing, as the minister required of the person who observed Sanders. Procedures can also be initiated by a governing body of the church. A special disciplinary committee appointed by the governing body first investigates the case;

then the prosecution and defense each present evidence and may object to evidence or cross-examine witnesses. If a verdict of guilty is returned, the moderator of the trial is to announce the verdict openly for each charge together with the degree of censure imposed.[8] Sanders could have been rebuked, temporarily excluded from membership, or permanently removed from membership by such a court. However, he was not tried at all, despite the submission of a written accusation from another church member, and instead was encouraged to continue treatment with a secular professional psychotherapist.

Sanders could have been tried; the proceeding would no doubt have revealed many milder analogues of the stark moral problems arising in the nonmainstream churches. Nevertheless, the mere existence of the court structure and its processes do not mean that the underlying practices and the moral issues they generate are the same. This is because, at root, the Presbyterian court system, like other court systems in mainstream churches, does not function to respond to confessional material. Of course, it could do so; it is possible in this system for a person to bring charges against himself, though he or she would be required to do so in written form.[9] Nor does it rule out the possibility that personal information, as in any secular court trial, would be brought to light against the wishes of the defendant and disclosed. Because confession itself is not part of Presbyterian practice, however, the Presbyterian court system does not function in any primary way to adjudicate issues of belief or behavior so raised—that is, because the member was expected or required to confess to church officials.

*High-Risk Choices.* With respect to the second of the three moral issues under discussion here, the mainstream denominations do not institutionalize or encourage high-risk choices and so do not engender the moral issues that informed consent raises in the shaping of these choices. Mainstream groups do not drink strychnine or handle serpents; they do not practice ritual self-crucifixion; they do not urge or require members to forego medical treatment or to rely on nonmedical healing. If they do recognize the curative power of faith, they do not take it to be incompatible with ordinary medicine. Consequently, since there are no practices involving high-risk choice, there is no superstructure of higher-order doctrinal teachings that encourage these choices, no doctrines that regulate how they are made, and no set of doctrinal excuses for the risks that fail. Nor are there any residual structures that might be seen as survivals from an earlier historical period in which the supervision and surveillance of members' individual choice making played a larger role in mainstream church practice. Perhaps the only vestigial risk-taking practice that has survived into contemporary times in mainstream Christianity is fasting—a holdover from earlier historical periods in which physical austerity and risk occupied a central role in medieval Christian religious observance. Obligatory fasting—not always a great risk, since the elderly and infirm were almost always exempt—has been virtually abandoned as a required, regular practice altogether. Only tokens remain: for Roman Catholics, partial fasting and abstaining entirely from meat are now required only on Ash Wednesday and Good Friday, and further abstinence from meat is required on the Fridays of Lent. Most mainstream Protestant denominations do not fast at all or only occasionally as a symbolic gesture in connection with such concerns as fundraising for the needy. Sustained fasting and associated forms of severe dietary restrictions are found in certain contemporary fringe groups, and Eastern Orthodox groups, especially outside the U.S., still encourage long periods of fasting, but in the American mainstream, where it occurs at all, fasting is so mild as not to pose physical risk. Thus, the moral issues generated by institutional influence on high-risk choice, while alive among intermediate and fringe groups that engage in practices such as faith healing and serpent handling, are now essentially extinct in the mainstream.

*Convert Seeking*. Not only do mainstream practices not raise issues about confidentiality or risk taking, but there are no dilemmas here about paternalism in aggressive convert seeking. In general, the mainstream groups no longer engage in direct conversion activities. While almost all of the mainstream groups do support invitational evangelism programs, both domestically and abroad, and welcome new expressions of faith, in general they no longer make a direct attempt to control or alter the religious beliefs of others. Those mainstream Protestant churches that maintained active, large-scale foreign and domestic proselytizing programs during the nineteenth century, as discussed in chapter 3, have for the most part discontinued or deflected these practices into other activities. Similarly, the Catholic church, in a change of policy articulated by Vatican II, has repudiated aggressive conversion tactics. Most mainstream denominations diverted earlier mission activities and resources into the founding of institutions, such as Methodist, Presbyterian, and Baptist hospitals, or Episcopal and Friends schools; these are now familiar institutions in contemporary life. Typically, however, they have very little or no proselytizing intent. Of course, many mainstream denominations still maintain medical, agricultural, and other aid missions, both domestically and in foreign countries, but unlike those of the evangelical groups, they are no longer conducted primarily as proselytizing enterprises. They do not isolate individuals or groups as targets for conversion. They do not make the provision of aid contingent on conversion or religious affiliation, conditions that are often coercive or manipulative, and they do not restrict aid only to those who are already members of the church. They are often conducted cooperatively among several denominations, rather than competitively to gain souls. Mainstream religious work in foreign countries now comparatively rarely involves sending American missionaries abroad, except when local churches in those countries request it, and the imperialist and intrusive aspects of earlier convert-seeking missions are studiously avoided. In fact, only a fifth of the U.S. missionaries abroad are from mainstream denominations; the majority are from the very rapidly growing evangelical and fundamentalist groups.

In general, then, mainstream denominations no longer practice active convert seeking and certainly not aggressive proselytism. Of course, many mainstream groups continue to have structures associated with active missionary work: for instance, the National Council of Churches maintained a working group on evangelism for a number of years, recently replacing it with a Commission on Worship and Evangelism, and many mainstream denominations either have continued or reestablished evangelism departments. In very recent years, there has been a resurgence of interest in evangelism among mainstream groups.

Vestiges of convert-seeking activity, though faint, may also be found in the outreach and mission programs of many mainstream denominations, for example, in the practice of inviting members to bring friends and neighbors to church. Outreach programs often represent major commitments in mainstream groups and serve both to extend welcome and to help those seeking religious affiliation. But such outreach programs are not aggressively "soul winning"; they are often milder than invitational convert seeking, a practice that is still conversion-oriented but whose methods consist in setting an example to be emulated, not in forcibly altering belief. Although outreach is typically welcoming in character and clearly welcomes conversion, it makes no attempt to impose change on others.

The abandonment of aggressive proselytism in the mainstream is, no doubt, associated with several factors. One of these may be the "universalizing" assumption characteristic of much of contemporary liberal Catholicism and Protestantism—that a truly loving God would not consign anyone to damnation. (Of course, this assumption tends to undermine the rationale and motivation of conversion efforts altogether.) Another factor may be the gradual rejection of the bipolar outcome schema associated with traditional views of the afterlife, what Martin Marty has called "the disappearance of hell."[10] It may even be, in part, a matter of good manners: the mainstream groups have generally been unwilling to "steal sheep," either from each other or from other groups. Not all mainstream groups uniformly exhibit these attitudes, and there has been a return to more conservative beliefs in recent years. Nevertheless, the changes have been profound in much of the mainstream. With them, it would seem, the practice and, therefore, the moral problems associated with aggressive convert seeking have largely disappeared.

It appears, then, that mainstream denominations simply either no longer engage in any of the three practices identified as the source of particularly compelling moral problems or do so only in extremely limited ways. Except for Catholicism, they do not generally practice confession; none practices physical risk taking; and if any convert seeking is found, it is only in the very weakest forms. If the mainstream does not generally engage in these practices, it will not confront the dilemmas these practices generate.

Of course, this may not be a permanent situation. Religious groups—including mainstream churches—undergo continual external and internal change. Denominational lines are constantly redrawn as groups undergo merger and fission. Groups migrate into and away from the mainstream, and the distinction between mainstream status and intermediate, marginal, or fringe status is still further blurred. As groups change in size and membership, they often change in character too. These factors are of considerable importance in influencing the practices of differing groups and in affecting the centrality or marginality of those practices. The virtual abandonment of confession, risk taking, and convert seeking in mainstream denominations could, therefore, be temporary, and a return to them possible in the future.

These changes aside, however, there is a more substantial issue. Even where there are vestiges in mainstream denominations of practices and residual structures associated with the three principal moral problems of concern here, it cannot be assumed that the mainstream's moral problems are simply weaker versions of the problems at the fringes. To suggest that if manipulation, coercion, deception, and so on, are found at the fringes, less pronounced, less conspicuous, and weaker analogues of these problems will be found in the mainstream supposes that any moral problems in the mainstream are of the same type but merely milder. This may not be true. There is a much more serious issue about moral problems in the mainstream, one that once more addresses our ongoing methodological concerns.

### Recognizing Fundamental Imperatives

The moral issues of the mainstream seem pale in comparison to the florid ones at the fringe. This does not mean, however, that the mainstream groups have confronted the basic moral dilemmas certain religious practices raise and have already found a solution; rather, mainstream groups simply do not engage in the practices that engender these issues and so need not confront them at all. The groups at the fringes do develop such practices; hence, they must confront the problems that these practices raise.

There may, of course, be good moral reason for avoiding specific practices and the moral issues they raise, reasons that, we might suppose, have been considered within these mainstream traditions over a long historical period. After all, the mainstream groups have a common history in the development of Christianity; Protestant groups can all be viewed as, among other things, protest movements against perceived excesses by the parent Catholic church or intermediate institutions. For instance, Protestantism's repudiation of auricular confession is clearly rooted in Martin Luther's view that confession—that is, mandatory private, auricular confession—was a tyranny practiced by a corrupt and domineering Catholic clergy over the faithful. Confession, as institutionalized in the Catholic church, did incalculable harm, in this Protestant view, harm that could not be justified by reference to some other principle. Furthermore, there were alternative ways to put into practice the fundamental mandate to confess—specifically, by stressing personal confession directly to God, without the interference of the clergy. Thus, confession became "privatized"—where it continued to exist at all—and the content of the confession, its specificity, and making confession at all became matters of individual conscience. Confession could no longer be observed or policed by officials of the church. By rejecting a required, detailed confession made individually to another person, the Protestant modification of confession mooted the issue of confidentiality. However, it also undermined the traditional practice of confession so completely that, for the most part, only formulaic, general confession in certain worship services has survived in contemporary mainstream Protestantism, where it usually takes the form of an abstract, general acknowledgment of sinfulness as the human condition, recited in a group setting without any real recounting or examination of one's own particular sinful thoughts and acts. In the move away from auricular confession to the privatized Protestant form and further on to the merely abstract acknowledgment of sin without explicit content, these denominations appear to have ceased to respond to the fundamental, 0-level religious imperative that requires the confession of sins.

The various Protestant movements also responded similarly, and for similar reasons, to practices involving risk. The medieval emphasis on bodily chastisements—many of which, like self-flagellation and severe fasting, had involved considerable risk of physical injury, deteriorated health, and even death—was lessened; they deemphasized physical austerities. None of the mainstream denominations now institutional-izes practices involving physical risk (with the very faint exception of occasional, largely symbolic fasting), even though they may respect personal choices involving real physical risk where they are undertaken for religious reasons. The mainstream groups still admire heroic, self-sacrificing action—as in rescues, martyrdom, actions of principle, and other expressions of religious faith—but they do not *institutionalize* these practices. On the contrary, Protestantism typically treats the pen-umbral fundamental imperative concerning risk—Christianity as a re-ligion of risk, in which one risks one's all for God—as a matter of mental, emotional, and cognitive risk: it is the leap of faith, not the physical risk, that is understood to be encouraged. Traditionalists would argue that this is not really to risk one's *all:* true risk taking involves being willing to take physical risks as well as mental ones. To this extent, the traditionalists would argue, the mainstream has ceased to give real recognition to the underlying imperative.

None of the mainstream Protestant groups, nor, for that matter, contemporary liberal Catholicism, has retained early and medieval Ca-tholicism's pronounced emphasis on conversion, though many did have such programs as recently as the nineteenth and first part of the twentieth century. In looking at the apparent moral problems that active, aggressive convert seeking poses, as we did in chapter 3, we find some of the reasons why conversion practices were abandoned: they involved manipulation, exploitation, deception, coercion, the destruc-tion of social units and cultures, and cultural imperialism. Of course, many other factors were also at work. But mainstream groups did come to see the ethical problems that aggressive convert seeking raised and this played a major role in their abandonment of aggressive conver-sion practices in favor of purely invitational evangelism. However, in abandoning the more aggressive practices, it appears that mainstream groups also abandoned any attempt to observe the mandate earlier recognized as requiring active efforts to convert: "Go therefore and make disciples of all nations."

As mainstream denominations have repudiated the developed practices of confession, risk taking, and aggressive convert seeking to avoid what they perceived to be moral excesses, they have ceased to respond to the allegedly fundamental imperatives that mandate these practices. The nature of the difference between mainstream groups and those further toward the fringe and the reason this difference raises moral questions become clearer. Mainstream churches simply do not observe some of the imperatives that are treated as fundamental by various evangelical, pentecostal, and fundamentalist groups that are also part of the Judeo-Christian tradition; this is why mainstream groups can avoid the more difficult moral dilemmas. It may be that the mainstream does not violate ordinary or professional moral norms and does not exhibit systemic moral dilemmas—or experiences only pale analogues of the more robust problems of the fringe groups. However, this cannot be immediately attributed to higher ethical standards but, perhaps, to the fact that mainstream religions avoid those practices that give rise to these problems.

## Moral Handprints

If the mainstream groups generally neither accept nor observe certain fundamental imperatives, it remains an open *moral* question whether they are thus culpable of still greater failings than those fringe groups that do attempt to observe them. The fringe groups attempt, however awkwardly, to observe fundamental imperatives but are caught in moral dilemmas that result from their manner of putting these difficult imperatives into practice. Mainstream groups preserve apparent moral acceptability by avoiding these practices but at the cost of failing to honor certain imperatives at all. This claim is roughly captured in the sentiment voiced by fringe groups that while mainstream denominations do not present many problems, they do not offer much "real religion" either. Only with the more problematic practices, this view holds, can people experience complete involvement in religion—for instance, like serpent handler Robert Grooms's experience in participating in serpent handling for the first time: "It was like a bucket of water pouring over me. I was tingling all over. I was so anointed with the power that I was just shouting. I was in *such* a fix!"[11] An expression of religious involvement as thoroughgoing as Robert Grooms's could hardly be found anywhere among the mainstream denominations.

These claims suggest a conclusion that is the opposite of the one intuitively assumed above. The analysis seemed to uncover comparatively few serious moral issues in the mainstream denominations because there were few serious moral issues to be found. In this view, the mainstream groups are the ones without moral failings, groups that should set the moral standard for the others. Certainly, common public attitudes (except among the fringe groups) reflect the assumption that the practices of mainstream denominations are morally respectable; those of the fringe groups are problematic. It is this assumption that journalists and writers trade on in "exposing" the "bizarre" practices of "cults" like the Moonies and it explains why it is so easy to turn public opinion against groups with practices like the Faith Assembly or the Children of God. However, given the problem of relativism confronted earlier, there is no firm antecedent basis for such assumptions and attitudes. Unless we have an independent, unbiased way of identifying which fundamental, 0-level imperatives, if any, a religious tradition should be observing, we cannot say whether a given group is failing to observe an imperative it should be or is observing a fictitious one it should not. This we cannot do without violating the commitment to neutrality.

Nevertheless, we can comment on the ethical character of both mainstream and fringe religious groups. Although neither 0-level imperatives nor background metaphysical beliefs can be evaluated directly, the choice to recognize or not to recognize a given directive as 0-level is not itself an 0-level matter. Whether a group recognizes a given imperative *as 0-level* is itself a *developed* practice and thus is open to ethical critique. It is, of course, intimately tied to the fundamental imperative. If we were to assign it a status in our schema, we might call it a ".5-order" doctrine to suggest that it is in principle distinct from the basic 0-level imperative, yet logically antecedent to the first-order doctrinal teachings that govern how to put that imperative, once recognized, into practice.

To speak of a religious group's *choices* in what 0-level imperatives it recognizes may seem to overlook the long historical and political processes that result in a group's honoring some imperatives but not others. With the exception of rare edicts and the sometimes comparatively rapid effects of the decisions of commissions and committees, a group's practices do not change overnight. Nevertheless, although religious traditions sometimes seem immutable, they are not. A tradition's acceptance of basic imperatives can undergo change; sometimes this change is gradual—as when mainstream denominations ceased to observe an imperative on convert seeking—and sometimes it is abrupt—as with the lifting of requirements of clergy celibacy and the discontinuation or privatization of confession at the time of the Reformation. Where the imperatives in question have been or become central and the change is abrupt, the disjunction is usually regarded as schismatic and the portion of the tradition that undergoes change is identified as a new church. Most change with respect to fundamental imperatives, however, evolves gradually, not abruptly.

Since a group's acceptance of a given imperative as 0-level can vary over time and since various groups are remarkably diverse in what they do accept, acceptance or nonacceptance of an imperative or constellation of imperatives as 0-level can itself be evaluated morally—this is to critique a sort of fundamental "moral handprint" of the group. Although it is difficult to differentiate this from critique of the 0-level imperatives themselves, they are, in principle, distinct. With this, we can state a fourth principle for the moral evaluation of religious practice generally: *the moral nature of a religious group is characterized not only by the practices it develops for observing fundamental imperatives but by those imperatives it recognizes and those it does not.* No group can possibly recognize all the potential imperatives that a scriptural text such as the Bible offers; it *must* be selective, but the pattern of its selectivity is an index of its moral character. Some groups recognize imperatives mandating convert seeking but not confession; some recognize imperatives mandating confession but not convert seeking, or confession and convert seeking but not risk taking. Some recognize neither confession nor convert seeking but do recognize imperatives that mandate the taking of risks. Given various potential 0-level imperatives, including those underlying practices not discussed here—preaching, baptism, religious education, ordination, regulation of sexual behavior and marriage, soliciting contributions, and so on—the range of possible permutations and combinations is clearly enormous. It is from these that we can draw conclusions about the extent to which a group's commitments violate moral norms.

There are, after all, some scriptural imperatives no group recognizes. Consider Matthew 18:8–9: "If your hand or your foot causes you to stumble, cut it off and throw it away; it is better for you to enter life maimed or lame than to have two hands or two feet and to be thrown into the eternal fire. And if your eye causes you to stumble, tear it out and throw it away; it is better for you to enter life with one eye than to have two eyes and to be thrown into the hell of fire." From time to time, people in what we assume to be psychotic states behave in this way, but no group in the Judeo-Christian tradition recognizes the imperatives in this text *as practices of the group.* A slightly macabre imagination can visualize the practices that could institutionalize imperatives requiring people to cut off a hand or pluck out an eye, as well as the upper-level excuses for the carnage that would result. Instead what we hear are excuses for *not* recognizing these imperatives: "They're only meant figuratively"; "The hand and the foot and the eye aren't what offend, it's the mind"; "That doesn't apply in the modern world"; and so on.

No group, mainstream or fringe, recognizes these imperatives as 0-level. This may seem to be a point in the moral favor of all groups that recognize the New Testament as scriptural, both mainstream and fringe; whatever else may be part of their fundamental ethical handprint, this cruel imperative, fortunately, is not. But since the morality of this alleged 0-level imperative cannot be assessed in itself, we cannot determine whether recognizing it is a morally good or bad thing. Although it is certainly cruel, there is no purely ethical basis—one that does not appeal to underlying theological commitments or their denial—for determining whether cruelty in this religious context is morally acceptable or not. We cannot say whether the imperative is ethically good or bad, or perhaps neutral in moral force, or whether recognizing it is to be commended or condemned. That no Christian group recognizes this imperative—neither the most literally fundamentalist groups, nor those that take otherwise sizable physical risks—does not answer the theoretical question here. This is the final barrier to further critique. By pursuing an analysis from the peripheral features of the practices of religious groups toward the center, from upper-level excuses and doctrinal teachings to the more basic first-order and even .5-order ones, we can use the categories of ordinary and professional ethics to identify systemic moral problems and even to characterize each group's basic moral handprint. However, we cannot, finally, decide whether it is the print of a clean or dirty hand. For this, we would need to decide the truth or falsity of the background metaphysical claims and the moral rightness or wrongness of the imperatives themselves. Thus, while the practices of mainstream groups seem not to generate systemic moral problems and while mainstream groups avoid adopting 0-level mandates that are coercive, deceptive, dangerous, or cruel, we cannot decide whether they lack serious moral problems or whether the absence of certain imperatives betrays grave moral problems, too.

This is an intractable issue, but fortunately it does not prevent us from pursuing the moral critique of religious practices at the levels of first- and second-order doctrines, as well as third-order excuses. Regardless of whether a doctrine, teaching, claim, excuse, or other religious assertion is rooted in a specific fundamental imperative or set of imperatives or whether it has developed independently, it is still a *developed* doctrine. Hence, how it attempts to resolve prior moral problems while avoiding new ones, or offers excuses, will be subject to ethical critique. If an upper-level doctrine appears to be rooted in an 0-level imperative but is not, it will be wholly and exhaustively accessible to critique with the apparatus of ordinary and professional ethics. If it does have such roots, then—insofar as its practices are developed, rather than directly dictated—it will be subject to ethical examination too, even though the underlying mandate that determines the basic nature of the practice cannot be so addressed.

## Identifying 0-level Imperatives:
### The Possibility of Alternatives

There is a final problem raised by attempting to resolve issues in organized religion in this stratified way. The analysis pursued here presupposes that it is possible to determine whether a group does or does not recognize specific 0-level imperatives. However, this presupposition may introduce complexities of its own. That there are difficulties in identifying 0-level imperatives does not change the results of the argument here but shows only that in identifying the basic moral handprint of a religious group, the practices of the group must be more carefully examined than at first supposed. In claiming that mainstream denominations no longer engage in practices that recognize the fundamental imperatives that mandate confession, risk taking, and convert seeking, we may be overlooking the development of alternative or substitute practices, practices that serve some of the functions of practices mandated by the 0-level imperatives but of which it is difficult to say whether or not they are rooted in those imperatives. Thus, we can consider three sets of practices now conducted in the mainstream as alternatives to or substitutes for practices viewed as problematic—that is, as differently developing practices rooted in the same fundamental mandates. The earlier practices were abandoned, we conjectured, in part for moral reasons; it may be that the new practices are simply alternative forms of already developed practices that serve the same ends without raising the same difficult moral issues. If so, these alternative practices would represent a moral advance: the goal is met but the problems are avoided.

*Pastoral Counseling.* First, we may observe the development of pastoral counseling within mainstream groups and consider whether it represents an alternative, less problematic form of confession. Pastoral counseling is by no means a new phenomenon, nor is it confined to the mainstream; members of most (but not all) religious groups have always been granted opportunities to confer with and confide in a spiritual advisor. Nevertheless, the growth, promotion, and development since the mid-twentieth century of pastoral counseling as a service institutionalized and formally offered by religious groups has been striking.

In mainstream denominations, pastoral counseling has taken on many of the trappings of secular counseling and psychotherapy. For instance, there is an American Association of Pastoral Counselors, headquartered near Washington, D.C., which—much like any secular professional organization—holds annual national and regional conventions, publishes a journal, issues a newsletter, and sponsors awards and prizes.[12] It offers training and continuing education courses for clergy specializing in counseling. It establishes standards for the certification of ministers, pastors, and other religious professionals who specialize in pastoral counseling, and it sets standards for accreditation of institutions that train pastoral counselors. The code of ethics composed by this organization promotes "the establishment of ethical standards in pastoral counseling" and, in a phrase that reinforces the parallels between pastoral counseling and professional psychotherapy, insists on "the maintenance of high standards of professional competence."[13]

As we shall see in detail in the next chapter, some forms of pastoral counseling reinforce structural parallels to secular psychotherapy and counseling. In many parish practices, for instance, the minister makes himself or herself available at regular hours, makes appointments, sees individuals on a repeating, regular basis, refers particularly troubled individuals to more specialized psychiatric services, and so on. Parallels to secular counseling in the psychological and psychiatric professions are also reinforced by the growing phenomenon of clergy malpractice insurance. Malpractice coverage is provided for ministers by many major denominations, and underwriters for many churches say that clergy malpractice actions would be covered under their general liability policies. To date, there have been few, if any, successful suits against clergy for malpractice (as distinct from, for example, personal injury or sexual misconduct cases), though as we shall see in the next chapter the much-discussed California case *Nally v. Grace Community Church* has increased fears of a new litigiousness directed at clergy. Some observers have accused the insurance industry, and particularly the Church Mutual Insurance Company, of deliberately fanning these fears.[14] Sam Ericsson, the attorney for the defense in the *Nally* case, accused his opponents and, by extension, the insurance industry of trying to "open a new product line."[15] Whatever the origins of the new phenomenon of clergy malpractice insurance, its increasing availability reinforces perceptions of similarities between pastoral counseling and counseling in the secular professions, perceptions already shaped by the similarities of office practice in psychiatry and psychotherapy. There may seem to be only two major differences between pastoral and secular counseling: much pastoral counseling, though not all of it, is free; and many people view counseling with one's minister as un-tainted by a stigma they associate with professional psychiatry and psychotherapy.

Thus, the first real issue here is whether modern pastoral counseling in the mainstream groups, with its extensive similarities to secular counseling, can also be recognized as a way of putting into practice what other groups recognize as the fundamental, 0-level imperative to "confess your sins." For those groups that do not practice auricular confession or related forms or that acknowledge confession only in a highly privatized form that does not institutionalize consultation with another person in an official role, does pastoral counseling function as an alternative practice that responds to the imperative? Certainly, it involves relating one's thoughts, feelings, fears, and experiences to an official of one's church. In these respects, it resembles traditional au-ricular confession; it involves the self-disclosure of matters that may be embarrassing or painful. On the other hand, for a person to seek assistance in sorting out what troubles him or her may not be the same as to confess things institutionally identified as sin. Here the problem lies not in characterizing pastoral counseling as a practice, but in dis-cerning its relations, if any, to a mandate to confess—or perhaps to some other fundamental teaching or mandate. This is not to say wheth-er observing or not observing a mandate to confess is, morally speak-ing, the more defensible course. What rides on this issue, rather, is whether pastoral counseling can be wholly and exhaustively examined with the apparatus of ordinary and professional ethics, or whether at its base there is a core imperative that cannot be critiqued.

If, as seems plausible, pastoral counseling does function as an alternative form of confession, then a second issue is raised: does this new form, as distinguished from the traditional practice, succeed better in resolving the moral issues that practice raises? There is much discussion among pastoral counselors and within the field's professional literature of familiar dilemmas of confidentiality in connection with personal, social, and marital problems; it would be premature to suggest that there is a consensus even among mainstream Protestant groups about how such matters should be handled. Should the minister inform child-protection authorities that a parent acknowledges child abuse? In some states, the law requires that the minister do so unless the confession has been made in the course of discipline enjoined by the rule of practice of the clergy's denomination—a privilege sometimes said, we saw, to apply only to ritual or sacramental confession; such protections rarely apply to secular counseling professionals. Should the pastor inform a company that an employee has been embezzling? Should the rabbi let one spouse know that the other has been having affairs? These remain live issues of confidentiality. The question for us now is whether the new professional-counselor variant of confession—as distinguished from the traditional sacramental ritual variety—is better able to resolve these issues. The secular counseling professions, following the *Tarasoff* decision, do allow certain violations of the general obligation of confidentiality—for instance, when death or serious harm to a third party would otherwise result—and many pastoral counselors understand their obligations of confidentiality to be limited in this way. Is this, morally speaking, a more defensible model for *religious* counseling? As argued in chapter 2 and as we will see in discussing the *Nally* case in chapter 5, wherever pastoral counseling is offered by a religious group and pursued by a member in a way intended to protect or serve the member's self-interests—for example, in personal, social, and marital contexts—and where it thus closely resembles what professional counselors and therapists do, it is subject to the same principle of fiduciary obligation as in secular contexts, even though the nature of pastoral counseling may involve encouraging a person to see his personal, social, or marital problem within the framework of a religious view. That pastoral counseling is subject to the same fiduciary obligation as secular counseling does not decisively answer the question of whether the religious professional should violate confidentiality to prevent a severe harm—after all, the strong opposition to the *Tarasoff* decision in the psychiatric profession has shown that this issue is by no means resolved in the secular professions either. However, it does entail that prima facie obligations of confidentiality are strong, even if in certain exceptional cases they can be overridden, and that the interests of the client are a central concern, not to be subordinated to the interests of others or of institutional needs. Although it may not wholly resolve the confidentiality problem, this answer will give some insight into the issue of the moral obligations of religious counselors toward their counselees. In the following chapter, a specific case of pastoral counseling is examined with these issues in mind. Even if an 0-level doctrine can be discovered at the basis of pastoral counseling and such counseling can be regarded as an alternative form of confession, there are still open issues about counseling as a religious practice.

*The Sanctuary Movement.* Except for vestigial fasting practices, mainstream groups do not observe the fundamental, though extrascriptural, mandate concerning risk taking—that one ought to risk one's all for God—and certainly do not interpret it literally in a physical way. We are not in a position to decide whether observing or not observing this imperative should be judged morally good or bad. There are, however, further difficulties: in some cases, it cannot be determined whether a practice should count as observing the imperative.

Consider, for instance, the recent sanctuary movement participated in by many mainstream and other groups, including in the greater Chicago area, for example, Catholics, Presbyterians, Congregationalists of the United Church of Christ, Jews, Unitarian Universalists, Quakers, and Mennonites. The sanctuary movement involves providing refuge in the United States for Central Americans fleeing political persecution in their homelands, even though the U.S. government considers them illegal aliens and sheltering them is a federal offense. Sanctuary workers in this country provide housing, food, and clothing, and make arrangements for refugees to speak about the political situation in their homeland; others assist refugees in coming to this country. Participation in the sanctuary movement carries substantial legal risk (though alleviated somewhat by recent acquittals) and may well also carry physical risk. As pointed out in a February 14, 1988 minute of the Pima, Arizona, Meeting of the Religious Society of Friends, or Quakers, requesting the help of a Volunteer Witness, "a person who helps refugees pass safely through the borderlands, who recruits clergy and congregations for sanctuary services . . . may have to endure a high-publicity trial . . . [and] should be aware that . . . there is nothing approximating due process in Mexico; providing sanctuary services can be physically dangerous."

The Quakers, like many other groups, mainstream and slightly outside the mainstream, provide support for sanctuary workers: for the position sought, the volunteer was to be provided with a personal stipend of $70 a month, travel costs and meals ($150 a month with a vehicle), telephone costs, health insurance, and travel home at the end of service. The position may involve substantial physical risk, including incarceration and perhaps danger of death, and certainly involves considerable physical hardship. Furthermore, volunteers are required to agree that if they are indicted, they will do no plea bargaining and will insist on a jury trial. Quakers who do sanctuary work thus expose themselves to considerable risk. Is this a risk-taking *practice*? Is it a practice of the group? If so, is it a practice that functions to respond to the 0-level imperative mandating risk? Or is it an activity that some Quakers engage in and that is supported by the Meeting for those who choose to do it, but which cannot be described as a practice of the group? These are not easy questions to answer, and they may be made more complex by subtle variations among different Quaker Meetings. It will be made still more complex by differences among other denominations that participate in the sanctuary movement. Whatever the details of a specific group's involvement, one can see the participation of religious groups in the sanctuary movement in several ways. On the one hand, it does involve encouraging church members to be willing to risk their safety, legal security, and lives in the service of a religious cause and, thus, raises the questions considered in chapter 2 about the ways in which such choices are shaped. On the other hand, it is not so clear that this practice is primarily a response to a fundamental imperative that mandates risk taking—though it certainly involves taking risks—but perhaps, instead, a different fundamental imperative such as "love one's neighbor" (including refugees) or "be charitable." Identifying the root imperative upon which a practice is most centrally based, if any, is a complex matter; it may be that a given practice responds to multiple fundamental mandates. Whatever the fundamental imperative a practice responds to, nevertheless, the upper-order teachings and doctrinal claims that support it are in any case subject to ethical review, though the analysis of the ethical issues raised must be pursued afresh. We cannot easily confirm our earlier assertion that mainstream groups generally do not recognize the risk-taking mandates; the sanctuary practices make it much less clear whether they do or do not, though in either case they are still subject to critique.

*Church Membership Augmentation Programs.* It is also not clear whether, in mainstream denominations, there is an alternative practice to that of convert seeking. Many of the mainstream energies of the nineteenth century devoted to aggressive conversion programs were diverted in the twentieth to founding institutions like hospitals and schools, but whatever the original ambition, these institutions now function with virtually no proselytizing intent. Modest resurgences of conversion activity occurred during the 1950s, stressing mass meeting campaigns and lay visitation, but these were eclipsed by the new social activism of the late 1960s and the 1970s. As religious concern turned to issues of racism, sexism, poverty, war, and other matters of social concern, conventional convert seeking fell out of fashion.

Now, however, new attention is being given to the matter of church membership, stimulated by pronounced declines in mainline Protestant denominations. Between 1965 and the present, membership in the United Methodist Church has declined 18 percent, from 11 million to 9.2 million; membership in the Presbyterian church has dropped 25 percent, from 4 million to 3 million; the Episcopal church has lost a staggering 28 percent, from 3.4 million to 2.5 million; and the United Church of Christ (which includes most Congregationalists) has dropped 20 percent, from 2.1 million to 1.7 million.[16] Some of these declines in membership represent losses to the evangelical and fundamentalist groups; some represent secularization. In either case, they reverse a steady pattern of growth that began in colonial times. The current decline in mainline membership is variously attributed to distaste for social-activist programs in the churches, to changing demographic factors, and sometimes to the churches' "loss of ability to respond to the basic human search for meaning."[17] Though there may be some very recent evidence of a slowing or reversal of this trend, it compelled Rev. Arie Brouwer, the former general secretary of the National Council of Churches, to wonder whether the mainline denominations can still be regarded as "mainline," or have become "old-line" or perhaps "side-line."[18] Furthermore, the Catholic church, although continuing to increase in overall membership, has suffered dramatic losses within certain populations: for example, while the Hispanic population in the United States has traditionally been solidly Catholic, somewhere around 20 percent have converted to evangelical Protestant denominations.[19]

Many mainstream denominations, including both Protestants and Catholics, have responded with active programs for increasing membership. At least until recently, however, membership drives have typically stressed denominational affiliation, not spiritual conversion. There has been some competitive membership seeking among the mainstream groups, where interdenominational transfer is frequent, but this has often involved such strategies as employing ministers with "better" personalities or greater "leadership" qualities, rescheduling services, and providing babysitting, than with attempting to convert prospective members to the denomination's theological beliefs. Various public relations practices of mainstream churches may also function as substitute or alternative practices to the more conventional ways of convert seeking; they function to improve the visibility or reputation of a given group and, hence, indirectly to increase membership, without actually aiming at conversion.

Some observers equate affiliation with a church with conversion to its beliefs and doctrines. For evangelicals like Peter Wagner, for instance, church membership is coextensive with the acceptance of Christ; thus, to promote "church growth" (to use the evangelical term) is to promote conversion to or personal rebirth in Christianity.[20] Many other commentators, however, recognize a variety of other psychosocial reasons for which individuals maintain membership in churches, including reasons of fellowship and belonging, security, and enhancing one's social status. These observers reject the concept of church growth as a synonym for conversion and do not equate increased denominational affiliation with the spiritual conversion of new members.

Clearly, the issue of church membership is a volatile one in ecclesiological circles at the moment. But if we wish to examine the *ethical* aspects of the various membership consolidation strategies that church augmentation programs use, we must ultimately be able to discern their relation—if any—to traditional imperatives of convert seeking directed at spiritual change. If such programs are not rooted in a basic, 0-level imperative, presumably that of convert seeking, but are simply management strategies for maintaining an institutional structure with a viable bottom line, then we can examine the ethics of these strategies in the same way as we would examine the ethics of membership promotion programs for any other secular enterprise, whether a health club, an investment scheme, or a street gang. On the other hand, if there is an underlying connection between church membership augmentation and convert seeking, then while the strategies employed can be scrutinized, we cannot critique the project itself in the same thoroughgoing way. The analogy with membership promotion strategies used by secular groups is useful; they may be similar in certain central aspects, and religious membership promotion strategies may be much like them. The secular groups typically not only appeal to self-interest, but also supply a definition of what self-interest consists in: for the health club, having a well-toned body; for the investment scheme, receiving a large financial return; and for the street gang, gaining protection from rival gangs and access to certain activities. In the secular enterprises, of course, we can not only examine the methods of membership promotion; we can also critique the underlying project of each. But this deeper level ethical critique is not possible for the imperative at the base of religious practices, even though the practices themselves are open to criticism. Hence, in assessing church membership augmentation programs, as in assessing pastoral counseling and projects like the sanctuary movement, we must consider what sorts of programs, at root, these are. As in cases in every other area of religious practice as well, it is with respect to the developed, upper-level, peripheral practices that ethical critique can be most acute, but ethical critique will be increasingly unable to challenge matters closest to the core. This is a far cry from subjecting religious practice to ethical critique altogether; but it is also a far cry from screening off religion as an area in which ethical critique cannot intrude.

The question in these three cases—pastoral counseling, sanctuary, and church membership augmentation programs—is whether they can be identified as alternative or substitute forms of more traditional practices, and if so, whether they resolve the moral problems presented by earlier ones. Of course, these practices are in a continuous state of flux and change; it may therefore be difficult to identify at one moment a practice that shortly later evolves into a clear-cut example. Is pastoral counseling an alternative form of confession? It is difficult to say, but the pressure put on these practices by cases like *Nally v. Grace Community Church*—as we will see—will force further development. Perhaps current pastoral counseling practices will evolve in a direction that will mark them as more distinctively religious and confessionlike, or perhaps they will evolve in a way that will reinforce their similarity to secular counseling (and in the process make them more obviously candidates for secular licensing and malpractice liability). Quite possibly, this development will take the latter route in the mainstream churches, but the former route in evangelical, pentecostal, and fundamentalist groups generally; certainly, for groups that entertain hopes of comparatively mainstream status but that have theological commitments closer to evangelical or fundamentalist views (including the church in which the *Nally* case was raised), this will be an acutely painful dilemma. However, it is in general too soon to see these developing practices very clearly.

The same is true for practices such as involvement in the sanctuary movement. As the Central American conflict finally subsides and fewer overland refugees seek safety in the United States, will American religious groups involved in this movement allow it to subside? Or will the characteristics of principled, religious risk have become so central in the practices of these groups that other occasions will be sought for its expression? Similarly, will the contemporary drive for membership evolve into something more evidently connected with the fundamental mandate characterized at the beginning of the century as "soul winning," or will it become evident that this is a practice related much more closely to the financial issues involved in maintaining a stable institutional church with a broad financial base, one having little or nothing to do with spiritual conversion? With respect to all of these issues, it is too soon to say; but they are all issues that invite continuous examination. This study has emphasized the importance of careful scrutiny of religious practices in evaluating them, both at the first-, second-, and third-order levels of developed practices and excuses and at the level of the nearly basic, .5-order, moral handprint of a group; we see here that answers, even when they are reached, cannot be firm. Since they address practices in flux, the answers will fluctuate too and will serve to remind us that an ongoing inspection of religious practices is a continuingly important task.

Thus far in this study, issues have been treated in a comparatively theoretical way; but we can also look at these issues in situ, by examining them as they arise in a single, concrete case. Doing so will also make it possible to see how the analytic apparatus developed here works in practice and how it can be systematically applied in a specific case. Let us turn to the difficult case of Ken Nally.

# CHAPTER 5

# Analyzing a Sample Case

## *Pastoral Counseling and the*

## *Death of Ken Nally*

Sometime over the weekend of April 1, 1979, twenty-four-year-old Kenneth Nally went to the apartment of a former roommate, took a twelve-gauge shotgun down from the wall where he knew his roommate kept it hanging, loaded the shells he had bought at J. C. Penney's that Friday afternoon, and shot himself in the head. He left no suicide note, but a three-by-five card with Bible verses scrawled on it was found under his body. One year later, his parents brought suit against the church of which Ken had become a member, naming four of its pastors; [1] they claimed that the kind of pastoral counseling the church had given Ken was responsible for his death. "I blame the church because they filled him up with guilt, guilt, guilt," said Ken's father, "so that when he had troubles he thought they were his fault and that he had sinned. He died a virgin, and they told him he had sinned." [2]

### *The Case of Ken Nally*

Ken Nally, baptized and raised a Catholic, had seemed an energetic and successful teenager with an active social life. He was active in the affairs of his parochial school; he was a debater; he was a basketball star; and, to his parents' considerable pride, he graduated second in his high school class. But his first quarter of college at the University of California, Irvine, was lonely and isolated and he soon transferred to the University of California, Los Angeles (UCLA). Here the friends he made were mostly religiously oriented students who attended a large, independent church in the San Fernando Valley area, Grace Community Church of the Valley. Ken joined the church in 1974, renouncing the Catholicism in which he was raised and describing himself as a born-again Christian.

From the beginning, Ken's new religious affiliation produced tension during his visits home. The visits "were like hell on earth," his father recalled. "He was always trying to convert me, and I didn't want to be converted."[3] Nevertheless, first Ken's mother and then both parents occasionally accompanied him to Grace Church. They were relieved to find it "a solid, middle-class, family-type church,"[4] not a cult.

During his years at UCLA, Ken became increasingly involved with Grace Church, not only attending services, but taking classes, participating in the church's jail ministry, and working at the church. He made the church the center of his social life and developed close relationships with several of the church's pastors. After graduating from UCLA, Ken attended the Logos Bible Institute, held at the church, and then entered the Talbot Theological Seminary, which held many classes on the church's campus. He began dating a fellow seminary student, Katie Thayer. He did janitorial work at the church to pay his seminary expenses and played basketball in the church's gymnasium with many of the church's pastors, including virtually all the defendants in the case that would be brought after his death.

But Ken suffered from emotional problems and pronounced depression. He often talked informally with his friends and with the pastors at Grace Church about his problems in dating and his conflicts with his family, about the absurdity of life, and occasionally about suicide. He had seen a Christian psychologist briefly at Shephard House in Van Nuys in 1975, but received no further formal counseling until 1978. Then, in January, he began a formal counseling program, called a "discipling" relationship, with one of the pastors at Grace Church, Duane Rea. Reverend Rea evaluated Ken as depressed; he observed that Ken cried frequently, looked despondent, hinted at suicide, and stated that he "could not cope" or "lead this life" (Appellants' Brief, 17). However, Rea found Ken an uncooperative counselee who would not follow his advice or "do his homework" in the counseling program; Rea terminated the formal counseling four months after it had begun. Ken also had three counseling sessions with pastor Rich Thomson, who directed the church's pastoral counseling program and was the author of the text used in training the church's counselors. During these sessions, Ken told Reverend Thomson about the depression he had had while at UCLA and a suicide attempt he had made while there. Ken was able to make some choices about his future—for instance, he decided to "serve the Lord through law" by becoming a "Christian judge"[5] and applied to and was accepted at a southern California law school for the following fall. Yet his depression did not lift and his emotional problems became increasingly acute. His mother arranged for him to see a general practitioner, Julius Milestone, M.D., who prescribed the tranquilizer Elavil. He saw another physician, Mary Oda, M.D., who believed his depression had a physical basis; she made an appointment for him to have a complete physical. However, he did not keep the appointment. His depression increased. On the night of March 11, 1979, while in his room at his parents' home, Ken took all the Elavil remaining in the prescription from Dr. Milestone. He was discovered unconscious by his parents the next morning and was rushed to Verdugo Hills Hospital.

That day, both head pastor John MacArthur and pastor Rea came to see him at Verdugo Hills. Ken told each of them separately that he was sorry he had not succeeded in carrying out his suicide. After Ken had been hospitalized for a week at Verdugo Hills, the consulting psychiatrist, David Hall, M.D., recommended to Ken that he commit himself to a psychiatric hospital. Ken refused. His parents, who had earlier asked the physicians to tell people Ken was being treated for pneumonia at Verdugo Hills, not a suicide attempt, refused to commit him involuntarily. Although they believed that psychiatric hospitalization would be appropriate, Dr. Hall and the attending physician, Dr. Evelyn, agreed to release Ken, in order "not to fracture the psychotherapist-patient relationship" and to avoid the possibility that Ken would reject future outpatient treatment (Respondents' Brief, 22, n. 58).

When he was released, Ken insisted that he did not want to go to his parents' home. Head pastor MacArthur and his wife Pat took Ken into their home for a week. During this time, Ken and MacArthur had numerous late-night conversations about Ken's troubles. However, the MacArthurs were leaving for a vacation in Scotland and after six days Ken returned to his parents' home. Ken's parents again contacted Dr. Hall, who again told them that he recommended psychiatric hospitalization, but Ken did not keep an appointment made for him with Dr. Hall. During the next nine days at home, the last days before his suicide, Ken saw two other physicians, one of them concerning his arm, which had been partially paralyzed since he slept on it while unconscious during his suicide attempt, as well as the dean of an institute of psychology and a psychologist's assistant. He also continued to see the pastors at Grace Church. Nevertheless, he remained extremely disturbed. He proposed to his girlfriend, Katie Thayer, but she said she could not marry him when he was like this and that he had to "put God first in his life." On Friday, March 31, he had yet another argument with his father and left home. He went to Katie Thayer's house and together they went shopping. They talked about Ken's condition and his thoughts of suicide; Ken told Katie he was thinking of walking up into the hills and shooting himself. Katie tried to dissuade him by pointing out that this would make "too much of a mess," and that it would be extremely disturbing, if, for instance, some children found the body. Nevertheless, as a saleslip found in a paper bag after the suicide later showed, Ken bought the shells for his former roommate's shotgun while he and Katie were shopping that afternoon. Ken's mother searched desperately for him over the weekend, but two days later he was found dead in his former roommate's apartment. That afternoon, as members of the church came to Ken's parents' house to offer condolences, they retrieved various tape recordings and literature from his room, which, they said, were church property.

The specific suit that Ken's parents, Walter and Maria Nally, brought against Grace Community Church and the four pastors, John F. MacArthur, Jr., Duane Rea, Rich Thomson, and Lynn Cory, was a wrongful death action, charging clergy malpractice, negligence, and outrageous conduct, including intentional infliction of emotional distress, in failing to prevent the suicide. Identified by the press as the first major "clergy malpractice" action, the case was widely watched. During the eight years the case spent in the California courts, it was brought, dismissed by the trial court, reinstated by the court of appeal, denied review by the supreme court, depublished, remanded to the trial court, dismissed again, reinstated by the court of appeal again, and finally reviewed by the supreme court, which late in 1988 affirmed the trial court's judgment of nonsuit on the ground of lack of evidence. Early in 1989, the Nallys' further pursuit of the case was brought to an end when the U.S. Supreme Court declined to hear it.

Virtually every major religious group in the United States contributed to Grace Church's defense, including both mainline and fundamentalist denominations. Even the Catholic church, which Grace Church head pastor MacArthur was alleged to have described as "evil," joined in supporting Grace Church's defense. Some forty denominations, said to represent 15,077 individual churches, filed amicus curiae briefs, as did the National Council of Churches and the American Association of Pastoral Counselors. Virtually all of those concerned feared that if the case were decided—regardless of whether the decision were in favor of the plaintiffs or the defendants—it would stifle religious counseling by (in the words of the trial court judge) "opening the floodgates to clergy malpractice litigation." *Newsweek* summed up these fears: "Four clergymen are being sued for malpractice—an action that, if successful, could render every minister, priest and rabbi in the United States vulnerable to state supervision."[6]

While the legal issues may have been settled with the U.S. Supreme Court's refusal to hear the case, *Nally v. Grace Community Church of the Valley* nevertheless provides a wealth of material for ethical analysis. It does so not only because the testimony is extensive, allowing a close look at actual practice, but because the case does not involve irregular or deviant behavior by the pastors of Grace Church, but the group's standard, accepted, ordinary practices. Ken Nally was counseled by Grace Church's pastors in precisely the way the church trains its pastors to counsel. (For this reason, the term "clergy malpractice," used by the plaintiffs in the statement of the case, is a misnomer: the pastors in this case were not performing the pastoral practices of the church badly or failing to perform them at all. On the contrary, with a few minor exceptions, they were performing the pastoral practices of this religious group exactly as expected.) It is this fact that makes the case of Ken Nally particularly suitable for the kind of ethical analysis being pursued here, since it focuses on moral problems generated by the usual, standard practices of organized religion, not on how some parties fail to conform to those practices. It might seem that the case would have little relevance to mainstream issues, since the church in which it arose is strongly evangelical and conservative, but close analysis will, I think, shed light on many other varieties of pastoral counseling as well.

## Pastoral Counseling at Grace Community Church

Grace Community Church regards pastoral counseling as an important part of its ministry. Its counseling operation is a sizable one: in 1979, at the time of Ken's suicide, Grace Church employed at least thirty salaried counselors for a congregation of over ten thousand.[7] The counseling service employed a secretary to coordinate appointments; it also provided counseling on an ad hoc or drop-in basis. It offered classes in biblical counseling, published books on how to counsel, and sold tape recordings, including tapes of counseling training sessions. About 50 percent of the counselees were members of Grace Church; the other 50 percent came from the surrounding community. The counseling service was clearly heavily used; at one point Reverend MacArthur testified that "the mass of people who pull at the pastoral staff of Grace Community Church is more than any of us can handle" (Appellants' Brief, 15), though he hastened to add that those counselors who had helped Ken with his depression had not been too busy to do a good job. Grace Church's counseling program was entirely funded by its general revenues (the church had a budget of about $8 million a year) and did not charge pastoral counseling clients a fee.

As in pastoral counseling generally, counseling at Grace Church involves using religious insights to address an individual's emotional or personal difficulties. In keeping with its fundamentalist, essentially Baptist theology, the type of pastoral counseling Grace Church offers is "biblical": it consists, as several of the pastors put it, in "applying the lessons of Scripture to a person's problems." At Grace Church, this means recognizing that man is inherently sinful and that the only real remedy for this is divine forgiveness. It also means recognizing that many, if not most, of man's problems—including his emotional or psychological problems—can be traced to sin. According to Reverend MacArthur, even the "deepest depression" is caused by sin and spiritual counseling is the only thing that can relieve it (Appellants' Brief, 13). The objective in pastoral counseling is to bring the counselee to understand this and to acknowledge the role of sin in his or her life, then to encourage the renunciation of sin and the acceptance of God's forgiveness.

This basic view of pastoral counseling is outlined in the text Grace Church used in training its counselors, pastor Rich Thomson's *Guide for Biblical Counselors*. Reverend Thomson, then director of Grace Church's counseling program, offered classes in biblical counseling not only to prospective counselors, but to members and nonmembers as well. Ken Nally had attended at least some sessions of Thomson's course. The training of counselors consists in the study of biblical texts and their application to personal problems; it does not involve training in crisis intervention, suicide prevention, psychology, psychiatric diagnosis or treatment, domestic, marital, or parent-child relationships, or other related matters, other than those provided in Thomson's book and other tapes and books on biblical counseling available from the church.

The conception of pastoral counseling as a remedy for sin is central to the techniques employed by Grace Church pastors. The immediate counseling objective is to get the counselee to recognize and acknowledge that he or she has sinned or is sinning; this is prerequisite to the healing that can then take place as the pastor offers forgiveness. Thus, in an initial appointment, the counselor might ask the counselee to describe the problem as he or she sees it and then try to get the person to see that these painful experiences are the product of sin. For instance, Reverend Rea testified that his first step in dealing with Ken, as with any counselee, was to "find out what sins are involved," and then to "make sure Ken knew without any mincing of words that his conduct had been sinful" (Appellants' Brief, 17). Reverend Thomson testified that "investigating the sin" is a "painful experience" for the counselee, (ibid., 19) and that when someone gives evidence of trying to "flee" or "escape," the counselor knows that the person is wicked. According to Thomson, the person "should be told that they are wicked" (19). Initial probing of the sins is followed by reading the Scriptures; this is done in order to achieve a proper biblical awareness of the nature of one's acts. Describing his informal counseling sessions with Ken, in which the issue of suicide had been raised, Rev. Fred Barshaw, another Grace Church pastor (though one not named in the suit), said his purpose in these sessions was to "show Ken the biblical standard for the behavior in question" (16). Reverend MacArthur, testifying concerning the late-night discussions he had had with Ken while Ken was staying at his home during the week after his release from Verdugo Hills Hospital, said that they had discussed guilt and "getting over depression by handling guilt in a biblical fashion" (25). MacArthur also submitted a six-page statement of his views on guilt, which included the claim that he "looks at guilt as a good thing" (25). Reverend Cory sent Ken a tape recording, together with a letter on the church's letterhead, saying "Our hearts are deceitful and wicked, and a tape like this is good to keep it in check" (Exhibit 60-A). The letter and the tape were found in Ken's room after his death.

While there are some differences in the individual style of the various Grace Church pastors who counseled Ken, it is possible to identify the central pattern of Grace Church's practices in pastoral counseling: to elicit from the counselee a description of his or her actions or concerns, to identify them as sin, to have the counselee acknowledge that they are sinful and that they are the root of his or her troubles, and (though this is emphasized only by MacArthur) to offer forgiveness for these sins. This schema describes the basic practice of this group in pastoral counseling. We can now ask whether, on moral grounds, this practice is a defensible one.

# The Professional and Ordinary Ethics Analysis
## of the Case of Ken Nally

An examination of the ethical issues in the case of Ken Nally and the pastoral counseling practices affecting his suicide begins by supposing that practices that satisfy both professional standards and the canons of ordinary morality are at least prima facie morally acceptable, while those that violate one or both are prima facie unacceptable. (This assumption should not lead us to think that accepted professional practices cannot themselves raise moral problems, that ordinary morality is not controversial, or that there cannot be conflicts between the two.) This is to begin by applying the two prongs of our pincer apparatus of professional and ordinary ethics. The view from professional ethics will be employed first—and more extensively—since it is particularly useful in a case where institutional religious practice is closely analogous to secular professional practice; we will also look briefly at ordinary ethics considerations. However, this double-pronged, pincer analysis is only a first move; once the initial professional and ordinary ethics analysis is complete, it must be supplemented and partially superseded under further principles of analysis.

### Professional Standards in Pastoral Counseling

Professional standards for counseling suicidal clients are fairly well established in the secular counseling professions. These standards include three basic requirements: (1) a requirement of adequate diagnosis, including a diagnosis of suicidal lethality; (2) a requirement of referral to appropriate treatment, if adequate treatment cannot be provided in the initial counseling situation; and (3) a requirement of notification to other parties who might be able to prevent suicide. While some rudiments of activity required under each of these standards by Grace Church's counseling program are evident, we must examine whether the counseling that the church provided Ken Nally satisfied any of these standards fully.

*Adequate Diagnosis.* Under these standards, the pastoral counseling that Grace Church provided Ken Nally clearly failed to diagnose Ken's condition adequately. In particular, it failed to ascertain the seriousness of Ken's suicidal threats. It may be true, as Paul Holinger claims in a recent study of pastoral care of persons with severe emotional disorders, that, paradoxically, pastors may often be confronted by more difficult diagnostic assessments than those faced by medical professionals; this is because individuals with more obvious psychotic symptoms are more likely to be seen first by psychiatrists or internists, whereas the more subtle cases of psychosis are seen by pastors.[8] But there was nothing difficult about diagnosing the fact that Ken was severely depressed and suicidal. Reverend Barshaw testified that in 1976 and 1977 members of the pastoral staff already realized that Ken might commit suicide. Reverend Thomson acknowledged that he took the possibility that Ken might commit suicide "seriously" (Appellants' Brief, 18). Reverend MacArthur discussed the subject of suicide with Ken and knew that this was a "real possibility" (ibid., citing R. T. 1424:7–1425:23). Rea did make one crude attempt at diagnosis: since he believed that "demonic activity" could cause suicidal ideation, he had made an effort to determine whether this was a factor in Ken's case and satisfied himself that it was not (ibid., 8). Nevertheless, although all of the pastors understood that Ken was suicidal, none of them made any attempt to apply standard diagnostic criteria or to assess the lethality of the threat. Reverend Rea "discounted" the possibility of suicide "because of Ken's intelligence" (ibid., 17, citing R. T. 584:12–22). although he later admitted that "he now recognizes that was possibly an important question and that it would have done Ken some good to talk about it" (ibid., 586:1–28). Rea never asked Ken directly whether he was thinking of suicide. While visiting Ken at Verdugo Hills Hospital, Reverend Cory overheard Ken say to Reverend MacArthur that he was sorry he had not been successful in his suicide attempt and that he wanted to try again, "not being able to live this life" (ibid., 22, citing R. T. 1325:1–10), but Cory did not raise the issue of suicide again.

Furthermore, not only did none of the pastors who dealt with Ken ask him directly about his intentions of suicide, none of them asked specific questions about what method of suicide he was planning to use. Professionals in suicide prevention employ direct questions of this sort to assess the lethality of suicidal intentions. This is a central technique in secular counseling and provides important evidence about how likely it is that someone who expresses suicidal feelings will actually commit suicide. For example, a response like "I intend to use the twelve-gauge shotgun my former roommate has hanging on the wall of his apartment, and I can buy shells for it at J. C. Penney" yields a much more dangerous lethality index than the vague, generalized "I intend to kill myself somehow or other, but I haven't thought of how" and mandates much more immediate intervention. On the Friday immediately before his suicide, Ken talked with his girlfriend, Katie Thayer, about different ways of committing suicide, including using a shotgun; this suggests that specific information allowing diagnosis of Ken's high lethality could have been elicited from him by the pastors in counseling sessions at that time.

That none of the pastors attempted to establish a more certain diagnosis or to determine the seriousness of Ken's suicidal intent might be explained by the fact that none of the written materials Grace Church used in training its counselors and counselees contained anything about how to investigate the seriousness of a person's intention to commit suicide (ibid., 14). People not trained in suicide prevention often believe, erroneously, that mentioning suicide or asking a person about his or her intentions or the methods he or she plans to use will trigger an impulse to do so. It is possible that the pastors were afraid to initiate such discussions, as persons not trained in suicide prevention might well be. But this does not exonerate the pastors; it simply underscores the fact that they did not have adequate training in dealing with suicidal persons—that is, training that would be considered adequate under secular standards of suicide prevention. Assessment of suicidal risk is a crucial step in the management of suicidal persons; all authorities in suicide prevention agree "that it is a grave error *not* to ask depressed or troubled persons about their suicidal thoughts or feelings."[9] Of course, the pastors did attempt to diagnose Ken's condition in the sense that they tried to "find out what [his] real sin was that was causing that guilt" (Respondents' Brief, Appendix, 12a). ("Yes. Yes," testified Thomson, "that's where diagnosis comes in, and listening compassionately") (ibid.). But attempting to identify the source of a problem is quite different from trying to diagnose suicidal potential. It is this latter effort that the Grace Church pastors did not make.

Not only did the counseling service not provide any way of assessing Ken's risk of suicide, it offered no mechanism for consultation among the pastors seeing Ken, either to compare observations about an appropriate diagnosis, to determine the seriousness of his suicidal state, or to coordinate ways of helping him. Nor was there any structure, formal or otherwise, whereby the various counselors would meet to discuss problem cases like Ken's. Even Reverend MacArthur did not know what counseling was being given Ken by Rea and Thomson. Indeed, MacArthur believed that Ken was the first member of the church ever to commit suicide, though at the trial he was shown documents indicating that other members of the church had in fact attempted or completed suicide.

It is clear, then, Grace Church's counseling program did not involve systematic diagnostic procedures for the identification of persons at risk of suicide or provide mechanisms for consultation and consistent supervision of such cases. It thus appears that by professional standards Grace Church's counseling program would be unsatisfactory in this respect and hence prima facie ethically indefensible.

*Referral.* Under secular standards for counseling with suicidal persons, Grace Church's counseling program also appears to have failed to meet a second condition in its treatment of Ken, namely that, given the inability of the program to relieve a client's depression or reduce the likelihood of suicide, it should have referred the client to appropriately trained psychologists or psychiatrists who could be expected to treat the condition effectively. This is just to say that the counseling program had an obligation to acknowledge the limits of its own competence and to refer where it could not effectively treat. As early as 1976 or 1977, Reverend Barshaw had discussed the possibility of referring Ken to a psychiatrist or psychologist, but did not do so. When Reverend Rea terminated formal counseling with Ken because Ken did not follow his advice or "do his homework" (specifically, Rea had advised him to "glorify God in all things" and to "rejoice" [R. T. 498:5–9]), he did not refer Ken to any other counselor or to a psychiatrist or psychologist. Reverend Thomson did not discuss the possibility of referral with Ken at all. Reverend Cory told Ken to see Rea or Thomson "because they were better qualified to deal with depression" (Appellants' Brief, 22), but Cory also did not refer Ken to a psychologist or psychiatrist.

Furthermore, not only was Ken not referred to a psychologist or psychiatrist, but, according to Dr. Hall, the psychiatrist who had examined Ken at Verdugo Hills after the suicide attempt in March, two weeks before his death—and who was the only psychiatrist Ken ever saw in the five-year history of his depression—Ken had been advised *not* to see a psychiatrist by his counselors at Grace Church. The reason for this apparently had to do with the perception that, as secular professionals, psychiatrists were not Christian and hence were incapable of dealing with spiritual problems. Thomson testified that he would not refer a counselee to a psychiatrist unless he believed the psychiatrist was "coming from the viewpoint consistent with the Scripture" (ibid., 20). He also admitted that not only did he not in fact know of any psychiatrist who agreed with his biblical philosophy, but had never attempted to find out if there were any. Thomson's *Guide for Biblical Counselors* teaches that "to settle for an answer from secular psychiatry or psychology or even from some of what is termed Christian psychiatry or Christian psychology is to settle for less than God's goal (ibid., 12). Rea testified that where psychology and psychiatry "parallel what God says in His Word" (Respondents' Brief, Appendix, 6a), they may be accepted, but where they run counter to it, one should not take their advice. One of Grace Church's attorneys, Samuel Ericsson, described the church's view that "the Bible can handle deep depression better than psychologists and psychiatrists" as a "sincerely held belief " (ibid., 8a). Apparently, with the exception of Reverend Barshaw, early in Ken's association with the church, it was not until *after* Ken's sublethal suicide attempt in early March, two weeks before he actually did kill himself, that any of the pastors considered the possibility of referring Ken to a professional psychotherapist or psychiatrist.

While Ken was staying at his home, pastor MacArthur did come to the view that Ken was so deeply depressed and suicidal that it was beyond his capability to deal with, and that proper care with a psychiatrist would do Ken more good than spiritual counseling. But by this time Ken had already absorbed an attitude of mistrust toward secular psychiatrists and psychologists. According to Rea, Ken was "negative toward 'shrinks'" (Appellants' Brief, 18, 25) and unwilling to pursue therapy that was not Christian in character. Dr. Hall, the psychiatrist at Verdugo Hills, reported that Ken had told him he would have to get permission from the church in order to continue to see him after his release from the hospital. Indeed, Ken's appointment with Dr. Hall was broken after he was released, with the explanation that the church had arranged for Ken to see a Christian therapist instead.[10] MacArthur acknowledged in testimony that he did not make a "major effort" to find a licensed psychiatrist or psychologist whose beliefs were consistent with Ken's theology. (Grace Church did not have any affiliation with licensed psychiatrists or psychologists to whom referrals might routinely be made.) On the Tuesday before Ken's suicide, Reverend Thomson did approve Ken's consulting a Dr. Mohline, also a member of the church, but incorrectly assumed that Mohline was a licensed psychologist, not, as was actually the case, the dean of administration at a school of professional psychology, a teacher of classes on biblical counseling, and the holder of only an honorary doctorate. The only actual referral made by any of the pastors at Grace Church to a professional practitioner was made by MacArthur a week before Ken's death: MacArthur suggested that Ken see Dr. John Parker, a general practitioner who was a deacon at the church and who had taken classes there in biblical counseling. It was actually Mrs. MacArthur who made the arrangement. Parker, who was neither a psychiatrist nor a psychologist, was not informed of Ken's history of depression and suicidal ideation and attempts, and he saw Ken for only a fifteen-minute physical examination.

At the trial, a psychiatrist serving as an expert witness, Dr. Stephen Wilson, testified that it would have been possible to treat Ken's depression in at least four ways: with psychotherapy, tricyclic antidepressants, monoamine-oxidase inhibitors, and electroconvulsive therapy. This is not to assume that referral to a licensed psychologist or psychiatrist and treatment with these methods would have saved Ken from suicide. Nevertheless, the one psychiatrist Ken did see, Dr. Hall, diagnosed Ken's depression as having a biochemical basis; if this was so, it might well have responded to medication. Thus, timely referral, making appropriate treatment possible, might well have substantially reduced the likelihood that Ken would kill himself.

According to accepted professional standards, thus, Grace Church's pastors clearly failed to meet the obligation of referral. However, this is an obligation established for counselors, therapists, and other clinical professionals. In the California Supreme Court's dismissal of the case, the court asserted that "nontherapist counselors" do not have a duty to refer to licensed psychotherapists, even when suicide is foreseeable.[11] Thus, in the court's majority view, those who provide counseling on a nonprofessional basis—not only pastors, but others who give advice, including personal friends—do not have the same duty to refer that professional therapists do. The supreme court viewed the court of appeal as having attempted to establish such a duty on the part of nontherapist counselors, but this, in the supreme court's view, ran counter to the legal principle that a person has no duty to protect another from harm except in a special relationship of custody or control. The concurring opinion in the same supreme court decision disagreed over the obligation to refer, arguing that given the relationship established in pastoral counseling, there is a duty of care; however, it claimed that in its view that duty had been satisfied. While these legal issues are complex, it is clear that Grace Church's pastoral counselors failed to satisfy the basic condition that secular professionals would be expected to meet in treating a depressed and suicidal person: referral to a party competent to treat the condition.

At the trial, the defense argued that during the last weeks of his life, Ken had been seen by no fewer than five physicians (Doctors Milestone, Oda, Evelyn, Bullock, and Parker), one psychiatrist (Dr. Hall), and two other mental health professionals (Dr. Mohline and the psychologist's assistant, Mr. Raup), and that the church had "arranged and encouraged" many of these visits. But it was a case of too little, too late. The possibility of a sustained therapeutic relationship with a psychotherapist or psychiatrist trained in the identification and management of depression and suicidal behavior had already been precluded. Clearly, the pastoral counseling program had in effect worked consistently against the possibility of referral, despite last-minute attempts after the Verdugo Hills hospitalization to get Ken to cooperate with doctors, insofar as it reinforced "antishrink" attitudes and made repeated theological claims that not only could emotional problems of any kind be resolved with biblical counseling alone, but that only this kind of resolution could be genuinely satisfactory. The issues of referral lie not simply in the church's failure to refer Ken to competent professionals, but in reinforcing attitudes that made it impossible for him to seek or respond to such help.

*Notification of Others.* If we examine the church's counseling program under the secular standards for counseling suicidal persons, it appears that it also failed to inform parties who might have been able to prevent Ken's suicide, including Ken's parents, the physician and the psychiatrist who had treated him in the hospital, and mental health or public safety authorities. None of the pastors who had been seeing Ken either informally or formally—Reverends Barshaw, Rea, Thomson, Cory, and MacArthur—ever informed Ken's parents that their son was suicidal, even though they all recognized that this was the case.

This failure to notify others had considerable impact on potential intervention to prevent Ken's suicide, especially that which could have been made by Ken's family. When Ken returned to his parents' home after spending the week following his release from Verdugo Hills with the MacArthurs, he saw Dr. John Parker, the general practitioner and member of Grace Church with whom Mrs. MacArthur had made an appointment. Dr. Parker gave Ken a physical, but also told him that he was a real threat to himself and should have himself committed to a psychiatric hospital. Ken's father, who was with him, testified that when Ken came out of Dr. Parker's office, he "had never seen Kenneth look more disturbed" (Respondents' Brief, 7, citing R.T. 1547-50). That evening Mr. Nally contacted Dr. Hall, the psychiatrist Ken had seen in the hospital, and told him that another physician had recommended psychiatric hospitalization. Dr. Hall again recommended that Ken be committed to a mental hospital; he volunteered to send an ambulance for Ken and to come himself to the Nallys' home to have them sign involuntary commitment papers. The Nallys refused. "No, that's a crazy hospital," said Maria Nally. "He's not crazy" (Respondents' Brief, 7).

However, although Ken's parents knew that he had made a recent suicide attempt and knew of the doctors' recommendations, they had never been informed of their son's long history of depression or his several suicide attempts prior to the one for which he was hospitalized. Nor did they know he had told two of the pastors that he was sorry he had not succeeded in committing suicide and intended to try again. On the contrary, the church's few contacts with the Nallys seemed to be intended to reassure them about their son. After Ken was released from Verdugo Hills, Reverend Thomson saw Ken's father and said, "Don't worry, Mr. Nally, I've been counseling him and he is all right" (Appellants' Brief, 28). Also after the Verdugo Hills hospitalization, Mrs. Nally met Reverend Rea in the back of the chapel at a funeral for someone else and told him that Ken had attempted suicide; he later testified that because she had "volunteered that information ostensibly in trust of me, . . . I tried to be warm towards her and assure her that things would be well and not to worry" (R.T. 446:3–11). While Ken was staying with the MacArthurs, Mrs. MacArthur phoned the Nallys several times to say that Ken was doing well and playing with the children. Reverend Cory had earlier introduced Mr. Nally to Reverend Thomson as a "psychologist that has been treating him or counseling him" (Appellants' Brief, 29), and, when Mr. Nally had burst open the door to Cory's office and seen Ken kneeling on the floor and crying, Cory had told him that Ken would be all right. After Ken's suicide attempt, Cory did not tell Mr. Nally what he had overheard Ken saying to Reverend MacArthur while he was still in the hospital, namely that he still wanted to commit suicide. Nor did any of the pastors contact either Dr. Evelyn, the physician who had treated Ken at Verdugo Hills, or Dr. Hall, the consulting psychiatrist, the doctors who authorized Ken's release, to let them know that Ken continued to be suicidal. Nor was Dr. Parker or Dr. Mohline so informed. Nor did the pastors inform any suicide prevention or crisis intervention workers, police, or others who might have intervened. In fact, throughout the case, only one person made any attempt to inform others who might intervene. After the suicide attempt which hospitalized him at Verdugo Hills, Ken's girlfriend Katie Thayer related to two of the pastors that Ken had been talking about "wanting to go home and be with the Lord" and had said he wanted to die (ibid.); again when Ken was staying at MacArthur's house, she reported to MacArthur that Ken had threatened to commit suicide if she broke up with him, a threat that she considered real.[12] However, the pastors did not relay this information to Ken's parents, who could have had him hospitalized, or to anyone else who might have intervened.

Insofar as Grace Church's counseling program appears to have failed to satisfy the three central standards of professional counseling for persons at risk of suicide—to pursue a diagnosis by exploring lethality, to refer for psychological or psychiatric consultation or treatment, and to inform those who might be able to prevent the suicide—it does not satisfy secular standards and therefore must be judged prima facie morally indefensible.

Nor do the practices of Grace Church satisfy the standards set by the American Association of Pastoral Counselors (AAPC),[13] the professional organization that sets standards for clergy counseling and provides training and certification for pastors specializing in counseling. The standards developed by AAPC incorporate those of the secular professions, though it recognizes that pastoral counseling also has a spiritual dimension and involves the application of religious insight to an individual's personal problems. According to AAPC, however, respecting the spiritual component in pastoral counseling does not exempt the counselor from meeting the basic professional standards, which, it asserts, are religiously neutral in character.

At the *Nally* trial, the plaintiffs called a number of expert witnesses in pastoral counseling to establish that Grace Church's practices failed to meet these professional criteria.[14] One of them, Dr. Bill Adams, was also asked to review Thomson's "Guide for Biblical Counselors," which served as Grace Church's primary statement of principles and techniques to be used in the counseling program. Adams testified that if the Guide reflected Grace Church's standards, it "completely violated accepted community standards" (Appellants' Brief, 37).

An initial analysis of Grace Church's counseling program, then, suggests that it violated professional standards for counseling with suicidal persons, standards recognized by both the secular psychiatric and psychological professions and also by the American Association of Pastoral Counselors. Of course, the standards themselves raise certain moral problems. First, for instance, the requirement that the diagnosis be pursued by assessing the lethality of the person's suicidal intent clearly presupposes that predictions of behavior will be sensitive and specific—that is, that assessments of lethality will both identify any person who will commit suicide and identify only those who will do so. So accurate a level of risk prediction is far from attainable using current psychodiagnostic methods. On the contrary, the standard that requires assessing lethality as a way of pursuing a diagnosis raises the familiar problems of false-positive and false-negative diagnoses, issues which loom large when treatment strategies such as psychotropic drug therapy and involuntary hospitalization are at stake.

Similarly, the second standard, which imposes a duty to refer persons judged suicidal to competent professionals, also brings with it a set of additional moral problems. These include problems of professional competency in general and of the referring party's oblig- ation to ensure that the client actually sees the professional to whom the referral is made. Some professionals may be more competent or more thoroughly trained than others; some are altogether incompe- tent. Furthermore, even when a referral is made, the client may find reasons to resist—as, given his "antishrink" attitude, Ken Nally surely would have. That professional standards require referral from a party not able to provide effective treatment to one that can be expected to do so does not put an end to the moral problems the standards raise.

Third, the standard that requires informing other parties that might be able to prevent suicide clearly raises ethical issues of confidentiality. Although there has been opposition within the secular counseling professions to the *Tarasoff* decision, it is now recognized in policy that violations of confidentiality are permissible where absolutely necessary to protect a client or patient from a serious risk of self-harm. At the same time, clergy privilege offers legal protection for not violating confidentiality. Among the issues presented by the *Nally* case was whether it would have been legally permissible for MacArthur, Rea, Thomson or Cory, all of whom counseled Ken, to have informed Ken's parents, the doctors Ken consulted, or anyone else about his continuing suicidal state.[15] There is, of course, a moral issue here as well as a legal one, but it is a moral issue that has been resolved in the secular professions in favor of carefully limited notification. Thus, although Grace Church's program seems to have violated professional standards for counseling and the moral norms accepted in the secular professions, this is not to say the program would not have given rise to moral problems had it followed these standards. It is for this reason that the church's failure to follow the standards can be said to be only prima facie morally indefensible, since the standards as well as the professional practices within which they develop also demand further scrutiny. The ethical problems they raise, however, will be the familiar moral problems characteristic of all secular counseling professions, issues that can be addressed outside the religious setting.

Grace Church's defense against the accusations consisted in part in attempting to show that it had satisfied the three criteria after all: that it had been sensitive to the nature of Ken's problems and had attempted to help him with them; that it had "arranged and encouraged" many of Ken's appointments with physicians and with the psychiatrist, and that notification of others was unnecessary because Ken's suicidal state was already "fully known" to his family and treating physicians (Respondents' Brief, 24). Indeed, the church's attorneys argued that "respondents did everything they could reasonably have been expected to do, in light of all the circumstances as known at that time" (ibid., 26). Justice Marcus Kaufman's concurring opinion for the California Supreme Court agreed with this claim, arguing that although the church and its pastors did owe a minimal duty of care to Ken, they fulfilled this duty. But while disagreement may continue about whether the church and its pastors did or did not satisfy professional standards for counseling with suicidal persons, this will be of restricted relevance in our ultimate assessment of the *Nally* case. There is more to the issue than can be decided simply by determining whether the church's treatment of Ken Nally met professional standards.

## The Standards of Ordinary Ethics

The *Nally* case may also be examined in the light of general principles of ordinary morality, the second prong of our pincer apparatus. These principles are not perhaps so well systematized as those of professional ethics in the contemporary literature, nor are they always distinct from them. They include many of the same elements, especially utilitarian, deontological, and virtue theorist components, variously requiring avoidance of harm, respect for autonomy, protection for human relationships, and so on. According to these principles of ordinary morality, some of the ways in which Grace Church treated Ken seem ethically commendable. For instance, one young woman member of the church who had known Ken said, "It's just all so sad. This church was Ken's life. These were his friends, all the people he loved and who loved him." Reverend Rea, testifying about an afternoon Ken had spent at his home helping him trim trees not long after his release from Verdugo Hills, said he had not thought of himself that day as a counselor, but "more as a father and a friend" (ibid., Appendix, 5a). Rea also testified that he prayed for Ken regularly. Such claims of love, friendship, and concern may be difficult to state or confirm in objective terms, but the general assertion is that the church and its members, in extending love and friendship to Ken and in being concerned for his welfare, were treating him in an ethically admirable way. Similarly, it is primarily as a matter of ordinary morality, not professional ethics, that we can scrutinize John and Pat MacArthur's taking Ken into their home for a week after his suicide attempt. Although their motivation cannot be known with certainty, it appears that they did so out of concern for Ken's welfare. Furthermore, while Ken was at their house, clearly still very disturbed, as a matter of course they "didn't let him out of their sight" (Appellants' Brief, 25). This too appears to be a case of appropriately paternalist interest in Ken's welfare and an attempt to protect him from suicide, not associated with professional roles but simply with human concern. Ken's parents apparently were grateful for the MacArthurs' care and expressed their gratitude with a gift: a set of serving trays.

However, fuller examination of the case from the point of view of ordinary morality might reveal many other aspects of the church's treatment of Ken, many of them indefensible. It might also reveal features of the case not part of the church's treatment of Ken, but which are still relevant. For instance, an ordinary ethics analysis of the way in which Walter and Maria Nally treated their son, especially with respect to their denial of his problem, would have considerable bearing on the case, as would an analysis of his behavior toward them. After all, as became clear in testimony, this was not an entirely happy family. While Mrs. Nally worked at a comparatively low-level job, Mr. Nally, who had been fired from his position during a scandal three years earlier and had not worked since, usually did not get out of his robe and slippers all day and did not sleep with Mrs. Nally. He spent substantial amounts of the family's resources maintaining another woman in an extramarital affair. Ken strongly disapproved of his father's conduct and his father's treatment of his mother. A full analysis of the case of Ken Nally would require careful examination of the way the people involved treated each other. It would also require an additional professional ethics analysis of the actions of the various physicians in treating Ken, especially those—like Doctors Parker and Bullock—who appear to have treated him without any attempt to assess his mental condition, or Doctors Hall and Evelyn, who released him from the hospital although they believed he was still suicidal. It would also focus further on Ken's friends, including his former roommate, Ernie Hauser, and his girlfriend, Katie Thayer, and their roles in responding to Ken's suicidal problems. Even Ken's own role in these matters invites scrutiny. As one of the pastors said, "Ken liked to get advice but he demonstrated an inability or a lack of willingness to carry it out" (R.T. 425:27–28, testimony of Rea). This pastor also hinted that Ken exhibited a kind of social and ethical immaturity by insisting that his girlfriends had to be blonde, blue-eyed, and tall, and that he "preferred a large bust" (R.T. 426:10–11, testimony of Rea), though this might also be understood as a reaction to his own Japanese heritage (Mrs. Nally was of Japanese ancestry) and partly Japanese appearance. But while this case is broad and complex and a full moral analysis would include scrutiny of the actions and attitudes of family, friends, physicians, and Ken himself, the focus here is whether Grace Church and its pastors, following the standard, accepted practices of the church, mistreated Ken in failing to prevent his suicide.

However, while Grace Church's treatment of Ken appears not to have satisfied professional standards and is thus prima facie morally unacceptable, even if it does seem to have satisfied certain principles of ordinary morality, approaching this moral problem with either the professional ethics prong of our pincer apparatus or the ordinary morality prong does not fully reach the heart of the matter. Thus, although a professional ethics analysis is of considerable initial utility in elucidating the case, the central ethical issue raised by Grace Church's counseling program is something which—while it must include the findings of a professional ethics analysis—remains much more difficult to assess.

The central ethical issue focuses on the fact that the biblical counseling techniques used by Grace Church address depression and suicidal intent as *sin*, not as mental illness, emotional disturbance, or other psychopathology. The secular professional ethics and ordinary morality views of counseling techniques like those used by Grace Church warn that not only do these methods fail to prevent suicides such as Ken's, but increase their likelihood. To conceptualize emotional problems as the product of sin, both views would argue, is to overlook possible physiological contributing factors and to reinforce the patient's hopelessness. To call a person suffering from suicidal ideation "wicked," as Reverend Thomson called Ken, is to exacerbate the sense of worthlessness from which that person already suffers and is likely to contribute to the suicide. It engenders feelings of rejection, isolation, and hopelessness. Certainly, the secular view from professional ethics and ordinary morality argues, the Grace Church program failed to prevent Ken's suicide by failing to assess his danger to himself, failing to refer him to competent professional help, and failing to inform his parents or physicians, but it also did Ken positive harm by intensifying his suicidal feelings. This is the basis of the charge of outrageous conduct brought by the plaintiffs against the pastors and the church. They had full knowledge of his past attempts at suicide, the charge claims, and either deliberately or recklessly aggravated his already intense feelings of guilt, knowing this might well lead to his death.

But while an analysis in terms of professional and ordinary ethics can point to this issue, it cannot really address it. It is at just this point that, it seems, the practices of religious groups cannot be scrutinized wholly in terms of professional standards or the professional ethics or ordinary morality concerns they raise. Grace Church can defend its practice by insisting that its claim that depression—and with it suicidal ideation—is *caused by sin* is a fundamental religious truth, though not, of course, one that is or can be understood by either the secular psychotherapeutic professions or by ordinary morality. "Sin" is a *religious* concept, this defense would continue, and is intelligible only in religious discourse and understanding; but while this concept cannot be understood in the secular world, its profound reality cannot be denied. Since the practices of the church are rooted in this fundamental religious claim, it can therefore insist, such practices are simply inaccessible to secular scrutiny.

Furthermore, the basic tenet that depression is caused by sin would seem to explain the deeper, religious reason for the counseling program's "failure" to observe the three basic professional standards for counseling suicidal people. (This, of course, would have rendered superfluous the church's defense that it did meet those standards.) After all, in the first place, to pursue a diagnosis in terms of lethality would be to focus on a biomedical model of suicide, not one that conceptualizes suicide as sin, since the very concepts of "diagnosis" and "lethality" suggest a disease process with a predictable prognosis. As the church's attorneys put it:

> The religious and spiritual counseling of the Church cannot be subsumed under an essentially *medical* model of psychotherapy, and treated as giving rise to quasi-medical duties to diagnose psychiatric problems and refer persons to psychiatrists. To be sure, both psychiatry and religion may deal with *human emotions* and *human problems,* but that no more makes religion a subspecies of psychiatry than psychiatry is a branch of religion. . . . They are different disciplines that operate on different premises (Respondents' Brief, 27, n. 62).

In the second place, in this view, to refer a suicidal person to secular psychologists and psychiatrists would be to encourage contact with professionals who would undermine that person's (correct) conception of himself as sinful. The effort would be to transform the patient's conception of the problem away from casting it as guilt or sin to one that reconceptualizes it as disease, thus displacing the responsibility that the pastoral counselor seeks to have the counselee assume. The effort in the pastoral counseling practiced at Grace Church is to help the counselee see that a person's troubles are the product of his or her own sinful choices and that by repudiating and repenting of these choices, the problems one is causing oneself can be resolved.

In the third place, in this view, to inform family or physicians might permit intervention by outsiders who also would bring an incorrect understanding of suicide to the situation; they would thus interfere with the spiritual progress made in pastoral counseling. Much as, according to the Christian Science view examined in chapter 2, treatment by medical doctors is believed to reinforce a person's misconception of the spiritual nature of man and hence the nonphysical nature of illness, so in the view of Grace Church's pastors, diagnosis or treatment of Ken's depression and suicidal tendencies by secular medical professionals would have reinforced the misconception that depression is an illness and not the product of his own sin. It would have thus inappropriately shifted the responsibility and the blame away from Ken. That depression and suicidal ideation are sin, it would be argued, is simply basic religious doctrine, a matter of faith and belief for Grace Church; therefore, the three standards set by professional ethics are altogether inapplicable. According to this view, the pastoral counseling Grace Church provided to help Ken cannot be critiqued even provisionally with secular professional or ordinary morality.

Given the analysis pursued in chapter 1 and throughout this book, this defense of Grace Church cannot easily be challenged. Under the assumption that a religious group is in general capable of identifying what it recognizes as its own most basic beliefs and theological commitments, it is not possible to dismiss the claim that depression and suicidal ideation are caused by sin without violating the basic requirement of our methodology, namely that no stand be taken on the veracity of background religious beliefs. It might seem, therefore, that it is simply not possible to challenge precisely those features of Grace Church's treatment of Ken Nally that appear to pose the most central moral problems.

This, however, is not the case. By applying the strategies of analysis developed in this book, the considerations of professional and ordinary ethics can be brought to bear on the practices of Grace Church—without violating the canon that basic, fundamental, 0-level religious imperatives not be challenged.

## The New Strategies of Analysis: A Further Look at the Practices of Grace Church

The analysis of a specific practice within organized religion with the criteria of professional and ordinary ethics—here, Grace Church's pastoral counseling practice—illuminates certain moral problems, but is only partially adequate. The additional principles of analysis developed in chapters 1–4 can be employed to extend this examination. Doing so requires that these additional principles be applied in the order in which they were developed in chapters 1–4; in the process, this will show why the principles are to be understood as nested in character, with the prior principle identifying those practices that are candidates for examination under the following principle.

Like any rich and interesting real-life case, the case of Ken Nally can be read in various ways, just one of which will be explored here. However, it should not be expected that this case or, for that matter, any other case will fit tidily into the analytic framework developed in this book. Nor should it be supposed that, despite the extensive deposition and trial testimony available, the evidence concerning the various aspects of the case is adequate. Nevertheless, this framework should supply a working sketch of how actual cases concerning ordinary, accepted practices within the various denominations of organized religion can be scrutinized in ethical terms, in a way that both makes use of and advances beyond what can be gained from an initial analysis in professional and ordinary ethics terms.

## 0-level and Upper-Order Doctrines
## and Practices

Following the procedure developed in chapter 1, the various teachings, doctrines, imperatives, and practices involved in a specific case may be distinguished. This will allow differentiation between those that function at the fundamental or 0-order level, together with elements of the background theology, and those that function as intermediate or higher-level developed practices and teachings. There is no easy procedure for making these discriminations; it is a matter of beginning both with a specific practice, together with any relevant historical material and a general account of a group's traditions and theological beliefs, in order to identify the underlying motivation or raison-d'etre for a practice.

Since Grace Church is an independent congregation and was not founded until 1956, it might be maintained that there is no relevant history for this group; it might also be asserted that the motivation for the development of its counseling program lay in its wish to imitate and compete with other successful religious groups. However, it is much more plausible to recognize Grace Church's essentially Baptist heritage and thus its origins in Protestant conservative traditions generally to identify the teachings and imperatives that may motivate this practice, thus construing the rationale for the church's counseling program in the most generous, least skeptical way. The first project, then, is to identify any 0-level imperatives and background theological beliefs that may be involved.

The background theology of Grace Church is much like that of other Protestant groups, but distinctive in one respect: it gives a particularly prominent role to the concept of sin. Reliably identifying the fundamental or 0-level imperatives that function as the basis of its pastoral counseling practice would necessitate extended discussion. For the sake of brevity, it may be conjectured that the basic imperative relevant in the practice is an amalgam of two distinct injunctions: the biblical command "confess your sins," discussed at length in chapter 1 and again in chapter 4, together with the obligation of *caritas,* or Christian love for others, expressed as charitable concern and aid. These fundamental religious imperatives are initially addressed to all believers and are perfectly general; they are basic, 0-level imperatives that, under methodological constraints, cannot be challenged, either with respect to the truth of the background theological beliefs on which they rest or with respect to their own morality.

To be sure, different readings of the Nally case can be explored by supposing that other 0-level imperatives lie at the base of Grace Church's practices. For instance, the pastoral counseling program might be construed as an expression of a fundamental imperative to preach and convert, rooted in the same basic doctrines considered in chapter 3. On this reading, the mission of the "counseling" program would be to promote affiliation with the group and to alter religious belief. The church's particular contact with Ken in offering him counseling would have served not so much to let him confide his troubles and to give him help in resolving them, but to bring about a change in his faith that would result in still stronger ties to the church. Some aspects of the church's practices and its counseling program suggest that this is not an implausible interpretation. However, since it will not produce as coherent a reading of the case as the interpretation explored here, it will not be pursued.

Assuming that the underlying imperatives are best identified as those of confession and charitable aid, the mechanism that has developed within the religious tradition for putting the imperatives into practice is that of personal interaction or consultation between the priest, pastor, or other religious official and the parishioner. This mechanism may be conceptualized as a first-order practice. Like any first-order practice, it introduces distinctive elements. Consultation between pastor and parishioner, even for the purpose of confession and charitable aid, already specifies and emphasizes certain features of the two initial 0-level imperatives. Specifically, it emphasizes the obligation to confess one's sins on the part of the parishioner or consultee and emphasizes the obligation of *caritas* on the part of the pastor or consultant. But it thus introduces asymmetries that are not part of the original perfectly general imperative, since by emphasizing some features it deemphasizes others. It preserves the obligation of the parishioner to confess to the pastor but does not oblige the pastor to confess to the parishioner.[16] It preserves the obligation of the pastor to give charitable aid to the parishioner, but not the obligation of the parishioner to help the pastor. Alternative mechanisms, while introducing other limitations, would not preserve these asymmetries but would create others. Inasmuch as the developed practice of consultation between pastor and parishioner specifies and interprets the underlying imperatives in identifiably restricted ways, it gives rise to classic moral problems associated with disparate relationships of power and vulnerability, many of which have already been considered here.

Disparate relationships of power and vulnerability raise basic questions, even at this abstract level, about the character of the interaction: it permits one party to control the interaction and thus, at least when not checked by fiduciary obligations or other constraints, to treat the other as it wishes. One party is in a position to be active; the other is cast in a comparatively passive, recipient role. The character of the particular interaction in any given case will be a function of the degree of disparity in power and of the degree to which, in the absence of constraints, the more powerful party exploits the disparity. There is, of course, an extensive professional ethics literature on this topic in the secular professions. However, the issue of disparate relationships of power and vulnerability is markedly more difficult in the context of religion because we do not know how to take account of the fact that one party in this unequal relationship is a pastor or priest, ordained within a religious group, and the other is a lay person.[17] The relationship, of course, bears many similarities to the disparities of power between doctor and patient or attorney and client; but the relationship between clergy and laity cannot be reduced to fit these models, except by engaging in unwarranted secularization of the issue. A preliminary conception of what issues are raised by the development of consultative relationships between pastor and parishioner can be reached by applying the categories of professional ethics, but this provides only a partial hold on the issue.

The issues are to some degree resolved in the second-order form in which the consultative relationship between pastor and parishioner is cast. Drawing on models from secular counseling and psychotherapy, it is formalized as *pastoral counseling*. This practice assumes many of the structural features that suggest a therapeutic or medical model: the scheduled session of fixed length, held in a private office with a closed door, arranged by appointment made in advance by the counseling program's secretary, repeated on a weekly or other regular basis, and so on. Interaction between pastor and parishioner to permit confession and render help could take a wide variety of forms, but this is the primary one found in the practice which has come to be known as pastoral counseling, employed not only by Grace Church but by most mainline and evangelical denominations.

This practice reinforces two features: that its objective is therapeutic, designed to relieve or ease the client's emotional distress, and that it is to be conducted through counseling, that is, by means of discussion and advice, rather than, for example, punishment, intimidation, or other measures. It therefore dictates how disparities in power in the relationship between pastor and parishioner are to be resolved—in a way that is therapeutic for the parishioner. However, this does not put an end to the issues raised, for this is not just counseling, it is *pastoral* counseling. As such, it has distinctive features not easily accessible with the categories of ordinary or professional ethics and not easily assessible with respect to how disparities in power are to be resolved.

After all, pastoral counseling involves the pastor/counselor's employing *religious* insight, perhaps as well as other principles of human psychology, to address an individual's emotional or other problems. But with this arises the occasion for the pastor/counselor to interpret or construct the parishioner's problem, as well as to identify what are to count as appropriate remedies. This occurs as the pastor draws on the religious group's doctrinal teachings and established practices, and will occur along the same general lines, with comparatively minor individual variation, for all of the clergy within a given group. The pastor, as it were, employs the group's theory as a filter or lens through which to discern the characteristics of the parishioner's problem and does not recognize that while this process highlights some features, it blurs others out of recognition. As Karen Lebacqz points out, "The primary role of clergy is rarely defined as 'the social construction of reality' or 'defining reality.' Yet this is precisely what clergy do."[18] It is in this way that the pastors of a given group emphasize some aspects of religious insight common to a larger religious tradition and at the same time eclipse other aspects. Just so, in the pastoral counseling offered by Grace Church, specific features grow particularly conspicuous: an emphasis on sin and reliance on prayer. Thus the pastor, working from a position of unequal power vis-à-vis the parishioner, constructs the parishioner's problem for him or her, as well as communicating what should be done to resolve it. The pastors at Grace Church all interpreted Ken's problem for him in the same way: it was a problem of sin and the guilt arising from sin, a problem that could be resolved only by repenting of sin and engaging in prayer.

The interpretation and construction of emotional problems as matters of sin and guilt to be remedied by repentance and prayer is thus distinctive and definitive of Grace Church's variety of pastoral counseling, as well as of many similar Bible-based groups. But this interpretation need not occupy a central role in all pastoral counseling. Other versions in other, rather different, denominations may emphasize quite different matters, such as compassion, love, grace, the redemptive value of suffering, or other basic teachings of Christian theology. Even with similar histories and with similar structural features, pastoral counseling practices are not and need not be uniform among various religious groups.

The variety of pastoral counseling developed within Grace Church is also distinctive in that, unlike forms practiced in many mainline groups, it does not give any role to such concepts as early childhood trauma, repression, transference, libido, social roles, or other concepts characteristic of the secular psychological, psychiatric, and sociological professions and so does not interpret the problem as one of psychopathology or disruptive social influences. Nor does it advocate supplementary psychological or psychiatric counseling as a remedy. Like all forms of pastoral counseling in various denominations, Grace Church's form of pastoral counseling is idiosyncratic and distinctive. It is this fact that allows us to see that Grace Church's pastoral counseling practices emphasizing sin and advocating reliance on prayer are *developed,* upper-level practices—even though their doctrinal roots may lie in measures intended to facilitate confession and to help persons in need.

Issues raised by the emphasis on sin and reliance on prayer in counseling persons with problems concern whether emphasis on sin, and with it guilt, can be therapeutically effective or has predictably negative effects. This is a hotly contested issue. For instance, in a spirited discussion at a conference session on pastoral counseling, Howard Sudak, a psychiatrist, referred repeatedly to the "morbidity engendered by the church," and Scott Sullender, a Presbyterian minister and pastoral counselor who was one of the expert witnesses in the *Nally* case, argued that "we need a concept of 'healthy' religion, since a lot of churches make people sick." In contrast, Newton Malony, a member of the faculty of conservative evangelical Fuller Theological Seminary, asserted that "while psychotropic drugs such as tricyclic antidepressants can reduce agitation, they cannot reduce guilt."[19] Guilt, in the view of the first two of these speakers, is a construct and symptom of underlying emotional distress; in the view of the third, guilt is the basic category, which is often expressed or exhibited as emotional distress. While the view from professional ethics allows us to see the degree to which the pastor constructs the parishioner's problem during the personal interaction between the two of them, it is nevertheless the case that the issue is closely tied to doctrinal matters about sin and guilt and their relation to secular conceptions of mental illness. Although professional ethics has a somewhat greater purchase at the second-order level of developed practice, its hold is by no means complete.

Similar pastoral counseling practices that emphasize sin and prayer are found in many different denominations, most of them comparatively fundamentalist in character. But each of them has distinctive features, as do the practices of Grace Church. The details of Grace Church's distinctive practices can be isolated more specifically by identifying that set of mechanisms that constitutes its counseling program and that enables it to put into practice the fundamental mandates of confession and charitable aid. These practices are already developed as involving a pastor-parishioner consultative relationship that emphasizes sin on the part of the parishioner and recommends that the parishioner resolve his or her difficulties through prayer; these distinctive details represent greater specifications of the upper-order practices, which—while they do not in this case seem clearly designed to resolve moral problems at the lower levels—provide further specificity of a practice. Two matters described in the case of Ken Nally come quickly to mind: the practice of using tape-recorded sermons and lectures as a supplement to counseling and that of assigning a set of biblical passages to the counselee to be used in prayer. These may seem superficial matters, but they play a central role in the way Grace Church conducts its pastoral counseling.

As the testimony showed, Ken frequently listened to tapes of Reverend MacArthur's sermons. On at least one occasion, Ken was sent a tape by one of the church's pastors. This was the tape sent by Reverend Cory with the covering letter saying "Our hearts are deceitful and wicked, and a tape like this is good to keep it in check." The tapes Ken listened to presumably also included those that the members of the church who had called to pay respects to his parents collected from his room after his death.

Grace Church's pastoral counseling practices also emphasized the use of scriptural passages to reply to the concerns a person might raise in counseling sessions. For instance, when Ken told Reverend Rea that he could not cope with his feelings regarding love and hate, Rea's response was to give him the appropriate scriptural passage; doing so was intended "to teach him God's standard that loving is giving," explained Rea (Respondents' Brief, Appendix, 5a). When Ken asked Rea what might be expected of him concerning his job, Rea's answers were, "Glorify God in all things" and "Delight in the Lord" (37:5). Ken was also assigned scriptural passages to use in prayer. It was apparently this practice that Reverend Thomson had in mind in terminating their "discipling" relationship, saying Ken "didn't do his homework" and was an uncooperative counselee. It is even possible that counseling assignments of this type were responsible for the Bible verses scrawled on the three-by-five card found under Ken's body after the suicide.[20] In any case, it is these quite specific, developed, upper-level matters that ultimately constitute the ways Grace Church puts its most basic imperatives, in particular those concerning confession from parishioner to pastor and aid from pastor to parishioner, into practice. Though seemingly trivial, these specific, concrete features of the church's practices are not.

After all, it is these superficial, developed practices at the uppermost levels that are most immediately vulnerable to professional and ordinary ethical critique. The use of tape recordings in counseling raises problems insofar as they are used outside the actual counseling encounter: Do they serve to reinforce whatever progress was made during the session, permitting the counselee to continue to reflect on his or her own problems and difficulties, or do they intensify the counselee's sense of isolation when listened to without the pastor/counselor's potentially comforting presence? The independent use of tapes leaves their interpretation open, since the pastor/counselor is not there to correct misunderstandings; in this sense, the home use of tapes might be said to lack adequate safeguards. This is an important consideration when tapes are used in counseling individuals who, like Ken, are severely disturbed. Other questions suggested by issues in professional and business ethics arise: How should the use of tapes for home listening be viewed in the light of the overwhelming client load on Grace Church's counseling program? Is this a realistic way of making pastoral comfort always available even when, as Reverend MacArthur said, "the mass of people who pull at the pastoral staff . . . is more than any of us can handle," and hence a responsible way of responding to a difficult distributive problem? Or, as one of many alternatives, should it be seen as a way of stretching the counseling staff's services in order not only to provide help for the 50 percent of its clients who were already members of Grace Church, but to encourage the other 50 percent to join? Of what relevance is it that Grace Church operated a bookstore and a thriving mail order business, the latter sending out seven thousand tapes a week, selling $500,000 worth of taped sermons a year? Were the tapes less a counseling aid than a market item? Was the counseling enterprise a way of creating markets for the tapes? Or, on the other hand, was it the case that the tapes and books functioned as a trustworthy extension of the therapeutic encounter, permitting counseling to progress more effectively than would otherwise be possible with limited, less flexibly scheduled visits? If the latter is the case, then counseling aids of this sort might well be a commendable, constructive addition to the counseling program. These questions can be addressed with the apparatus of professional and ordinary ethics, including business ethics, largely independently of underlying doctrinal beliefs and imperatives. As upper-level practices, they are the ones most wholly accessible to normative critique. Whatever conclusion is ultimately reached as to the ethics of conducting counseling using tape-recorded sermons and lectures, it will not be an adequate response to say simply that doing so is a religious practice, a practice treated as standard and basic to a particular denomination and thus immune to critique. Grace Church's pastors were practicing what they preached, but as in religious groups generally, this is not always an adequate defense.

In distinguishing among levels of practice in this way, we may also expect to find third-order "excuses"—teachings, doctrines, and practices intended to excuse residual moral problems not resolved in the development of lower-level practices. Excuses are not particularly prominent among the teachings and practices of Grace Church or in the testimony presented in *Nally*, but then there is little evidence of awareness on the part of the pastors of the moral problems their practices generate. They remained unaware, for instance, that any of their other members had committed suicide. If anything resembles an excuse in the discussion of *Nally*, it is Reverend MacArthur's insistence that the counseling pastor must not only investigate the sin but offer forgiveness. This obligation might seem designed to mitigate the harshness of a practice that makes emphasis on sin central in approaching human problems. To insist that counselors also offer forgiveness might be understood as acknowledgement of the blunt, negative impact of continuing emphasis on sin and the way such emphasis reinforces feelings of unworthiness and hopelessness, but also as suggesting that this negative impact can be softened and mitigated by other important features of developed pastoral counseling practices. Here, and here alone, the pastors may have deviated from the obligations Grace Church's practice imposed on them: while they may have believed that the strongly negative impact of emphasizing sin is to be excused because forgiveness, with its strongly positive emotional impact, can be offered at the same time as a remedy, there is little evidence that they offered or emphasized such forgiveness in counseling Ken.

In examining a practical case such as that of Ken Nally, we could have begun at either end, so to speak, either by first (conjecturally) identifying the underlying imperative(s) and then using these to identify the features of the superficial levels of actual practice, or by beginning with these superficial practices and using them to discern the underlying imperatives at their roots. The most satisfactory, extended analysis will no doubt do both, working back and forth from both ends at once in attempting to construct a coherent, accurate, sensitive picture of the case. At each deeper level the value of an analysis conducted in the categories of professional and ordinary ethics is less tight and the problems are less accessible. Yet this is not a failure of method, but rather the success of a method that allows the (partly) nonsecular nature of religious practice to be seen.

### Fiduciary Responsibilities

An initial principle of differentiation to scrutinize the practices of organized religion was developed in chapter 1; it was then suggested in chapter 2 that the range of upper-level practices open to ethical scrutiny could then be examined under the fiduciary principle, namely, that religious professionals have an obligation to protect or further the interests in connection with which the parishioner seeks help. This is to emphasize those features of organized religion that are more strongly analogous to those of the secular professions—where clients or patients seek the services of professionals such as lawyers or doctors to protect or further certain interests, such as their legal rights or their physical health—and thus to draw again, though only partially, on a professional ethics analysis. To apply the fiduciary principle in reviewing Grace Church's upper-level counseling practices, we must ask what interests Ken sought to protect or further in seeking help and whether the services provided him could reasonably be expected to do so.

It may seem clear from the testimony why Ken initially sought help from the counselors at Grace Church. He was having continuing problems in maintaining relationships with women; he suffered periods of depression; and he was also plagued by ideas of suicide. In fact, Ken had been seriously depressed since 1975. According to a review of his medical records, notes, and correspondence conducted at the time of the trial by Stephen Wilson, M.D., a board certified psychiatrist, the appropriate DSM III diagnosis for Ken was major affective illness, depression, of a recurrent type.[21] It may thus seem obvious that what Ken sought was relief from depression and help in avoiding suicide. However, the church's defense insisted that what Ken sought was "religious guidance, counsel and comfort" (Respondents' Brief, 27), and this may seem to be a rather different thing. Why Ken sought help from the church might seem to be an empirical question which, since it is no longer possible to question Ken, it is impossible to answer. However, as seen in chapter 2, the emergence of a religious group's fiduciary obligation to a member or user of its services arises not simply from what the client seeks from the group, but what the group offers the client. What interests the client can expect to have furthered are not simply a function of what the client wants, but of the way in which the church announces or represents itself. While it is not possible to be certain why Ken sought help or what kind of help he sought, the plausibility of our speculation as to his motives is increased by considering what type of help Grace Church offered.

The counseling service, described in the church's 1978 annual report as "organized in six teams of compassionate, competent counselors" (Appellants' Brief, 14), appears to have made extensive claims about the kinds of problems it could handle. Thomson's *Guide for Biblical Counselors,* which the service used in training its counseling staff, told counselors and prospective counselors that they could handle a wide range of personal difficulties, including "someone's extreme problem like suicidal tendency or a nervous breakdown (ibid., 12). The scope of the counseling service was a matter of some dispute; head pastor MacArthur insisted that "we don't run a counseling center as such. We aren't paid for that, and we don't solicit that. We just respond as pastors, so what we do is on a spiritual level, and a biblical level, or a prayer level" (California Supreme Court, majority opinion, 4). The majority opinion delivered by the California Supreme Court accepted this claim, asserting that Grace Church did not have a professional or clinical counseling ministry. On the other hand, the concurring opinion of Justice Kaufman, though agreeing with the lower court's judgment of nonsuit and dismissal of the action, countered that the Grace Church pastors "expressly held themselves out as fully competent to deal with the most severe psychological disorders, including major depression with suicidal symptoms," and also that they "developed a close counseling relationship with Kenneth Nally for that very purpose" (ibid., concurring opinion, 2). The picture that emerges from the record, according to the concurring opinion, "is decidedly *not* that of a small band of simple pastors who offered occasional counseling on minor matters to the faithful few" (ibid., 3).

This may seem to be a minor factual quibble between the five justices supporting the majority opinion and the two signing the concurring, minority opinion, a quibble of interest only in interpreting California's basic principle of appellate review that when reviewing a judgment of nonsuit the court must accept as true the evidence most favorable to the plaintiff. The minority concurring opinion complains that the majority has reversed this legal principle, violating it repeatedly throughout its opinion, and that the majority "quite inexplicably" overlooks the "substantial evidence" adduced by the plaintiffs (ibid., 2–3). While there is an important issue concerning the legal principle of evidence here, the issue under discussion is central to the ethical issue. What is crucial is how Grace Church announced and advertised its counseling services and how this would be understood by someone in serious need of counseling, including someone in Ken Nally's situation. Of course, different members of the church, as well as different attenders and nonmembers, may see the counseling offered by the church in different ways, and hence they will regard it as appropriate to approach the counselors for help with different needs. Given Ken's extreme difficulties with depression and thoughts of suicide, however, the claims made by the various pastors and by Thomson's *Guide for Biblical Counselors* could have been expected to have a particular, predictable impact: they would tell him the pastors could help.

Furthermore, not only were the counselors announced as competent to treat a full range of mental illnesses, expressly including depression, they also were trained to regard themselves as competent to treat these conditions. Thomson's *Guide* asserts that unless the client's problem has a physiological cause, such as a brain tumor, "every emotional

problem" is within the competence of the counselor to handle—
including "drug abuse, alcoholism, phobias, deep depression, suicide,
mania, nervous breakdown, manic-depressive [disorder] and schizo-
phrenia." The *Guide* contains discussions of a number of these, with
hypothetical questions and answers interspersed throughout the text.
The exchange on suicide reads:

> [Question] "You mean *I* could counsel with an extreme prob-
> lem like a suicidal tendency or nervous breakdown or something
> like that?"
> [Answer] "With the proper understanding of God's Word to
> diagnose and treat the problems, this could not only be done
> occasionally but could become the rule."[22]

It is clear that Grace Church announced itself as being able to provide the kind of help Ken could be expected to seek during his suicidal
crises. While, according to the majority opinion in the supreme court
decision, the pastors "in essence . . . held themselves out as *pastoral*
counselors able to deal with a variety of problems—not as professional, medical, or psychiatric counselors" (California Supreme Court,
majority opinion, 4), they also specifically claimed to be able to deal
with the kinds of problems professional, medical, and psychiatric
counselors do. They advertised themselves as pastoral counselors, but
as pastoral counselors able to treat depression and suicidal ideation—
precisely what Ken sought. It is this interactive relation between the
interests for the protection or furtherance of which a member approaches the church (though these may never be fully clear) and the
interests the church announces itself as able to protect or further, that
gives rise to the fiduciary obligation incumbent upon the church. In
the view of the concurring supreme court opinion, the pastors "pat-
ently held themselves out as competent to counsel the mentally ill"—
"inviting" a relationship that "contains elements of trust and dependence." like that "in the therapist-patient context" (ibid., concurring
opinion, 14, 19, 14, 14, respectively). They offered Ken what looked
like psychotherapeutic help for his problems, although the content and
underlying assumptions of this help were different. In this sense the
church's pastoral counseling program functioned as a kind of alterna-

tive psychotherapy (much as Christian Science functions as an alternative medical care system) and engendered the same fiduciary obligations. To the extent that Ken came to the church's counseling program at its express invitation for help with his emotional problems and to prevent suicide, the church had an obligation not to take advantage of him or to otherwise fail him in protecting these interests. But this obligation, it seems, the church failed to meet.

Of course, the fact of Ken's suicide does not establish that the church failed to observe its obligation. To secure this claim, it would need to be established that the church could have prevented the suicide but did not do so, or at least that alternative forms of treatment that would have been successful were not supplied by the church or made available by referral. It may be that the pastoral counseling that Grace Church supplied Ken in fact kept him from suicide for several years before his final act. However, the evidence does not suggest this, given his increasing disturbance and the greater lethality of his later attempts. In any case, it is clear that the counseling program did not refer Ken to psychologists or psychiatrists presumably able to treat his problem, or inform his parents or others who might have hospitalized him or otherwise prevented his suicide.

In what might be a still greater violation of the fiduciary principle, the form of counseling that Grace Church provided may also have exacerbated Ken's suicidal urges. Dr. Stephen Wilson, asked what he thought the effect of treating depression as "caused by sin" would be—especially when continued over a period of years with various counselors—testified that it might have no effect, that it might make it worse, or that it might make it better, but that he believed that in the case of Ken Nally, it had made it worse. Ken's parents clearly believed that Grace Church's particular form of biblical pastoral counseling had caused his death. That Ken actually did commit suicide is not proof that the type of counseling performed by Grace Church increases suicidal tendencies; only a sustained study of suicide rates in matched subjects receiving counseling at Grace Church versus standard psychiatric treatment (and perhaps versus an untreated control group) would establish this. Samuel Ericsson, one of the church's attorneys, did claim in his opening statement before the court that Reverend Thomson had counseled "well over two hundred seriously depressed individuals" (R.T., vol. 1, 58), and that Nally was the only one who had killed himself. This was an attempt to establish comparative data, although it turned out that Nally was not the church's first suicide. Nevertheless, the type of counseling Grace Church offers might actually be more effective than conventional therapy in preventing suicide. Much as in Christian Science, however, a church that holds out its religious treatment as effective in resolving human problems—whether physiological or emotional—incurs a duty to ascertain whether its practice *is* effective. None of the records suggests that any attempt was made to determine the effectiveness of Grace Church's biblical counseling methods; the mistaken claim that no other member of Grace Church had ever committed suicide underscores its lack of conscientious self-examination. The fiduciary obligation is not better satisfied by using unproved methods (especially those that preclude proved methods) than by using methods actually known to be ineffective. By using methods for which it had no evidence of efficacy in treating Ken's suicidal crises—effectively blocking referral to other, established methods—Grace Church failed to satisfy the fiduciary duty it assumed toward Ken in announcing that it was able to help.

There is an additional complication in the story, one that renders the case still more difficult to assess. Though it appears that Ken originally came to the pastors of Grace Church seeking help with his depression and suicidal tendencies, as the counseling progressed Ken's aims seems to have shifted to "getting right with God" and were no longer focused on lifting depression or avoiding suicide. If this is so, the church's defense (though it provided no evidence for this claim) that Ken came simply for "religious guidance, counsel and comfort," as distinct from specific help in relieving depression and avoiding suicide, becomes more plausible. It is, of course, impossible to know what Ken really wanted in the months and weeks before his suicide or what help he sought. But he did begin to describe himself as wanting to "be with God." It might be conjectured that he used pastoral counseling to find out whether suicide would permit or prevent his achieving his ultimate aim, and it is a plausible conjecture insofar as it concerns someone living in a religious culture where personal aims concerning one's relationship with God are central. In rejecting Ken's proposal of marriage, Katie Thayer told him, "You've got to put God first in your life," and although Katie presumably had no such intention, it could be that—in his intensely disturbed state—Ken had begun to see suicide as a way of satisfying her admonition. If Ken's aims in approaching Grace Church's counselors did undergo a shift of this sort, it would be an example of a phenomenon analogous to the reevaluation of outcome states discussed in connection with Jehovah's Witnesses in chapter 2— a reevaluation that, because it substitutes distinctively religious ends for the ordinary personal interests with which people often first approach religious institutions, has the effect of removing the matter from the scope of the fiduciary principle. Such a shift in values may be part of the point of pastoral counseling, inasmuch as its objective is helping people in difficulty approach their problems in a *religious* way. As the California Superior Court put it, "Pastoral counseling is shepherding the people into a deeper level of faith, to instill Christian realities and values" (Respondents' Brief, 11, citing R.T. 2050). When it substitutes distinctively religious ends for those dictated by ordinary self-interests, pastoral counseling also alters the way in which it is itself subject to the fiduciary principle.

The shift in Ken's interests, if it occurred, renders Grace Church's treatment of his difficulties after this point still more difficult to critique using the professional ethics apparatus. Nevertheless, if the shift occurred, it was presumably the result of the teachings of the church— including those put forth in pastoral counseling. If the effect of pastoral-counseling practices in promoting a person's reevaluation of his or her own ends is to make the way he or she is treated under these practices less susceptible to moral criticism, the practice becomes self-insulating against criticism. This fact, however, raises the third basis on which we can assess such practices.

### *Off-scale Claims*

Chapter 3 developed a third principle for assessing the practices of organized religion: that the use of unprovable, self-interest-gratifying, off-scale claims about the afterlife is to be viewed as suspect, especially in situations within the scope of fiduciary responsibility, when they are used to influence behavior or to excuse policies that do. Off-scale claims of this type are inaccessible to and uninterpretable within ordinary professional situations. Yet such claims appear to have played a substantial role in the counseling of Ken Nally. According to the plaintiffs, they also played a causal role in his suicide.

On repeated occasions (as documented in both deposition and trial testimony), Ken acknowledged that he "couldn't cope" or "couldn't live this life," and otherwise made it clear that he was considering suicide. He repeatedly told Katie Thayer that he wanted to "go home and be with God." On several occasions, he asked Grace Church's pastors what would become of a person who committed suicide. For example, during a session with Reverend Thomson after he was released from Verdugo Hills, Ken asked whether Christians who committed suicide would go to heaven. Thomson replied to this question by telling Ken that once a person was saved (which, in accordance with the group's born-again theology, Ken presumably believed himself to be), he was always saved and would go to heaven no matter what. Thomson testified that he also told Ken that he should not be thinking in this way. If Ken's conception of his own interests had shifted to "getting right with God" instead of relieving depression and avoiding suicide, however, it may be that—in his extremely disturbed condition—the effect of Thomson's answer was to lead him to believe that committing suicide would not jeopardize his relationship with God or preclude his going to heaven. The effect of these claims, like those discussed in chapter 2, may be described as altering his "risk budget," thus altering his risk behavior: Ken would no longer seek to avoid suicide. This, I think, is the intuitive basis of his parents' claim that the church *caused* Ken to kill himself.

Particular dispute during the supreme court's consideration of the case concerned the admissibility of a tape involving this issue. The tape presented one of Reverend Thomson's pastoral counseling lectures (described by the defense as having a "rambling, classroom give-and-take quality" [Respondents' Brief, 51]), and was produced and sold by the church. At one point in this tape, Thomson described suicide as God's way of calling sinners home: "Suicide is one of the ways that the

Lord takes home a disobedient believer. . . . Suicide for a believer is the Lord saying, 'Okay, come on home. Can't use you anymore on earth. If you're not going to deal with those things in your life, come on home'(Appellants' Brief, 43). Since the tape was not recorded until 1980, eighteen months after Ken's death, Ken could not have heard it; the plaintiffs, however, contended that the tape represented the kind of view Reverend Thomson held of suicide and that Ken surely would have been counseled by him in the same fashion. Since the legal issue was one of proximate causation in Ken's death, the tape was not admitted into evidence. But the reason for the volatile disagreement about it may well have to do with the particular nature of the claim: if Ken had ever heard such a claim, its effect might well have been to *encourage* him to commit suicide. It clearly makes an afterlife promise, one that is clearly self-interest gratifying: it would suggest to Ken that he could be "home" with God in heaven, even if he did commit suicide. The inducement may be stronger: the claim that "suicide is God's way of calling disobedient believers home" might well have suggested to Ken not only that he would be received in heaven if he did kill himself, but that God *wanted* him to do so—that is, that the suicidal urges he was experiencing were God's way of telling him, sinner that he was, that it was time to come home. The pastors had repeatedly told him what a sinner he was. What other inference, it might seem to Ken, was there to make? Thus, Ken could easily have understood such claims as the off-scale, unprovable, ultimate self-interest-gratifying claim that God expected him to kill himself. We cannot of course know whether Ken actually did understand these claims in this way, but such a conjecture, in the context of Ken's new interest in "getting right with God" and his possible reevaluation of his interests, is not implausible. This is not to say that the church taught that suicide was permissible (a misrepresentation it vigorously denied in the trial court) but rather that the teachings it did convey—that a person who was already saved would go to heaven, even if he or she did commit suicide—would expectably be understood in this way by someone in Ken's condition. We cannot assume that these off-scale claims are false; however, when viewed in their function of removing from its scope practices that would otherwise be covered by the fiduciary principle, we must at least regard them as suspect.

Another unprovable, off-scale claim—though not involving afterlife matters—played a role in the *Nally* case. During the suicide attempt that had hospitalized Ken at Verdugo Hills, he had apparently lain on his arm while unconscious, injuring and partly paralyzing it. Two weeks later, at the end of the week he spent at his parents' home and on the last day they saw him alive, Ken had an argument with his father. Mr. Nally attempted to resolve the argument by saying, "Look, let's go away somewhere. We'll play ball like we used to." Ken replied that he could not play ball because of his injured arm, and that the people at the church had told him it was "God's punishment" for his suicide attempt (California Supreme Court, majority opinion, 10). This claim would seem to operate against suicide, rather than for it; but it is nevertheless an unprovable claim of the same type. It is even possible that Ken understood it as a claim that God was punishing him for failing to succeed in his suicide attempt. In any case, whether this claim operated for or against suicide, off-scale claims clearly played a substantial role in the church's treatment of Ken—as they do in the practices of many or most other churches too.

As said in chapter 3, afterlife claims—whether about the fate of the suicide, God's will, divine punishment, or any other matter—cannot be assumed to be either true or false, since they are closely connected to matters of background theology and basic doctrine. Strictly speaking, it cannot even be assumed that it was an unfortunate thing that Ken did commit suicide—even though it is highly likely that his death could have been prevented with adequate antidepressant medication and therapy—for it cannot be assumed that claims about afterlife outcomes, and specifically about being called home by God, are incorrect. But this only highlights the potentially influential, even coercive role such claims can play in the treatment of an individual. It is not implausible to conjecture that not only did the pastoral counseling practices of Grace Church fail to prevent Ken's suicide, but that they actually provided inducement for it. Whether the pastors themselves were aware of the effect such afterlife claims might have on someone in Ken's condition is not clear from the record; but whether or not they were, it is clear that they should have been.

## *Moral Handprints*

Finally, in examining the ethical issues presented by a particular religious practice, it is also possible, as argued in chapter 4, to identify the "moral handprint" of a given group. To identify the complete pattern of basic 0-level doctrines and imperatives accepted, as well as those common in other Judeo-Christian groups but rejected by this one, would require a lengthy excursion into Grace Church's theology, but it is already clear that part of that handprint will reveal the centrality of claims about sin. These claims are articulated in its doctrines and reflected in its entire range of practices, including pastoral counseling. To this extent, the handprint of Grace Church already differs from those of most mainstream groups, including liberal Catholicism and Protestantism,—even from contemporary Protestant groups of Calvinist origin. While mainstream groups for the most part accept teachings on original sin or human nature's capacity for sin, they do not accord it the central, emphatic role in either doctrine or practice that Grace Church does.

Looking at the extensive evidence provided in *Nally* provides a way of sketching what is involved in the ethical scrutiny of organized religion. It also shows how ethical scrutiny is different from an examination of legal issues and why the California Supreme Court's dismissal of the case should not for a moment lead us to think there are no further ethical issues here. Even had the case been ruled protected by the First Amendment—an issue mooted by its being declared a nonsuit on the ground of insufficient evidence—this would not show that the case is immune to ethical argument. Quite the contrary, where the walls of legal separation of church and state must remain highest if freedom of religion is to be preserved, ethical scrutiny—which carries only moral force, not the coercive power of the state—becomes most appropriate. The supreme court dismissed *Nally* at least in part, as its majority opinion clearly shows, out of a refusal to create a new duty to refer for nontherapist counselors, including but not limited to pastoral counselors. It feared that the creation of a legal duty to refer might "stifle all gratuitous or religious counseling" for fear of the liability to which such counseling would expose clergy or others (ibid., 28). But moral criticism does not impose legal liability; thus, gratuitous and religious counseling can be protected from the litigiousness prevalent in other areas of professional activity while still exposing it to the kind of criticism it sometimes fully deserves.

Some things have changed at Grace Church since the *Nally* case was first brought over a decade ago. Duane Rea left Grace Church in 1982 and is now a minister in Westport, Washington. Lynn Cory is the pastor of a small church in Laguna Beach, California. Rich Thomson moved to Houston; he is the pastor of Grace Bible Church of Mission Bend, another independent congregation, where he distributes his *Guide for Biblical Counselors*. Thomson's *Guide* is no longer used by Grace Community Church; in any case the section on suicide has been deleted, pending "future inclusion."[23] John MacArthur remains head pastor at Grace Community, which now has twenty thousand members and holds services for ten thousand on an average Sunday. Mac-Arthur's office reports that, while they do make ongoing efforts to encourage people with physiological problems who are under the care of a physician to keep taking their medication, no changes have been made in the church's practice of biblical counseling: "We weren't doing anything wrong, so there is nothing to change. . . . After all, people go to a church because it is a place of refuge. We try to help them."[24]

How, then, should we assess the practices Grace Community Church exhibited in counseling Ken Nally, whether or not they still continue? What result or conclusion can we reach? This may be the wrong question to ask. It is a ubiquitous misconception, especially among observers of applied ethics, that applied normative ethics *solves* ethical problems. This is not always the case; on the contrary, careful ethical analysis often lets us see why a case is difficult, even when we may not have noticed the difficulty before. Applied ethics is a way of making trouble, not avoiding it, and showing where complacency about received, ordinary practices is unwarranted. The considerations advanced here do not resolve the case of Ken Nally; instead, they show us why there is a difficult moral problem in pastoral counseling, both for Grace Church and for other denominations that offer pastoral counseling, whether "biblical" or not. Yet even if it makes trouble, the analysis pursued here may help us distinguish what features of the practices at hand give rise to this trouble and what features are comparatively immune to moral critique.

The pastoral counseling of Ken Nally is just one case among many. Even at that time, Grace Church was scheduling appointments for at least thirty salaried counselors. There are about four hundred and fifty thousand churches in the United States and between 1½ and 2 million pastors.[25] Two major national studies, one in 1957 and one replicating it in 1976, have shown that more people turn to their ministers for help with personal problems than to any other professional.[26] While there has been a small decline in the utilization of clergy in this period, the pastor is still almost twice as likely to be consulted for a personal problem as all nonpsychiatric physicians, one-third more likely to be consulted than a psychiatrist or psychologist, and almost twice as likely to be consulted as other mental health sources.[27] There is some variation among groups: Jews, Episcopalians, and Congregationalists are the least frequent users of clergy counseling; fundamentalists and, to a lesser extent, Catholics are the most frequent users.[28] Nevertheless, the proportion of people turning to their clergy remains extremely high: nearly 40 percent of all Americans who seek help approach the clergy. That pastoral counseling is not tainted with the stigma often associated with psychiatric treatment and that it is often free are only two of the many reasons for the extensive use of pastoral counseling; perhaps most important is the fact that clergy are persistently viewed as effective. Some 80 percent of people who have consulted clergy describe them as "helpful" or "very helpful"—more than any other profession.[29] Not all pastoral counseling has outcomes as tragic as that of Ken Nally; and much of it takes very different forms. Like secular psychological and psychiatric counseling, however, it is also an arena of potential moral problems, one conspicuous example of which has been explored here.

# The Ethical Analysis of

# Organized Religion

This inquiry began with a curious fact: that while applied professional ethics, as a contemporary field of moral philosophy, has spread from medicine to law, engineering, business, education, and a huge range of other professional and semiprofessional fields, the vast institution of organized religion has remained virtually unexamined. This seemed to be a function of a variety of factors, including our tendency to separate the religious from the secular, our traditional respect for the integrity of the clergy, and our frequent assumption that ethical norms derive from values received in religion—all factors that have been taken as reasons for thinking that organized religion is not subject to ethical critique. But there were other considerations: that organized religion resembles secular professional institutions in many clearly identifiable ways; that we are heavy consumers of services provided by religious organizations; and that we are familiar with the quick, intuitive moral judgments we already make in response to literary exposés and media scandals about religious practices. These provided reasons for thinking that organized religion and the practices that constitute it *can* be criticized on ethical grounds.

Thus, I have proposed to see whether the concerns of applied professional ethics, including business ethics, used together with the insights of ordinary ethics in a kind of pincer apparatus, could be used to critique the operations of organized religion. Three general practices have served as examples for exploring the characteristic problems they raise—confession, risk taking, and convert seeking. However, while professional ethics provided entry to these problems, it proved far from adequate for resolving them. Further strategies of analysis were needed, none of which professional or ordinary ethics could provide: first, a method of differentiating among various orders of doctrine, making it possible to distinguish between fundamental imperatives, developed practices, and excuses; second, a way of appealing to a version of the fiduciary principle, identifying the obligations of the religious professional or spiritual provider to the person who seeks help; and third, a position asserting that unprovable, off-scale, self-interest-gratifying claims should be treated as suspect. These further principles allow areas of religious practice to be distinguished to which professional and ordinary ethics could be applied. Thus, while that set of considerations and perspectives germane to professional ethics, together with the insights of ordinary morality, has served admirably as a starting point for these inquiries, it has not allowed us to finish the job. The question, then, is what this approach can be expected to yield in examining other issues presented by organized religion.

However, this question cannot be answered without noticing one further thing. The three general issues examined here are quite different in kind; for this reason, the bearing of professional ethics on them is not the same. This is not only a matter of whether the professional ethics literature is adequately developed with respect to these issues or whether a given problem has been exhaustively examined in the secular professions, but a matter of the types of problems that professional ethics is in general able to consider.[1]

## A Typology of Problems

Generally speaking, three quite different types of problems arise within the scope of professional ethics. In looking at three issues raised by organized religion—confession, risk taking, and convert seeking, treating them as problems of confidentiality, informed consent in decision making, and paternalism, respectively—we have been looking at one of each.

*Stock Issues.* The first major practice, confession, poses what can be described as a *stock issue.* A stock issue is one that occurs in virtually every secular institutional setting addressed by professional ethics; it does so because it arises from characteristic structures common to virtually all professional institutions. These structures include such things as patterns of contact between practitioners and clients, codes regulating professional behavior, and mechanisms for transferring money or other resources from clients to practitioners or to the practitioners' institutions. These are the structures first observed in pointing out similarities between the secular professions and organized religion. Where organized religion exhibits structures similar to those of the secular professions, we can expect to find ethical issues similar to those confronting the secular professions. Although an analysis of stock issues in religion is more complex than in the secular professions, since in religion these issues concern practices governed by doctrine and doctrinal excuses, the basic dilemma of a stock issue remains the same.

Confidentiality is one such stock issue. In some secular professions, the practitioner comes to know sensitive information about the client because it is part of the nature of the interaction between professional and client for the client to tell the professional this information. This is the case in psychiatry and law and, to a lesser extent, in medicine and various other fields. These practices are not called "confession" in secular contexts, but parallels to the religious practice of confession—especially direct auricular confession to a religious professional, as in Catholic practice—are nevertheless close. Somewhat differently, in other secular professions—for instance, accounting, education, architecture, financial management, and medicine—the professional comes to know damaging or embarrassing information about the client by observation during the course of other transactions, although the client is not expected to volunteer it. Certain aspects of religious practice in Mormonism bear a strong resemblance to these ways in which the professional comes to know or believe information about the client: observations of domestic and personal life made by the bishop or home teacher in his efforts to assure the spiritual and material welfare of those in his care. Still differently, in some secular professions the professional comes to know certain things about the client because of surveillance or reporting systems: psychiatry and psychotherapy are sometimes confronted with such situations, as are education, journalism, and criminal corrections, among others. These bear obvious parallels to the pursuit of rumor and subsequent extraction of confession, as evident in the Collinsville Church of Christ's discipline of Marian Guinn.

What is common to all of these situations, both in the secular professions and in religious settings, is that the practitioner comes to know material about a client that would prove harmful or embarrassing to the client if revealed. The product of developed, upper-level practice, it is this abstract structure—a structure whereby the professional knows the client's secret, the client wishes the secret not to be revealed, and the professional has the power to reveal it or not—that is common to both secular and religious situations. Furthermore, in both secular and religious situations, whether the material is revealed may have substantial consequences not only for the individual but for third parties as well. It is this abstract structure that gives rise to the familiar moral dilemma of whether the professional should ever break confidentiality. That this abstract structure is common to so many professions, including religion, and has such similar features, marks it as a stock issue.

There are many other stock issues. For instance, most of the issues associated with church organizations are stock issues, very much like those in other professions. These issues are generally the products of upper-level, developed practices, practices that have evolved as religion has taken institutionalized forms. The issues of church organization include institutional secrecy; the management of finances and other resources by the organization; the allocation and disbursement of funds and other resources to various projects; the collection of payments (or, in religion, "contributions") from the recipients of services; and fairness in employment and access to earning credentials. The current disputes over the ordination of women in the Roman Catholic and Episcopal churches are textbook examples of the stock issue of access in employment and credentials, which is made much more complex than its analogues in the secular professions (as virtually all stock issues in organized religion are) by further questions of the bearing of doctrinal claims.

*Counterpart Issues.* The problem of institutional influence on decision making under risk is an example of an issue that is both critical in religion and has counterparts in other professional areas, but where the similarity is not close enough to allow it to be called a stock issue. It has been treated here as an issue in informed consent; this allows us to see that the matter of influence or control over decision making is central, as are issues of information, impairment, and altered value rankings. These issues clearly arise both here and in various practices within secular institutions, including consent to medical treatment, to therapeutic and nontherapeutic medical experimentation, to strategies of legal representation, and to engineering, architectural, and business contracts, and so on. However, these problems in religion also include features that either have not been noticed or have not been noticed distinctly in other professional areas, and that suggest that they may not be such close analogues after all.

For instance, one salient, central feature of institutional influence on risk-taking choice in organized religion involves the way a *group* of persons—the members of a particular religious denomination or sect—tends to make similar choices, even though their choices involve risks that other people typically would not take. Informed consent issues in medicine, law, engineering, and other secular professions are not usually understood in this way; on the contrary, the usual emphasis is on individual differences among patients or clients in giving consent, rather than any commonalities they exhibit. Thus, our observation about patterns of decision making in organized religion and the ways they are influenced by religious groups invites us to consider whether there are commonalities in risk-taking behavior among "groups" consisting of the clients of other professionals. For example, do the clients of doctors or lawyers or financial-management services characteristically take risks that fall outside the risk budgets of most ordinary people not just because they are ill or in legal jeopardy or wish to set their finances straight, but also because those professions have distinctive ways of influencing the risk-taking choices of their clients? Even within professions, are there differences in the ways different specialists—internists and surgeons, for example—can and should influence the risk-taking choices of their patients? Or are the canons of informed consent uniform throughout medicine? Ought we think of the canons of informed consent as uniform across professions, different only in details of content but not in structure? If so, does this include religion? Or instead, do our observations about religion suggest there is a more substantial disanalogy here and that we cannot fit choice making in religion under a secular model? As a case in point, we argued in chapter 2 that the use of anecdotal evidence is problematic in Christian Science since it does not meet the canons of informed consent for medicine; but this also invites us to look at the extent to which anecdotal evidence is nevertheless pervasively used in clinical medicine to persuade patients to make certain choices (even though it is at the same time disavowed in research medicine) and perhaps to reconsider whether it is actually unwarranted here. Answering this question requires reexamining *both* the practices of organized religion and of the relevant secular profession. This way of looking at informed consent issues in other secular contexts has not been explored much by philosophers working in professional ethics, but it is clearly suggested by looking at its counterpart in organized religion.

Although adequate discussion would require a full-scale examination of the issues, matters like religious education and persuasive preaching are probably also best treated as counterpart issues. But it cannot be simply assumed that a given practice is a counterpart practice, rather than a stock one, since many usages that appear to be different actually involve quite close similarities that are cloaked only by thin differences in terminology or other superficial matters. To say that an issue is a counterpart issue, rather than a stock one, is to insist that the analogues between the various professions in which it arises are comparatively loose, not really reducible to a common abstract structure found in similar underlying form across many seemingly different fields—though to establish that the analogues are not thus reducible also requires sustained, careful work.

*Unique Issues.* The third general issue considered here, convert seeking, is either essentially unique to organized religion or at least occurs in religion with very much greater force than in the secular professions. Although attempting to convert persons to a religious faith exhibits some parallels to secular professions that involve persuasion and the deliberate alteration of values and beliefs—for instance, education, psychotherapy, and criminal rehabilitation—these parallels are stretched. Our examination of the issues of convert seeking has made extensive use of the concept of paternalism and its relation to the principle of autonomy, but at the same time we were forced to acknowledge that although the concept of paternalism provides initial access to the issues raised in convert seeking and a way of conceptualizing them, it does not resolve them very well. Applying the considerations developed in secular professional-ethics discussions of paternalism was quite difficult: in the end, distinguishing between soft and hard paternalism in any intelligible way was not possible, the distinction between supererogatory and required actions slipped away, and the problem of off-scale values turned out to be largely insoluble. Thus, though the conceptual schema of paternalism, a staple of discussion in secular professional ethics, seemed to be the most appropriate tool for examining the issue of religious convert seeking, it did not really prove adequate to the task. But since the issue of convert seeking is central to religion, the failure is a significant one. The issue of converting others might be described as the most fundamental *moral* problem in organized religion generally, even though many groups, especially in the mainstream, try to avoid the issue by downplaying aggressive proselytism, substituting merely invitational missionary work or eschewing conversion-oriented activities altogether. The conceptual apparatus provided by secular professional ethics is not, in the end, adequate for addressing this unique problem, even though it is the best tool we have. It is a problem that cannot be resolved at the upper levels of developed practice, but that demands attention to the underlying imperative; but this is, of course, precisely what makes it intractable.

While the ethical issues arising in organized religion include many stock and counterpart problems, the genuinely unique issues are comparatively few. Baptism might be said to be one of them. It is a practice that raises unique issues not so much because it is understood as an initiatory rite, but because in at least some religious groups it is alleged to alter a person's metaphysical standing: the baptized person becomes saved or a candidate for salvation, but thereby also becomes accountable for his or her actions in a way that—in these belief systems—the unbaptized person is not. Baptism thus imposes liabilities as well as benefits. Another example of a unique problem in religion, though it is not currently practiced (except perhaps in Satanism) in contemporary religious groups, is human sacrifice. Here, the issue has to do with whether it is appropriate to subordinate the interests of some human beings not to the interests of other human beings or human institutions (a question that professional ethics would be capable of addressing), but to the interests of a suprahuman entity, God. This might be called, to use the Kantian phrase, the problem of the kingdom of ends. The problem of whose interests count, and whether this includes divine and semidivine beings as well as humans, are issues of major significance in religion since so many of its practices, including some extremely problematic ones, are said to be justified on the basis of the way in which they serve God. Professional ethics has no background for addressing this question of the kingdom of ends and no conceptual resources that would be useful in exploring these issues.

This rough distinction—it is not intended as a rigid categorization—among basic types of problems also provides insight into the fit between issues in organized religion and the apparatus of professional ethics that is employed to examine them. *Stock* issues, typically arising in connection with developed, upper-level practices, can draw most directly and heavily on the sustained considerations and literature of professional ethics. This is where professional ethics can tell us most about organized religion since it is able to draw on considered insights into strongly similar, perhaps virtually identical problems in other areas of professional practice, as well as proposed resolutions. This is possible, no doubt, because in the West religious and professional institutions have, in many respects, developed in parallel ways. Of course professional ethics will always come up against a final barrier, where it can go no further without announcing a commitment to the truth or falsity of the underlying metaphysical teachings. Nevertheless, it can reveal a great deal about the structure and scope of particular problems along the way. *Counterpart* issues in religion must draw less directly on the established literature and conceptualizations of professional ethics because the parallels among problems are much less close. Thus, the fit between the issue to be explored and the apparatus for exploring it is considerably less neat. Consequently, the risk of misunderstanding issues is much greater here. However, while professional ethics may provide less successful analyses of the counterpart problems in religion, it is here that religion can tell most about the shortcomings of professional ethics since it alerts us to features of problems not yet noticed in the secular professions. *Unique* issues are the most intractable: these are the cases in which the problems arising in organized religion have only tenuous counterparts in other professional areas, if any, and where *professional* ethics has little, if anything, to offer. Professional ethics may be able to isolate and identify the peripheral structures of the problem, but it cannot get to the core. Professional ethics is incapable of understanding the very issue itself in these unique cases; and ethical analysis is forced to rely more and more on ordinary moral intuition—though this, too, proves inadequate in the end. The practical lesson of this typology of problems is clear: when exploring issues in ecclesioethics, it is best to begin with the stock issues, then move to the counterpart issues, and save the unique issues, if one has courage for them at all, until last.

One must thus be careful to avoid blanket generalizations about the applicability of professional ethics to issues in religion. Professional ethics is indeed quite useful in illuminating certain sorts of problems; but it is considerably more useful for some types of problems than others. To predict how useful a professional-ethics analysis will be in any given case, one must first identify the problem and determine whether it is most nearly a stock problem, a counterpart one, or unique. Complex problems may have different components—as is evident in the complex, real-life case of Ken Nally—and in these cases, discerning what these are may provide much of the challenge at hand, even before detailed analysis can begin.

Neither professional ethics nor ordinary morality is adequate for a complete critique of religious practice in general. It has served as an initial pincer, to fix problems and permit the examination of them to begin, but it must then be supplemented by the further principles of analysis developed here. These further principles have the effect of delineating the territory within which professional and ordinary ethics considerations have their greatest purchase, and showing where, in general, they cannot penetrate very far. This is not a counsel of despair, but one of prudence in addressing issues that are often very subtle and profound.

## *Justifications*

Whether the pincer apparatus of professional and ordinary ethics provides a perfect fit or not, however, it has identified an astonishing range of what appear to be clear moral abuses. We saw deception and failure to prevent harm in Catholicism's response to the issue of confidentiality in confession; promise breaking, manipulation, and deceit in the Mormon version; and promise breaking, coercion, invasion of privacy, and deceit in the Collinsville Church of Christ's discipline of Marian Guinn. In examining religious practices involving risk, we saw coercion in the Faith Assembly, impairment of rationality among the serpent handlers, the deceptive use of misleading evidence in Christian Science, and inducements with off-scale claims among the Jehovah's Witnesses. Groups practicing various active conversion techniques provided a third range of apparent moral abuses: deception of the bait-and-switch merchandising variety in the Campus Crusade for Christ; a variety of distortions of ordinary human relationships in Dr. Trumbull's soul winning, the Moonies' disguised approach, the Boston Church of Christ's befriending; and religious prostitution in the Children of God's flirty fishing. These practices all involve deception, manipulation, promise breaking, and the specific use of self-interest gratifying, unprovable claims as inducements for belief. We did not find them exhibited in mainstream practice, or at least not at all vividly, though we did see many elements of these problems in the case of Ken Nally.

Lying, ignoring harms, promise breaking, manipulation, deceit, and the distortion of ordinary relationships are accusations not to be directed lightly to practitioners in the religious professions, nor to the religious institutions themselves. But it is important to notice that similar activities, though perhaps weaker in form, are countenanced in the secular professions as well. In numerous situations, ordinary moral rules are overridden in the interests of enabling the secular practitioner to provide the service that it is the function of his or her profession to provide; these are then understood (though not always by members of the profession) as prima facie wrongs, which are justified in the interests of a greater good. Professional ethics recognizes this as the "dirty hands" problem; it devotes considerable attention to issues of when practices involving prima facie wrongs can be morally justified, especially if they are the normal operating mode of the profession. For instance, the ordinary rule of truth telling is said in medicine to yield before a more weighty rule, special to medicine: that the physician shall always promote cure or, if cure is not possible, relieve pain. On this basis, it is argued, while patients ordinarily ought to be told the truth, even if they are dying, information may be withheld from patients whose recovery it might seriously jeopardize or for whom it would cause severe, fruitless suffering. Put more crudely, although lying is prima facie wrong, sometimes the physician may—indeed, *ought*—to lie.

Similarly, the practice of law countenances violations of ordinary moral rules against the concealment of information. The attorney is expected to reveal only information about the client's case that is favorable to the case, to withhold information that is incriminatory, and to deny that the client is guilty unless the client enters an explicit guilty plea, even when the attorney knows the contrary to be true. Such advocacy involves a form of deception, but it is institutionally favored and held essential to the provision of adequate legal defense. In still another area, the business executive who designs marketing strategies that "get people to buy" by engendering wants that are not genuine needs may be practicing an obvious form of manipulation. Yet it is so much a part of contemporary economic life that we barely recognize it at all and do not object to it when we do notice. If, then, we find lying, promise breaking, deceit, coercion, manipulation, and other prima facie wrongs apparently justifiably embedded in the practices of secular professionals—as the continuing inquiries of secular professional ethicists have allowed us to see—it may be the case that they are justifiably a part of the practices of religious professionals too.

In each of the secular professions, practices that involve violations of ordinary moral rules can be said to be morally justified only if they are necessary to provide that morally important service that is the function of the profession—in medicine, cure or relief of suffering; in law, defense of a client's legal rights; in business, the conduct of commerce. The violations of ordinary moral rules must not produce greater harm than the profession's service provides good; the morally problematic practice must be necessary to achieve the appropriate functioning of the profession; and there must be no alternative way of providing the service that is both practically possible and avoids violating moral norms. To provide similar justification for the violation of moral norms in the context of organized religion, then, we must be able to identify the "service" organized religion provides—that is, the aims or goals that are the objective of this institution—and we must show that this is an important service that cannot be provided in any way involving less serious violations of moral norms. Doing this, of course, would involve us in a very long dispute, a dispute as old as the scrutiny of organized religion itself. Some parties to this dispute would support a traditional characterization of the function of organized religion—to facilitate and promote the individual's spiritual development, both in order to approach God and to make possible the attainment of salvation. Others would insist that supernatural goals are not the primary function of institutional religion, but rather that it serves to regulate social behavior, teach morality, provide individuals with a sense of meaning and purpose in life, and to strengthen the human community. Still others would assert that the services that organized religion provides offer neither supernatural nor social or personal benefits, but function only to promote a self-aggrandizing institution, one that confers no real benefits at all.

Needless to say, to propose an answer to this ancient quarrel is not the purpose here. But it is precisely at this point that the lessons of secular professional ethics are so useful: they show that we *must* answer this question if we are to assess the morality of violations of moral norms in the practices of organized religion. As in other professions, violations of moral norms will be acceptable only if they are necessary to enable the religious practitioner to perform his or her central function in providing the institution's services; and only those institutional practices will be acceptable that are effective in providing the profession's services with a minimum of violation of moral norms. Furthermore, these must be aims that cannot be accomplished by any other (secular) profession, if they could be achieved with fewer violations. Thus, the only real way to answer the question of whether the practices examined here are morally justified—and the startling violations of moral norms many of them involve excused—is to address the issue of the aim and purpose of organized religion generally.

Certain features of this issue can be identified by examining the same issue as it arises in the secular professions.[2] If we look at the three principal areas of professional ethics that have emerged in recent years—bioethics, business ethics, and ethics of the practice of law—we see that despite their generic similarity, there are also some striking differences. These may make it clear how we must go about answering the question of moral justification in organized religion.

If we look carefully at the institution of medicine, for instance, we see that its central purpose is *cure*. Characteristic moral problems in medicine arise largely in situations where cure cannot be achieved. These problems are of two general types and generate two different kinds of moral issues. First, in some situations cure cannot be achieved because the disease process is (given the current state of the medical arts) ineluctable; here, the characteristic moral issues concern the treatment of the individual who is dying or who is chronically or incurably ill. These are primarily issues about autonomy, quality of life, consent, and prognostication; they arise in applied circumstances like abortion of defective fetuses, nonresuscitation of defective neonates, refusal of treatment, euthanasia, suicide, and "allowing" someone to die. The second situation where cure fails to be achieved is where there is a scarcity of resources, medical personnel, or funds; the characteristic moral problems here are issues of distributive justice. These concern problems like deciding which of two patients will get the single respirator or dialysis machine, whether there should be a ceiling on medical care expenses, and whether research funds should be allocated for rescue or for preventive medicine. However, in medicine, the "standard situation" or "central act"—the physician curing an ill patient—

does not inherently involve these problems. Medicine aims at the universal distribution of an undoubted good, cure, in a maximally effective way.

If we turn to the normative issues in the practice of law, we see that the standard situation or central act involves *defense,* that is, the attorney's defense of his or her client's rights in an adversary situation. Lawyers do much (such as tax advising and intercorporate negotiation) that does not fit this model, just as physicians do much (such as research and preventive medicine) that does not fit the model of the bedside healer promoting a cure. Nevertheless, defense is the model that lies at the heart of the legal enterprise. Here, some of the issues that arise are strikingly similar to those in medicine. For instance, how does the attorney accurately inform the client, in a comprehensible way, of his or her legal rights and chances in the courtroom? May the attorney override the client's wishes in conducting the defense in order to protect the client's rights, win the case, or both? May the attorney allow the client to lie? What duties of confidentiality does the attorney have in protecting the client's admissions? Some of these problems also occur in medical ethics, but in law they assume a much larger role and constitute characteristic moral issues in the practice of law. This is because they are all involved in defense, which often involves protecting the interests of those who have in fact committed the crime of which they are accused. The moral problems arise, then, as such practices are said to be justified in protecting the interests of someone who has committed an offense, who has harmed someone else's interests, and who may commit similar offenses in the future. In some cases, the protection that the attorney's defense provides for this person's interests may actually enable him or her to repeat the offense in the future. The issues in defense involve cases both where third-party interests have already been violated and where other third-party interests are jeopardized in the future; this is not the standard situation in medicine. The practice of law generates moral issues at a deeper, more central level than medicine.

When we look at the institutional practice of business, the situation seems to be still different. Here, the standard situation involves *selling* and, in particular, the making of a profit by serving someone else's wants or needs. Business also involves the use of another person's labor, the acquisition of capital, competition with intent to outdo other businesses, secrecy in research and manufacturing processes, and manipulation and inducement of unnecessary wants by means of advertising. Many or all of these practices may seem to involve prima facie harm, though as we said, they are so basic a part of our economic life that we barely notice them. Yet it is possible to criticize the very foundations of the institution of business, including its assumptions about the moral acceptability of private property, of the profit motive, of competition in a market economy, and so on. Thus, the institution of business is open to still more fundamental critique than is that of medicine or even law.

Once we see that the characteristic normative problems that arise within medicine, law, and business differ because the central enterprise of the various areas differs, we can begin to ask about characteristic normative problems in the ethics of the practice of religion. The doctor cures, the attorney defends, the businessperson sells. Which of these central acts do the religious professional's characteristic activities most closely resemble, and why? What is the central act of the religious practitioner—is it to inculcate belief, to perform ritual, to counsel, to encourage right behavior, or to increase the strength of the church in the world? To say, as one might have earlier in the century, that it is the "cure of souls" does not answer the question, at least not without some further explanation of precisely what this activity involves. Furthermore, answers may differ from one religious group to another. But it is a particularly important question, given the seemingly flagrant abuses of the norms of professional and ordinary morality uncovered here— deception, coercion, failure to prevent harm, and so on. We may be tempted to claim that the institutional practice of religion is most like the institutional practice of medicine, less like law, and least like business, in that its central act is more like curing or safeguarding health— here, spiritual health—than defending or selling. Yet this cannot be too easily assumed, nor can it be assumed that it is uniform across the immensely varied spectrum of religious groups.

Recognition of these seemingly flagrant abuses also raises the question of whether the law should regulate the practices of organized religion at the higher-order levels where they are most accessible to ethical critique. Reminding ourselves in the case of Ken Nally that to decide the legal issues is not to resolve the ethical ones, we gave a very short answer to this very large question: if the walls of legal separation of church and state must remain high to preserve freedom of religion, ethical scrutiny becomes doubly appropriate. Ethical scrutiny carries with it only moral force, not the coercive power of the state. First Amendment protections are designed to prevent only state interference, not ethical criticism; yet our cultural tendency to screen off the religious from the secular seems to have produced both. This obscures the distinct nature of two different questions: first, whether the law should intervene in what are the standard, regular, accepted practices of a group, practices that affect only willing believers, where these practices clearly involve what professional and ordinary ethics would identify as abuses of the believers involved; and second, whether and to what extent moral criticism of such practices should be encouraged. My own view is that the law should, in general, stay out of it; but it is also my view that the applied ethicist should rush right in. The ethical critique of religion is best pursued by ethicists, not lawyers and judges, though it may nonetheless be as relentless as the ethical critique of medicine, business, and law has become. Since it can appeal to the ordinary moral intuitions of a broad public—a public already familiar with primitive versions of such critique—it may serve to alert those who are associated with various religious groups, from the fringe to the mainstream, to be a little more sensitive to complex ethical issues in how their own groups treat them. This does not quite recommend the consumerist attitude toward organized religion of psychiatrist Eli Chesen, who observes that "people take more care in selecting dog food and motor oil than their religion,"[3] but it is not far from it in urging careful ethical scrutiny—under appropriate methodological constraints—by both participants and observers of the religious institutions with which they are involved.

The ethical critique of organized religion is important for one final reason as well. Religion is often praised for such contributions as giving a sense of meaning to life, inspiring charity, exhibiting models of self-sacrifice and courage, serving as a force for good and unity, and so on; such claims often appear in characterizations of the aim or purpose of religion. These are claims of moral *commendation*. But moral commendation is itself a form of moral critique, and it, like moral denunciation, presupposes that it is possible to conduct ethical assessment of its subject in the first place. Those who are perhaps least likely to welcome the possibility of negative moral evaluation of religion may be those most likely to praise the importance and positive value of this institution. This, however, is an incoherent aim. If it is not possible to pursue the moral critique of religion, then all possibility of moral praise of organized religion must also be dismissed. In attempting to see in this inquiry how negative moral critique is possible, we have discovered how praise is possible, too.

# NOTES

## INTRODUCTION

1. There is one notable exception: Karen Lebacqz's *Professional Ethics: Power and Paradox* (Nashville, Tenn.: Abingdon Press, 1985) is an extended exploration of confidentiality issues in the mainstream ministry.

2. The term is Alan H. Goldman's. See *The Moral Foundations of Professional Ethics* (Totowa, N.J.: Rowman & Littlefield, 1980) for the classic discussion of whether professional morality involves distinct principles.

3. See the first part of Margaret P. Battin, "Applied Professional Ethics and Institutional Religion: The Methodological Issues," *The Monist* 67(4):569–88 (Oct. 1984), for a discussion of organized religion as a profession.

4. Dudley Clendinen, "Cult and Child Beating: Defense and Accusation," (*New York Times* July 1, 1984), Y10. Also see coverage in this and other papers beginning July 23, 1984, when Vermont state police raided the sect and briefly seized all of its children under the age of eighteen, some 112 of them.

5. Constant H. Jacquet, Jr., ed., *Yearbook of American and Canadian Churches* (Nashville, Tenn.: Abingdon Press, 1988), 287, 253, and 286, respectively. Church membership as a percentage of population was 58.7 in 1987 (down from 59.3 in 1986); attendance figures are for 1986.

## CHAPTER 1: TELLING CONFESSIONS

1. See "Murder Case Debate on Priest's Duty," *Times* (London), (Dec. 16, 1967), 1; "How Secret the Confessional?" *Time* (Dec. 22, 1967), 51; "Magie mit Versen," *Der Spiegel* (June 27, 1966), 32–33. Bartsch was arrested in June 1966 and sentenced Dec. 16. In addition to the four murders, he also confessed to seventy other attempts.

2. *Salt Lake Tribune* (Jan. 10, 1986), B1.

3. Sources for discussion of professional ethics, in addition to Goldman, *The Moral Foundations of Professional Ethics,* include Michael D. Bayles, *Professional Ethics* (Belmont, Calif.: Wadsworth, 1981); Joan Callahan, *Ethical Issues in*

Professional Life (New York: Oxford University Press, 1988); and Peter Y. Windt, Peter C. Appleby, Margaret P. Battin, Leslie P. Francis, and Bruce M. Landesman, *Ethical Issues in the Professions* (New York: Prentice-Hall, 1989).

4. *Tarasoff v. Regents of the University of California*, 551, P.2d 334 (1976).

5. This is the text and renumbering of the new code of canon law that went into effect in 1983.

6. Edwin F. Healy, S. J., "The Seal of Confession," *Review for Religious* 2(3):176 (May 15, 1943).

7. John R. Roos, *The Seal of Confession*, Catholic University of America Canon Law Studies No. 413 (Washington, D.C.: Catholic University of America Press, 1960), 1.

8. Church of Jesus Christ of Latter-day Saints, *General Handbook of Instructions* (Salt Lake City, Utah, 1989), sec. 10, p. 3 (10-3) (hereafter cited in text as *General Handbook*).

9. At the time, excommunication for homosexuality was mandatory.

10. From a confidential letter to the author.

11. William Harold Teimann and John C. Bush, *The Right to Silence: Privileged Clergy Communication and the Law* (Nashville, Tenn.: Abingdon Press, 1983).

12. Fred L. Kuhlmann, "Communications to Clergymen—When Are They Privileged?" *The Journal of Pastoral Care* 24(1):44 (1970).

13. For an account of these practices, see R. C. Mortimer, *The Origins of Private Penance in the Western Church* (Oxford: Clarendon, 1939), drawing on the earlier work of O. D. Watkins and B. Poschman.

14. See *New Catholic Encyclopedia*, 1967 ed., s.v. "confession, auricular," (vol. 4, 132).

15. This development is traced in B. Poschman, *Die Abendlaendische Kirchenbuesse im Ausgang des Christlichen Altertums* (Munich, 1928), in English as *Penance and the Anointing of the Sick,* trans. and rev. F. Courtney (Freiburg: Herder, 1964); see also Mortimer, *The Origins of Private Penance,* 3.

16. See, for instance, Count C. P. de Lasteyrie's *The History of Auricular Confession* (London: Richard Bentley, 1848), espec. vol. 1, chapter 2, "Seduction of Women in Spain, by Means of Confession."

17. I thank Michael Quinn for much of the information in this paragraph.

18. *New Catholic Encyclopedia*, 1967 ed., s.v. "secrets" (vol. 13, 29).

19. Sissela Bok's chapter on confessions in her *Secrets: On the Ethics of Concealment and Revelation* (New York: Pantheon, 1982) raises many related points.

20. Roos, *The Seal of Confession,* 2–3.

21. "How Secret the Confessional?" *Time* (Dec. 22, 1967), 51, quoting pastor Christian Schulze of Hamburg.

22. The first mention of confidentiality is in the supplement to the *General Handbook* for 1979; the fuller policy is made increasingly explicit in the editions of 1983, 1985, and 1989.

23. See Roos, *The Seal of Confession*, 73: "[the confessor] actually has no human or communicable knowledge about the information being sought"; and *New Catholic Encyclopedia*, 1967 ed., s.v. "confession, seal of" (vol. 4, 134).

24. Roos, *The Seal of Confession*, 73.

25. See Lester E. Bush, Jr., "Excommunication and Church Courts: A Note from the *General Handbook of Instructions*," *Dialogue: A Journal of Mormon Thought* 14(2):78 (Summer 1981).

26. The details of Guinn's story are based on a variety of accounts, including the decision in *Guinn v. Collinsville Church of Christ* (Case no. CT-81-929, District Court, Tulsa County, Oklahoma, March 15, 1984, *appeal docketed*, no. 62, 154, Okla., Apr. 16, 1984) and the Reporter's Daily Transcript, covering trial testimony for March 12–15, 1984; Christopher S. Heroux, "When Fundamental Rights Collide: *Guinn v. Collinsville Church of Christ*," *Tulsa Law Journal* 21(1985) 157–82; Lynn R. Buzzard and Thomas S. Brandon, *Church Discipline and the Courts* (Wheaton, Ill.: Tyndale House Publishers, 1986); a variety of newspaper accounts at the time, especially those in the *Daily Oklahoman* for March 13, 14, 15, 16, and 19, 1984; and two fundamentalist tabloids, *Christian Worker* 70:3 (March 1984) and *Christian Chronicle* 41:4 (April 1984); and finally, the Oklahoma Supreme Court decision, no. 62, 154, Jan. 17, 1989. These accounts differ in certain minor details; where this is the case, the trial transcript is preferred.

27. Heroux, "When Fundamental Rights Collide," 158.

28. Reporter's Daily Transcript 69:19–23.

29. Reporter's Daily Transcript 555, Plaintiff's Exhibit 1.

30. While Churches of Christ do not generally dictate the Bible translation that must be used, the King James version would probably have been most familiar to the members of the Collinsville church. Matthew 18:15–17 reads: "Moreover if thy brother shall trespass against thee, go and tell him his fault between thee and him alone: if he shall hear thee, thou hast gained thy brother. But if he will not hear thee, then take with thee one or two more, that in the mouth of two or three witnesses every word may be established. And if he shall neglect to hear them, tell it unto the church: but if he neglect to hear the church, let him be unto thee as an heathen man and a publican."

31. Reporter's Daily Transcript 556, Plaintiff's Exhibit 2.

32. Buzzard and Brandon, *Church Discipline,* 12.

33. The jurors apparently misunderstood the judge's instructions, and had intended to award Guinn more than twice this amount.

34. In an interview, Ted Moody, one of the three elders, explains that "we recognize that there is a universal body of Christ which one enters by the new birth and cannot resign from. There are also local congregations in which people come and go at will. We did not accept the resignation of Marian Guinn because we had been working with her for two and one-half years to encourage her to repent. About ten days before withdrawal was to occur, she gave us the letter of resignation. We did not believe, and we do not now believe, that a member has the right at this point in a discipline process to resign. As shepherds, we felt responsible not only to help her face the life she was living but also to let the community know that the Collinsville Church of Christ did not approve of that kind of conduct. To accept her resignation at the point in which she offered it does violence to the teachings of Jesus in Matthew 18:15–18." (Interview by Howard Norton, *Christian Chronicle* 41:4 (April 1984), 21.) There are several peripheral arguments here; the central one is a biblical claim functioning not as an 0-level imperative, but as an excuse.

35. Buzzard and Brandon, *Church Discipline,* 13–15.

36. Support for the Collinsville Church of Christ's position has been extensive. According to Ron Witten (telephone communication, June 25, 1988), as of June 1988 the church had received over $1 million from other churches to fight the *Guinn* case.

37. Bill Hearn, preacher, Downtown Church of Christ, Salt Lake City, Utah, telephone communication with author, June 25, 1988.

38. *Daily Oklahoman,* March 19, 1984, 2.

### CHAPTER 2: HIGH-RISK RELIGION

1. Charles Fried, *An Anatomy of Values: Problems of Personal and Social Choice* (Cambridge: Harvard University Press, 1970), 167.

2. See Thomas C. Johnsen, "Christian Scientists and the Medical Profession: A Historical Perspective," *Medical Heritage* (Jan/Feb. 1986):70–78, for a loyal account of the historical background; also see Robert Peel, *Spiritual Healing in a Scientific Age* (San Francisco: Harper & Row, 1987), for a loyal attempt to address scientific issues.

3. Arnold S. Relman, M.D., "Christian Science and the Care of Children," *New England Journal of Medicine* 309(26):1639 (Dec. 29, 1983).

4. Nathan A. Talbot, "The Position of the Christian Science Church," *NewEnglandJournal of Medicine* 309(26):1641–44 (Dec. 29, 1983). See espec. p. 1642.

5. Talbot, "The Position of the Christian Science Church," 1642.

6. On the distinction between mechanical procedures and other medical treatment, see Arthur E. Nudelman, "The Maintenance of Christian Science in Scientific Society," in *Marginal Medicine,* ed. Roy Wallis and Peter Morley (New York: Free Press, 1976), 42–60; also see William E. Laur, M.D., "Christian Science Visited," *Southern Medical Journal* 73(1):71–74 (Jan. 1980). See espec. p. 73.

7. Rita Swan, "Faith Healing, Christian Science, and the Medical Care of Children," *New England Journal of Medicine* 309(26):1640 (Dec. 29, 1983).

8. Constant H. Jacquet, Jr., ed., *Yearbook of American and Canadian Churches* (Nashville, Tenn.: Abingdon Press, 1988), 42.

9. See the pamphlet supplied by the Watchtower Bible and Tract Society of Pennsylvania, "Jehovah's Witnesses and the Question of Blood" (1977).

10. Some Witnesses will also accept closed-loop extracorporeal recirculation of their own blood during surgery and in hemodialysis.

11. See, e.g., J. Skelly Wright's decision in "Application of President and Directors of Georgetown College," 311 F.2d 1000 (D.C. Cir.), certiorari denied, 377 U.S. 978 (1964).

12. Jim Quinn and Bill Zlatos, series of stories beginning May 2, 1983, in the *Fort Wayne News-Sentinel,* Indiana; see, also, Ron French, ibid., Aug. 25, 1987, and June 8, 1989.

13. Quinn and Zlatos, story in *Fort Wayne News-Sentinel,* May 5, 1983, 1.

14. Robert W. Pelton and Karen W. Carden, *Snake Handlers: God-Fearers? or, Fanatics?* (Nashville, Tenn.: Thomas Nelson, 1974), provides a useful pictorial essay on these practices.

15. *Swann v. Pack* 527 S.W.2d at 105. This case notes that Hensley died of a diamondback rattlesnake bite during a prayer meeting in 1955.

16. Nathan L. Gerrard, "The Serpent-Handling Religions of West Virginia," *Trans-Action* 5(7):23 (May 1968).

17. Pelton and Carden, *Snake Handlers,* p. 12 of Appendix.

18. Gerrard, "The Serpent-Handling Religions of West Virginia," 23.

19. Weston La Barre, *They Shall Take Up Serpents: Psychology of the Southern Snake-Handling Cult* (Minneapolis: University of Minnesota Press, 1962), 19–20.

20. Findlay E. Russell, *Snake Venom Poisoning* (Philadelphia: J. B. Lippincott, 1980), 527.

21. *Swann v. Pack* 527 S.W.2d at 100.

22. *Fort Wayne News-Sentinel,* June 2, 1984, 6A.

23. Gale E. Wilson, "Christian Science and Longevity," *Journal of Forensic Sciences* 1 (Jan.–Oct. 1956):43–60.

24. CHILD is an acronym for Children's Health Care Is a Legal Duty. The organization's address is Box 2604, Sioux City, Iowa 51106.

25. See J. Lowell Dixon and M. Gene Smalley, "Jehovah's Witnesses: The Surgical/Ethical Challenge," *Journal of the American Medical Association* 246(21):2471–72 (Nov. 27, 1981).

26. Dixon and Smalley, "Jehovah's Witnesses," 2472.

27. William Franklin Simpson, "Comparative Longevity in a College Cohort of Christian Scientists," *Journal of the American Medical Association* 262(12):1657–58 (Sept. 22/29, 1989). An extended critical analysis of the statistical methods of this study, by Prof. David Nartonis, is available from the church.

28. Pelton and Carden, *Snake Handlers,* 29–30.

29. Members of the Holiness churches insist that serpent handling is not to be understood as a "test of faith" in the sense that reciting a creed might be, but that it is a "confirmation" of God's word. Glossolalia, serpent handling, strychnine drinking, and similar practices are the "signs following" belief in God but are not evidence for it. See Pelton and Carden, *Snake Handlers.*

30. Merrily Allen Ozengher, *Christian Science Journal* 101(9) (Sept. 1983).

31. Footnote appearing at the beginning of the "On Christian Science Healing" section of testimonials in each issue of the *Christian Science Journal.*

32. Talbot, "Position of the Christian Science Church," 1642; see, also, *A Century of Christian Science Healing* (Boston: The Christian Science Publishing Society, 1966) for the church's account of this history. The figure is from the Committee on Publication's 1989 paper "An Empirical Analysis of Medical Evidence in Christian Science Testimonies of Healing 1969–1988," First Church of Christ, Scientist, 175 Huntington Avenue, Boston, Mass. 02115.

33. Talbot, "Position of the Christian Science Church," 1642.

34. See, e.g., Daniel Kahneman, Paul Slovic, and Amos Tversky, eds., *Judgment Under Uncertainty: Heuristics and Biases* (Cambridge: Cambridge Univ. Press, 1982).

35. Nudelman, "The Maintenance of Christian Science in a Scientific Society," 49.

36. Base-rate and related information could presumably be accumulated if Christian Scientists as well as non-Scientists were routinely examined and diagnosed by physicians and if medical records of all procedures as well as records of

healing by prayer were kept. Of course, this is not generally the case. Neither could the kind of persuasive evidence supplied by controlled clinical trials be obtained on the efficacy of Christian Science healing since it would not be possible to *randomize* subjects into groups, one of which would (sincerely) perform Christian Science prayer and the other of which would not pray but have confidence in conventional medicine alone. The closest one could come to designing such a trial would be to randomize believing Scientists into groups that use prayer and those that, denied the services of a Christian Science practitioner, are offered only conventional treatment or to randomize nonbelievers into those who use conventional medical treatment and those who go through the motions of prayer.

A recent study cited in the *Hastings Center Report* (vol. 19, no. 3, May/June 1989, pp. 2–3) reports a randomized, double-blind study of the effects of intercessory prayer on hospitalized patients ("Positive Therapeutic Effects of Intercessory Prayer in a Coronary Care Unit Population," *Southern Medical Journal* 81(7):826–29 [1988]). Of course, this study did not randomize patients who prayed for themselves, but patients who were prayed for by others; nevertheless, it did conclude that the group prayed for exhibited fewer complications than the control group.

37. Nicholas Rescher, *Risk: A Philosophical Introduction to the Theory of Risk Evaluation and Management* (Washington, D.C.: University of Press of America, 1983), 132.

38. Lois O'Brien, "Prayer's Not a Gamble," letter in *U.S. News & World Report,* April 28, 1986, 81.

39. Contrast the symposium articles in the *New England Journal of Medicine* 310(19):1257–60 (May 10, 1984), with subsequent letters to the editor.

40. Rita Swan, letter to the editor, *New England Journal of Medicine* 310(19):1260 (May 10, 1984).

41. George Mills and Richard Grove, *Lucifer and the Crucifer: The Enigma of the Penitentes* (Colorado Springs Fine Arts Center, The Westerners, 1956), 21, citing Mary Austin.

42. Rev. Rodney Dorsey, Pocatalico Community Full Gospel Church, Sissonville, West Virginia, telephone communication with author, Sept. 20, 1989.

43. Pelton and Carden, *Snake Handlers,* unnumbered last page of Appendix.

44. Charles Fried, *Medical Experimentation, Personal Integrity and Social Policy* (New York: American Elsevier Publishing Co., 1974), 33.

45. By the turn of the century, Christian Science was viewed by the medicalestablishment as an alternative (and bogus) school of medicine, not as a religion. See Johnsen, "Christian Scientists and the Medical Profession," 72.

46. Johnsen, "Christian Scientists and the Medical Profession," 73. As Johnsen also notes, a unanimous opinion of the Rhode Island Supreme Court affirmed in 1898 that prayer in Christian Science could not be mistaken for the practice of medicine in any "ordinary sense and meaning" of the term.

47. Alan Brinkley, "The Oral Majority," *New Republic* (Sept. 29, 1986), 31.

### CHAPTER 3: MAKING BELIEVE

1. Charles Gallaudet Trumbull, *Taking Men Alive* (New York: Young Men's Christian Association Press, 1908), 103.

2. European Parliament, Committee on Youth, Culture, Education, Information and Sport, *Report on the Activity of Certain New Religious Movements within the European Community.* Rapporteur: Richard Cottrell. Document PE 82.322/fin, 22 March 1984.

3. David G. Bromley, and Anson D. Shupe, Jr., *"Moonies" in America: Cult, Church, and Crusade* (Beverly Hills, Calif.: Sage Publications, 1979), 173.

4. Richard Delgado, "Religious Totalism as Slavery," 54.

5. Bromley and Shupe, *"Moonies" in America,* 172.

6. Edd Doerr, "Church and State," *The Humanist* 46(2):41 (March-April 1986).

7. Quoted in Rasa Gustaitis, "Hard-Sell Religion," *Nutshell* (Fall 1983), 76–77. The church was formerly called the Lexington Church of Christ.

8. Deborah (Linda Berg) Davis with Bill Davis, *The Children of God: The Inside Story* (Grand Rapids, Mich.: Zondervan Publishing House, 1984), 118.

9. Roy Wallis, "Sex, Marriage, and the Children of God," in *Salvation and Protest* (London: Frances Pinter Ltd., 1979), 75.

10. Wallis, *Salvation and Protest,* 79.

11. Davis, *The Children of God,* 119.

12. Ibid., 23.

13. Phidellia P. Carroll, *Soul-Winning: A Problem and Its Solution* (New York: Eaton & Mains; Cincinnati, Ohio: Jennings and Graham, 1905), 77.

14. This practice took place while T. Bowring Woodbury was mission president and considerable emphasis was placed on increasing the numbers of converts. Anson Shupe and John Heinerman, "Book of Mormon and Baseballs: Mormon Missionizing Techniques," paper presented at Sunstone Symposium 11, August 26, 1989, Salt Lake City, Utah.

15. *Decree on the Missionary Activity of the Church (Ad Gentes),* in *The Documents of Vatican II* (America Press, Association Press, 1966), 600.

16. Richard N. Ostling, "The New Missionary," *Time* (December 1982), p. 44.

17. James T. Richardson, "Paradigm Conflict in Conversion Research," *Journal for the Scientific Study of Religion* 24(1985):119–236.

18. Richardson, "Paradigm Conflict," 168, quoting John Lofland.

19. Rev. Edward Storrow, *Popular Objections to Foreign Missions* (London: John Snow, 1889), 31.

20. *Encyclopedia of Theology: The Concise Sacramentum Mundi* 1982, s.v. "mission," 968.

21. Gaylord Noyce, "The Ethics of Evangelism," *Christian Century* 96(32):974 (Oct. 10, 1979).

22. Aylward Shorter, *Theology of Mission* (Notre Dame, Ind.: Fides Publishers, 1972), 20.

23. For an example, see Richard Ostling's discussion of the Dani, "The New Missionary," 43.

24. Quoted in Rev. John Liggins, *The Great Value and Success of Foreign Missions, Proved by Distinguished Witnesses. . . .* (New York: Baker & Taylor, 1888), 72–73.

25. Daniel Wikler, "Persuasion and Coercion for Health: Ethical Issues in Government Efforts to Change Life-Styles," in *Paternalism,* ed. Rolf Sartorius (Minneapolis: University of Minnesota Press, 1983), 57.

26. See Bernard Williams's discussion in *Moral Luck* (Cambridge: Cambridge University Press, 1981), 94–100; and Ian Hacking's account, "The Logic of Pascal's Wager," *American Philosophical Quarterly* (April 1972).

27. Blaise Pascal, *Thoughts,* trans. W. F. Trotter (New York: P. F. Collier & Son, 1910), 233.

28. Ostling, "The New Missionary," 40.

29. Wikler, "Persuasion and Coercion for Health," n. 11.

30. Williams, *Moral Luck,* 98.

31. Church of Jesus Christ of Latter-day Saints *General Handbook of Instructions* (Salt Lake City, Utah, 1989), 10–1.

32. Ibid.

33. Ibid.

## CHAPTER 4: MORAL PROBLEMS

1. "Book of Order," Part 2 of *The Constitution of the Presbyterian Church (U.S.A.)* (New York: The Office of the General Assembly, 1981, 1985), para. D-7.0300 (hereafter "Book of Order").

2. These systems are surveyed in Carl H. Esbeck, "Tort Claims against Churches and Ecclesiastical Officers: The First Amendment Considerations," *West Virginia Law Review* 89(1):1–114 (Fall 1986).

3. Ibid., 69.

4. *The Book of Discipline of the United Methodist Church* (1980), para. 16, art. 1, p. 25.

5. Esbeck, "Tort Claims against Churches," 75.

6. J. Pendelton, *Baptist Church Manual* (1966), 141.

7. "Book of Order," para. D-7.0900.

8. Ibid., para. D-8.1200–.1500.

9. Ibid., para. D-7.0300.

10. See, e.g., his Ingersoll Lecture, delivered at the Harvard Divinity School, November 15, 1984, entitled "Hell Disappeared—No One Noticed."

11. Robert W. Pelton and Karen W. Carden, *Snake Handlers: God-Fearers? or, Fanatics?* (Nashville, Tenn.: Thomas Nelson, 1974), 29.

12. The association's address is 9508 A Lee Highway, Fairfax, Virginia 22031.

13. "Code of Ethics," *American Association of Pastoral Counselors Handbook,* rev. April 1988.

14. See Maury M. Breecher, "Ministerial Malpractice: Is It a Reasonable Fear?" *Trial* (July 1980), which recounts the claim that Church Mutual circulated a fictitious story to stimulate the purchase of such insurance.

15. Neumeyer, "The Church That's Being Taken to Court," 158.

16. Peter Steinfels, "National Council of Church Plans Restructuring to Resolve Divisions," *New York Times,* May 22, 1989, A8.

17. James H. Smylie, "Church Growth and Decline in Historical Perspective," in *Understanding Church Growth and Decline: 1950–1978,* ed. Dean R. Hoge and David A. Roozen (New York: Pilgrim Press, 1979), 70.

18. Ari L. Goldman, "Church Council, Losing Appeal, Adopts Changes," *New York Times,* Nov. 4, 1988, Y9.

19. See Roberto Suro, "Switch by Hispanic Catholics Changes Face of U.S. Religion," *New York Times,* May 14, 1989, A1.

20. See C. Peter Wagner, "Church Growth Research: The Paradigm and Its Applications," in *Understanding Church Growth and Decline: 1950–1978,* ed. Dean R. Hoge and David A. Roozen (New York: Pilgrim Press, 1979), 270–87.

## CHAPTER 5: A SAMPLE CASE

1. The account of the case provided here is based on the following documents: *Nally v. Grace Community Church of the Valley,* Los Angeles Superior

Court No. NCC18668B, CA 2d 2 civ. 67200, June 28, 1984, by Dalsimer, J., Hanson, J., dissenting; California Court of Appeal No. B015721, Appellants' Opening Brief (hereafter "Appellants' Brief"); California Supreme Court No. S002882, Respondents' Brief on the Merits (hereafter "Respondents' Brief"); California Supreme Court No. S002882, Nov. 23, 1988, Lucas, J., Kaufman, J., concurring (hereafter "California Supreme Court Majority opinion" and "California Supreme Court concurring opinion," respectively; and the daily Reporter's Transcript (hereafter "R.T.") of the trial.

2. Kathleen Neumeyer, "The Church That's Being Taken to Court," *Los Angeles,* November 1980, 155. This magazine article is the most extensive of the media treatments of the case.

3. Neumeyer, "The Church That's Being Taken to Court," 154.

4. Ibid.

5. Respondents' Brief, Appendix, 6a, citing testimony given outside the presence of the jury.

6. Kenneth L. Woodward with Janet Huck, "Next, Clerical Malpractice?", *Newsweek,* May 20, 1985, 90.

7. According to the California Supreme Court's majority opinion (p. 3), there were thirty salaried counselors; the concurring opinion (also p. 3) put the number at fifty. Most observers estimated the size of the church membership at the time at about ten thousand; however, in an open letter to "Members and Friends of Grace Community Church" dated April 15, 1980, Thomas Lovejoy, chairman of Grace Church's Board of Elders, asserted there were over fifteen thousand who "actively identify."

8. Paul C. Holinger, M.Div., M.D., *Pastoral Care of Severe Emotional Disorders: Principles of Diagnosis and Treatment* (New York: Irvington Publishers, 1985), 53.

9. M. Robert Wilson, and Nancy Britton Soth, "Suicide," in *Psychiatry, Ministry, and Pastoral Counseling,* ed. A. W. Richard Sipe and Clarence J. Rowe (Collegeville, Minn.: The Liturgical Press, 1984), 319.

10. There is some dispute about who broke the appointment; Dr. Hall's office testified that the voice on the phone identified himself as Ken's father, though Mr. Nally denied doing so.

11. Supreme Court, majority opinion, 2; see also 14.

12. However, Katie Thayer later testified (R.T. 1727:17) that she did not recollect telling MacArthur this.

13. In an editorial in the American Association of Pastoral Counselors *Newsletter* (vol. 28, no. 2, Spring 1989, p. 3), W. B. Matthews and C. Roy Woodruff, the AAPC executive director, claim that Grace Church's pastoral counselors

"acted in Kenneth Nally's best interests and sought to get him to professional help." While the counselors may have taken themselves to be acting in Ken's best interests, the record does not suggest that, except at the very end of his life, they made any attempt to get him to professional help.

14. James Long, M.D., a board-certified psychiatrist and for eight years anordained minister in the United Methodist Church, who is also a member of the American Association of Pastoral Counselors and psychiatric consultant to two pastoral counseling centers in Los Angeles County, testified that the examination of deposition and trial testimony by Reverend Rea led him to conclude that Rea had violated the three basic professional standards of treating suicidal individuals, the duty to investigate suicidality seriously, the duty to refer to other specialists, and the duty to cooperate with family and doctors (Appellants' Brief, 34). Rev. Scott Sullender, then president of the Pacific region of the American Association of Pastoral Counselors, also testified that these three standards govern counseling with a suicidal person. (Appellants' Brief, 35). Dr. Lawrence Majovski, a licensed psychologist with a private practice in Pasadena, did not mention a duty to inform family, but otherwise concurred with these standards. Dr. Bill Adams, a licensed clinical psychologist and for fifteen years the minister of the Trinity Bible Church in South Gate, also agreed with the standards. His review of Thomson's deposition and trial testimony led him to the opinion that Thomson's care did not comply with the generally accepted standards that apply to counselors who deal with suicidal people; he added that to say Thomson did not comply "would be an understatement" (Appellants' Brief, 36–37).

15. It is worth noting that none of the pastors on trial in *Nally* asserted clergy privilege or defended himself on these grounds (Appellants' Brief, 14).

16. As Peter Appleby points out, certain religious practices—e.g., the formula said by the Catholic priest at the beginning of Mass—involve the clergy's confession to the community. This, however, is not apparent in pastoral counseling.

17. As noted earlier, however, Karen Lebacqz's *Power and Paradox* does an excellent job of examining some of these issues.

18. Lebacqz, *Professional Ethics: Power and Paradox*, 119.

19. From a panel on pastoral counseling, meetings of the American Association of Suicidology, April 1989, San Diego.

20. Nothing was made of the card at the trial. Ken could have been holding it as he shot himself or it could simply have been lying on the floor of the storage closet where he shot himself, a place where he was accustomed to storing his belongings when he lived in the house.

21. *Diagnostic and Statistical Manual of Mental Disorders III.*

22. Rich Thomson, "Guide for Biblical Counselors" (photocopied booklet, unpaginated). The "Guide" is available from Biblical Counseling Ministries, 13307 Verbena Lane, Houston, Texas 77083.

23. Rich Thomson, "Guide for Biblical Counselors," see table of contents.

24. Telephone interview with office staff, April 4, 1989.

25. Testimony of Sullender, R.T. 777:6–16.

26. Joseph Veroff, Richard A. Kulka, and Elizabeth Douvan, *Mental Health in America: Patterns of Health Seeking from 1957 to 1976* (New York: Basic Books, 1981), 83.

27. Ibid., 134.

28. Ibid., 179.

29. Ibid., 147.

## CONCLUSION

1. I thank Leslie Francis for pointing out some of these differences.

2. The several paragraphs that follow are drawn from Margaret P. Battin, "Professional Ethics and the Practice of Religion: A Philosopher's View," in *Ethical Issues in the Practice of Ministry,* ed. J. Boyajian (Minneapolis, Minn.: United Theological Seminary of the Twin Cities, 1984).

3. Eli S. Chesen, M.D., *Religion May Be Hazardous to Your Health* (New York: Macmillan, 1972), 82.

# INDEX

130898

## DATE DUE

| | | | |
|---|---|---|---|
| | | | |
| | | | |
| | | | |
| | | | |
| | | | |
| | | | |
| | | | |
| | | | |
| | | | |
| | | | |
| | | | |
| | | | |

**Ohio Dominican College Library**
**1216 Sunbury Road**
**Columbus, Ohio 43219**

DEMCO